GUIDE FOR
THE CHRISTIAN ASSEMBLY

THIERRY MAERTENS – JEAN FRISQUE

GUIDE FOR THE

CHRISTIAN
ASSEMBLY

REVISED EDITION

ADVENT — CHRISTMAS

First Sunday of Advent —
First Sunday of the Year

Notre Dame, Indiana 46556

TRANSLATED FROM THE FRENCH BY THE MONKS OF VALYERMO

Nihil Obstat: V. Descamps
can. libr. cens.

Imprimatur: J. Thomas, *vic. gen.*
Tournai, March 12, 1969

LCCCN: 72-114245

ISBN: 0-8190-0001-9

2773

PREFACE TO THE NEW EDITION

With the introduction of the new lectionary we have undertaken a complete revision of the *Guide for the Christian Assembly*. The purpose is twofold. We want to provide a manual which studies the new formularies in depth, and to indicate in our commentary how the Word of God proclaimed in scripture is complemented by his word elsewhere — the word, that is, which mysteriously informs actual happenings in the world and in the history of the Church.

We have entirely reworked our material and hope that our readers will find it a useful source for personal meditation and prayerful lives as Christians. In order to take account of everything the new lectionary provides we decided to revise the structure of the commentary. We concentrate almost exclusively on the readings, and do not provide extensive treatment of other material such as prayers or hymns. Greater liberty of choice, and some improvisation, is to be expected in that area.

Consequently the old headings of *Liturgical Analysis* and *Biblical Theme* have been eliminated, and commentaries are divided simply in two parts: exegesis and doctrine. We have however incorporated all the former material in one or other of our present divisions.

A. EXEGESIS

The reader will first find a brief exegesis of the readings for each Mass of the liturgical year. This is a minimal requirement if the thought of the inspired author is to be respected. Pastors who wish to comment on the text or lay people who seek to penetrate its content do not always have a ready means at hand of finding the exact meaning, and may resort to dubious expedients. In recent years there has been considerable development in the field of exegesis, but pastors and laity encounter isolated items only. Our function is to make the work of the specialists available for them.

It should be clear however that the function of exegesis is preliminary; it does not cover everything. It keeps us from following false trails or seeking verification in the text for *a priori* views. But it does not exhaust the possibilities of the text in deepening our understanding of the liturgical celebration. Another sort of study is necessary.

Specifically, the exegetical part comprises three paragraphs. The first places the reading in its context and provides the critical material necessary for interpretation. The second gives the exegetical commentary proper, the various themes, the really central message, out of which a homily can be built. Some doctrinal, moral or liturgical comments will be found in the third, which relate the biblical text to the whole context of life in the Church and in the world today.

B. DOCTRINE

The doctrinal discussions are centered on the Sunday formularies. Usually there are two for each Sunday, which consider the principal themes of the exegetical commentary. For the weekdays there is, strictly speaking, no doctrinal commentary, but in the course of the exegetical commentary we have suggested avenues of doctrinal reflection.

A word of explanation about the method followed in doctrinal exposition. We do not really study an isolated theme in purely analytic fashion. Theological reflection should be centered on the eucharistic celebration because this is the essential act of the Church's life, involving the whole mystery of both Christ and the Church. Because various approaches are necessary to gain insight into the totality of the mystery, eucharistic formularies, in an attempt to indicate the totality, will utilize various themes. The different themes however do converge, and in this convergence lies the key to deeper understanding. The living relation which unites a man with Jesus Christ crucified and arisen, the one mediator of salvation for everyone, is shaped more than anywhere else in the eucharistic celebration. It begins at that extraordinarily complex historical moment of baptism, which brings a man from unbelief into faith. It is developed as the liturgy of the Word initiates him into salvation history, the thread of growth, at once continuous and discontinuous, which links Adam with Jesus by way of Abraham. The thread always lies in the background of every formulary, reminding us where we stand and whither we must go. It is important for each one to know throughout life where he stands on the road that leads to Christ, what is still pagan in him, what still remains at the stage of Jewish man.

Whoever is admitted to the Eucharist is a member of the Church. In the mystical body he has his essential role, the implications of which he should constantly weigh. It requires him to cooperate in the building of the Kingdom, in the always actual shaping of salvation history. It ought to dominate his life, because it is in the warp and woof of actual living that the Church has the mission to bear witness for men to the salvation acquired once for all in Jesus.

Considerations such as these determine our style of reflection. Our treatment of each theme has two broad angles. First there is question of clarifying the continuous-discontinuous line from pagan man, ancient and modern, *via* Jewish man to Jesus Christ. The progressive consciousness that we find traced in scripture is somehow normative for all time and we must discern its tenor. It is essential that the Christian have a full appreciation of what coming to the faith means, and the steps he must take to achieve recognition of the man-God. Secondly, the light derived from consideration of the mystery of Christ is cast upon the mystery of the Church and the new state that Christian life in the Church means. So we go on to show how the liturgical theme being treated clarifies the missionary dynamism of the Church and of all authentic Christian life. All that remains is to point out how the day's eucharistic celebration, by the appeal made in the Word proclaimed, brings the assembled faithful to realization of their active role.

As we reflect on each formulary we shall attempt to follow these broad lines. It is a method, we think, that furnishes pastor and people with a tool that is fairly easy to handle, and that contributes to a continuous deepening of their faith under the sign of Christ and the Church.

A METHOD OF TEAM PREPARATION

The materials made available in the new volumes of the Guide for the Christian Assembly do not lend themselves to immediate use in the conduct of the celebration, or the homily. What we have sought to provide, for layman and pastor, is a cultural instrument, and it should be clear that this kind of study can be further developed on the pastoral level. The pastor will derive items of information and ideas, we believe, that give him a suitable perspective for preparing his homily and commentary according to liturgical tradition.

Furthermore the materials are suitable for teamwork. We should like to describe the kind of treatment we have ourselves frequently attempted. To begin with, all listen to the readings of the liturgy about to be celebrated. In that God himself is speaking, and people are properly disposed for hearing his will, the subsequent work will be inspired by the Spirit. Then a member of the team presents the exegesis and liturgical analysis. We might call this the "objective part." The commentary is discussed, and care is taken to isolate the central point that emerges from all contributions. Once this is agreed, another team member reads some relevant biblical passages.

Now comes the "reflective part." The section we entitle

Doctrine is presented by the person who best combines the qualities of pastor and theologian, always with an eye to the concrete situation of the particular assembly. This is a delicate task. The priest's habitual style of meditation is not readily developed into articulate reflection on the lived life of the Church.

It is possible at this point for the joint work to proceed. All that has taken place enables each one to say how he sees the Mass of the coming Sunday as a new stage in salvation history. The stage can only be reached by having recourse to the mystery of Christ. Again, with regard to the principal theme of the celebration, he might state the questions with which, in his opinion, the Church could be confronted by the world. It is important to linger over this discussion, even though it is time-consuming in the beginning.

Finally the team comes to grips with the actual pastoral procedure for the Sunday. Here, obviously, there is no need to be concerned with each detail of the matter considered. During the course of the celebration the homily and commentary will be developed with full consideration for their functional laws. Once again, the homily is not an exegetical or doctrinal discourse; but exegesis and doctrine are a good preparation for the sort of homily and commentary that will meet actual needs.

At the end the meeting should determine suitable chants. These, entrance hymn, communion chant and recessional, should be chosen to illustrate the theme selected. All these are merely suggestions. Trial and error will enable us, whether individually or in teams, to develop our own method.

CONTENTS

FIRST SUNDAY OF ADVENT

A. THE WORD

I. Isaiah 2:1-5
1st reading
1st cycle

The poem actually consists of verses 2-4 only. Verse 1 is simply a title added later to the whole group of poems in Isaiah 2-5, and verse 5 a transition between this poem and Isaiah 2:6-21. In Mi 4:1-3 we find a similar version of verses 2-4, which guarantees their authenticity. The verses however seem more natural in Isaiah than in Micah, since Isaiah always took an optimistic view of the future of Jerusalem. He was keenly aware of universality in the "times to come" when knowledge of God would be bestowed in its plenitude.

a) The first theme, the *exaltation of Mount Zion* (v. 2, cf. Ps 48) constitutes a challenge to the tower of Babel (Gn 11:1-9) and other "high places" of religion. However arrogant, man alone cannot in his pride ascend to God: only Yahweh can confer religious value on cults or places. From the exaltation God will derive more glory than Jersualem itself; because it is God who will be exalted (Is 2:11, 17), who will be a true temple for his own (Is 8:14), a temple erected on the faith of his Messiah (Is 28:16-17).

The Jerusalem contemplated is symbolic, shorn of historical and geographic context as verse 3 indicates, a point which is also emphasized by the disciple of Isaiah who composed Isaiah, 26:1-6. The idea suits the general "Remnant" theology of Isaiah, where the Remnant is no longer geographically rooted in Israel, but purely a religious community.

b) Corresponding to the exaltation of the symbolic city is the *universal call* to her liturgy. Once withdrawn from the particularism of Zion, Yahweh becomes accessible to all peoples, who are "numerous" (v. 3). The epithet suggests the multitude for whom centuries later (Is 53:11-12: Mk 14:24; 10:45) the suffering servant will offer his life. The "numerous" nations were promised to Abraham and Jacob (note the expression "God of Jacob"); and the promises of Gn 12:3 and 27:9, applied for the first time to Zion, will enable her to become, on the very eve of her destruction, a new city open to all humanity.

c) However, the nations will direct attention more to the Word, to God's Law and the knowledge of his designs, than to the temple of Jerusalem. This is no longer the center of the bloody sacrifices of the old covenant, but a place where everyone learns to obey the will of God (Ps 39/40:7-9; Rm 12:12). Yahweh's true temple is then to be distinguished from the temple of stones, against which Jeremiah (Jr 7) and Jesus (Mt 21) will revolt. As they ascend the new Zion, the nations will discover a *spiritual temple,* built upon faith (Is 8:14) and on worship in spirit (Jn 4:23-24).

Such thinking puts Isaiah several centuries ahead of his time. His universal ideas were gradually adopted by his disciples (Is 56:1-8; 66:18-21); but the notion of a spiritual religion capable of uniting all men will not be accepted until much later, practically in New Testament times. The knowledge of Yahweh already implies a desire for peace (v. 4; cf. Is 11:1-9 and 32:1-5): men will renounce any recourse to arms (cf. Is 2:7; 3:25) because their relationship with God will eliminate all antagonisms (cf. Ho 2:20; Ez 34:25).

An interesting feature of the reading is the association of faith and religion with so profane a matter as the quest for peace. No true peace can exist without knowledge of the Word of God made flesh in Jesus. It is his living resurrected person which replaces the temple where all nations are gathered together. The universal mission is linked with that of a "little remnant" as if to indicate that the anguish of finitude and suffering is a necessary preliminary to absorption in a power capable of supporting all beings. Our assembling round the blood offered "for the multitude," our willingness to bear witness to the Jerusalem envisaged by Isaiah, means that we must know properly how to work with the nations of today in the search for peace and happiness.

II. **Isaiah** **63:16b-17;** **64:1, 4-8ab** *1st reading* *2nd cycle*   The collection known as "Third-Isaiah" is an anthology of pieces of varying literary genre which was made between 530 and 475 BC. It illustrates the doctrine and piety of the first century after the exile. Today's passage is taken from a long prayer (Is 63:7–64:11), a sort of lamentation song (like Pss 73/74 or 78/79) composed in 587 at the moment of Jerusalem's fall. The first returning exiles sang it on the occasion of an expiation ceremony of the reconstruction of the temple (cf. Is 63:18; 64:9-10). The song begins (63:7) with thanksgiving and recollection of marvels in the past (vv. 8-13). After verse 15 comes the epiclesis which continues to 64:11, calling for divine intervention in the present crisis. The form then is a traditionally Jewish one, to which the majority of Christian anaphoras are indebted.

a) Our liturgical reading has only a portion of the epiclesis, where God is addressed by two titles, novel at the time: *Father* and *Redeemer* (v. 16). "Our fathers" Abraham and Israel (father of the northern tribes) seem careless of the promises of which they are the custodians. Consequently God takes to himself this fatherhood that has become precarious, and in the patriarchal sense of fatherhood (v. 16a) becomes the real father of the people. The term "Redeemer" (*goel*) originally signified a member of the clan whose duty it was to rescue a relative from slavery. The *"goel"* function becomes that of God himself, because the exiled Jews, with the whole clan in slavery, could no longer count on a family redeemer. So the very collapse of patriarchal and family structures in Israel makes for a deeper knowledge of God. Here we have a typically Jewish concept of salvation: God intervenes directly at the very moment when men come to realize the frailty of their own means. The Christian attitude is not altogether this: God intervenes, but by human intermediaries, by those at least who are servants of Christ. Most important is the change from the classical father or *"goel"* to God the Father and Redeemer. It shows how the Jewish people abandoned the security of their stable classical norms in order to project themselves into a new life of incident and the unexpected event, and thus became the Chosen People of God. Theirs was the first conception of faith.

b) But if God is more "father" than the patriarchs, more "redeemer" than one's own family, why does he permit the trial (vv. 18-19) and the disobedience (v. 17)? It is the eternal problem of human liberty and the origin of evil. The prophet does not give an explanation. He simply proclaims the intervention of a God who will sunder the heavens, accomplish prodigies and marvels upon earth, and decree the chastisement of his enemies (63:19b–64:4a). Man must then turn to God because he is himself too puny to cope with misfortune.

Similarly, the Christian recognizes God as Father and Redeemer. He affirms that the solution to sin and evil lies in the plan of God, whom he hopes one day to join. Since God has sent his own son among men, the Christian no longer awaits the intervention of a *deus ex machina,* or counts on a "sign from heaven" (compare Is 63:19b with Mt 12:38-40). He realizes that God's fatherhood is manifested by means of the human nature of his Son, that the "Redeemer" does not perform miracles but works through man's freedom.

Of course the Mass can be regarded as a manifestation of God, when in a world that is turned to sin and evil, the compunction of converted hearts and fraternal union makes actual the sign of God's paternal and redemptive functions. The sign is so much more efficacious than the Jerusalem envisaged by Third Isaiah.

III. Jeremiah The theology of this reading, an extract from
33:14-16 a passage introduced into the book of Jeremiah
1st reading (Jr 33:14-26) at a fairly late date, is derived
3rd cycle from Zechariah 4:1-14 (end of the 6th century,
after the first exiles returned to Palestine).
The author is commenting on an ancient oracle of Jeremiah (Jr
23:5-6) and he modifies some details. A comparison between the
original and the commentary will clarify the points of doctrine
in either case.

a) The condemnation launched by Jeremiah against the line
of Jehoiakim, king of Jerusalem, and against his son Coniah
(Jr 22:24-30), does not question the principle of davidic kingship
(2 Sm 7:8-16: Is 7:10-14). Note that the prophet foretells a
seed for David, even though it springs from a branch of the line
other than Jehoiakim's (Jr 23:5). The commentator takes up this
oracle, which has in the interval become *messianic* (cf. Zc 3:8;
6:12), and insists on the motif of the "seed," concentrating there
the whole doctrine of a "remnant" which escapes the trial.

b) According to Jeremiah the future king will impose justice
(Jr 23:5) in a land that too often has been delivered to the dis-
honesty of its shepherds (Jr 7:3-6; cf. Ps 71/72:1-7), and he will
obtain justice for the people from the nations (Jr 23:6a). He will
be called "Yahweh-our-justice," an ironical allusion to the then
king Zedekiah, whose name means "Yahweh-my-justice."

The commentator retains the figure of the just king; but he
juxtaposes with it the theme of Jerusalem (v. 16), to which he
transfers the title "Yahweh-our-justice." Salvation then will spring
from both the king and the temple (cf. vv. 17-26 and the theme
of the two anointed in Zc 4:14; 6:13). Enlarged thus to include
the city, the royal expectations include the temple too and the
priesthood. The action which will "justify" the people will be
that of a priest as well as a king. Thus the knowledge of justice
moves away from too mundane a definition and becomes the

healthy relationship between God and man in the intimacy that Christ's sacrifice confers.

c) The original oracle had foretold also the reunion, thanks to the justice of the future king, of the twelve tribes, and the reconciliation of Israel and Judah (v. 6a). It was characteristic of Jeremiah (3:18; 31:1) to give the messianic future an "ecumenical" dimension. The commentator however, more concerned with the future splendor of Jerusalem than with such unity, substitutes the word "Jerusalem" for "Israel" in Jr 3:16, thus obliterating the other motif. He does however retain some of his master's message when he addresses his oracle to both houses, Israel as well as Judah.

Jesus took on both royal power and sacrificial priesthood: both functions are combined in the worship rendered to his Father by the man-God. The liturgical assembly finds its justification in that worship and merits in turn the title "Yahweh-our-justice." In a more real sense than Jerusalem, it constitutes the royal and priestly people, and is a sign of universal unity in the justification given by God (Heb 12:22-24; 1 P 2:4-10).

IV. Romans   Compiled about 57, the letter to the Romans
13:11-14   rejects the means of salvation offered by the
2nd reading   Law in favor of collaboration with the Spirit,
1st cycle   the object of the ancient promises. Worship
                   too is emancipated from the temple, because
it is now spiritual, rooted in Christian involvement and moral performance (Rm 12:1-2).

Chapters 12 and 13 describe this new ethic in terms of particular needs in the Roman community. It consists in charity towards brothers, towards all men, even enemies, and obedience to civil authority.

At the end of this discussion comes a summary, giving the fundamental reason for Christian attitudes. Since the last times have begun, every hour of our life ought to demonstrate our passage from night (darkness) to day (light).

a) Paul is very attached to his concept of this *time* which stretches between the historical coming of Christ and his manifestation in glory. The period set aside for the conversion of men (Ac 3:19-21; Rm 11:25; 2 Co 6:2) and the testing of the faithful (Ep 6:13) is already charged with the time of God, given for the living of eternity.

The images he uses are interestingly nuanced. "Darkness" has always a pejorative sense in scripture: it denotes the effect of evil, from which only the grace of God and conversion can deliver us, by leading us to the "light" of salvation. "Night" on the other hand merely denotes the time of man, not necessarily pejoratively. This is a time which passes, which ought to give way to the time of God, the "day" inaugurated by the coming of Christ.

Consequently while the first image (darkness − light) is moral, the second (night − day) is temporal. A combination of the two enables the reader to give a temporal dimension in history to his moral performance.

b) Just because the Christian's moral effort has this time-aspect, sometimes the word "waking" (cf. Mt 25:1-7; 1 Th 5:4-8) is used, sometimes "watchfulness" (Lk 12:39-40; Col 4:5; Ep 5:16; Ga 6:9-10). The time of night is passed, and during the day we should not seem still to sleep. Again *stripping* and *reclothing* denote the necessity for conversion implicit in the Christian moral attitude.

Christian involvement then has both a moral and an eschatological dimension: it takes place during a time which provides opportunity for conversion and encounter with God.

Because each instant of our time contains the eternity of God, the hour has come. This is no time for depending solely on temporal wisdom like the pagans, or awaiting a divine intervention in the future like the Jews; salvation is here and now. Every decision now between light and darkness is a sign of the coming of the Son of Man. The Eucharist is indeed this coming of the Lord among his own because it is the source and flowering of all such choices.

V. 1 Corinthians
1:3-9
2nd reading
2nd cycle

Paul's first letter to Corinth gives answers to the problems of a young Christian community "dispersed" in a pagan and immoral environment. As in the majority of his letters, after the usual greeting he makes a sort of act of thanksgiving (vv. 4-9) which contains in germ the theme of the whole epistle.

a) For Paul it is in the *common union of all in Christ* (v. 9) that the solution to the community's problems can be found. Members must be "of Christ" (vv. 6-7) and "in Christ" (v. 5; cf. 1 Co 1:10-30; 4:10-15; 7:21-22, 39; 15:18-22, 31). This union secures us God's grace (vv. 1, 4, 7), a salvation which is purely gratuitous; it secures us his riches (v. 5), in particular his Word and the knowledge of God. Word and knowledge enabled Paul to classify properly charisms like tongues and discernment, in which the Corinthians took such pride (1 Co 12-14). In making the gratuitous gift of God the object of his thanksgiving, he is preparing to launch those diatribes (1 Co 1-4) against the wisdom of the world, which presumes to have in itself the secret of salvation.

b) The witness to Christ which he bore (v. 7) in the Corinth community was particularly solid precisely because he did not depend on frail human wisdom (1 Co 3:12-15) but on God's own action (1 Co 2:4-5; 4:15; Ga 4:19) and on the power of the resurrection. This allusion to the role of apostolic ministry in the transmission of God's graces has its point, because in the course of his discussion he will in fact be concerned to place the charisms so dear to the Corinthians under hierarchical supervision (1 Co 12:27-30).

c) God's gifts do not bring salvation once for all: on the contrary they are a ferment meant to "increase," "to keep steady and without blame" (v. 8). They come at the beginning of a process which will be accomplished on the *Day* of judgment and resurrection (cf. 1 Co 5:5; 3:13; 11:26), the day of "revelation" (v. 7) and triumphal manifestation of Christ and his Church. Every grace is then a first fruit of glory and kingship, of resurrection and of life totally in Christ (1 Co 15:24-28). Later he will discuss the final resurrection at greater length (1 Co 15:35-53); but even here he insists that one cannot share in Christ's glorious return if one is not already with him in faith through the gifts he dispenses. God is faithful (v. 9) and what he communicates here and now constitutes the fruits of Christ's life and glory.

d) The Corinthians had much experience of the problem set up by *dispersion of Christians* in the world. Jews had managed to sustain this in hope of the *Day* which would see Jerusalem reestablished at the center of the nations (cf. preceding readings). Not having such a concrete rallying-point, the Corinthians were tempted to rely on the wisdom of the world which surrounded them. Paul shows them their true city: the person of Jesus Christ and the "Day," already here, of his glorification.

VI. 1 Thess.
3:12-4:2
2nd reading
3rd cycle

Paul ends the first part of his letter to the Thessalonians with a prayer. Previously he has recalled their evangelization and conversion (1:2-10) and stressed the difference between the conduct of the apostles and that of false missionaries (2:1-16). The time is 51 and he is far from Thessalonika. He fears the consequences of false preaching and of persecution, and is not wholly reassured even by Timothy's news (2:17–3:10). Accordingly he prays to God that he may have the joy of seeing them again and enabling them to make progress unceasingly in the faith.

The prayer has a precise structure. Verses 10-11 mention the faith of the Thessalonians, verse 12 their charity and verse 13 their hope. His principal concern then is with the theological virtues, the foundation of the Christian life.

a) The community's *faith* is frail; Timothy's report has probably revealed shortcomings. Paul actually had to leave Thessalonika before completing the necessary catachesis (Ac 17:1-10). He begs God to remove the obstacles that have until now prevented his return.

b) The second petition is for an increase in charity, among brothers, but also towards all men, even persecutors of the community (Ga 6:10; Rm 12:10-21). Paul feels responsible and hopes the degree of mutual charity among them will correspond to the love he himself showed them (same attitude in 2 Th 3:7-9; Ph 3:17; 4:9; 1 Co 4:16; 11:1).

c) Firm faith and charity will insure an irreproachable "holiness" among the community. But this ought to grow unceasingly in the hope of the Lord's Parousia (1 Th 5:23; 1 Co 1:8). He shares of course the ideas of his time about the Parousia, that it would come at the end of the persecutions. Perhaps the tribulations of the Thessalonians are the prelude?

Christian holiness is not static: it grows unceasingly because of the hope that one day we shall find ourselves in the presence of the Father, with the glorified Lord and all the saints.

VII. Matthew
24:37-44
Gospel
1st cycle

In a passage that is unique, and quite apocalyptic, Matthew gives the teaching of Christ concerning the coming of the Son of Man and the end of the holy city. Terms derived from different discourses of Christ about the fall of

Jerusalem or about the last things are used in the description. But how to recognize the signs heralding these happenings? To provide an answer Matthew juxtaposes three parables: that of the fig-tree announcing summer's approach (Mt 24:32-35), that of the deluge (Mt 24:36-41), and finally that of the householder and the thief (Mt 24:42-44). Today's gospel gives us the last two only.

a) The figure of the "days" of deluge only has point if the "day" of the coming of the Son of Man coincides with the fall of Jerusalem, and with the destruction of the temple, which has been already supplanted as the religious center of the world by the very person of the risen Christ (Mt 23:38-39; 26:61-64). In the fall of the city there will be the same discrimination as in the days of the deluge. One shall be taken and the other left (vv. 40-41; cf. Mt 24:19-22), and the "Remnant" of saints will form the new people, as Noah's family constituted the new humanity.

Mention of the deluge stresses too the uncertainty of the disciples, and of Christ himself (v. 36) concerning the time of these events. However, such uncertainty should not lead to the negligence of Noah's contemporaries (vv. 38-39). There was need for sufficient discernment to see the significance of the temple's destruction, and a sufficiently universal outlook not to regret the passing of a Jerusalem that was over particularist. Only thus can one belong to the "Remnant" which reads in these events the coming of the Son of Man.

b) The parable of the householder and the thief possibly alludes to some such incident known to Jesus' listeners. The coming fall of Jerusalem will surprise the careless Jews (1 Th 5:2-4; 2 P 3:10; Rv 3:3) as the thief surprised the careless householder. For those who "keep watch" however, awaiting the first signs of the kingdom, Christ will appear as a friend (Rv 3:20-21).

c) The fall of Jerusalem actually enabled the Church to free herself from Judaism, to initiate at last a spiritual cult and embrace her universal mission. Is not this a sign that the process can be looked upon as a *coming of the Son of Man?* To the uneasiness of the apostles before the onset of a catastrophe Jesus opposes watchfulness, a quality which discerns in the turn of events the on-going Kingdom of the Risen Lord.

This Christian watchfulness implies a missionary spirit. Through all vicissitudes of peoples and cultures the advent of the Risen Lord makes itself apparent, and in the eucharistic sacrifice, which offers a guarantee of brotherhood to all men, the missionary spirit is displayed.

VIII. Mark   In the vigilance parables of the synoptic tra-
    13:33-37   dition there are individual features. In Mt
    Gospel   24:42-44 the father of the family, had he been
    2nd cycle   vigilant, would not have been surprised by
                    the thief. So too with the careless Jews at the
fall of Jerusalem.

In Luke 12:35-40 the servants keep watch, waiting to give an account to their master, which suggests the judgment at the end of the world (Mt 25). In Mark's version, only the doorman watches while the rest remain at work, and the master on his return does not require an account. It could be that this version is inspired by some reflection concerning Peter's (the doorman) primacy.

Mark's omission of any calling of people to account suggests that there is no question of the watchfulness necessary to prepare for judgment, but rather of a special watchfulness, which is the duty first of Peter, then of every Christian (v. 37), and which means sensitivity to the signs of Christ's Lordship implicit in the approaching fall of Zion (Mk 13:14-32). Peter is charged to watch and strengthen the faith of his flock (Lk 22:32); for he is the rock on which Christ erects a temple more solid than that of Zion, which is destined for destruction (Mt 16:18). Mark's teaching on watchfulness then has a particular bias. It shows the part played by the hierarchy in the Church's sensitivity to signs of the Lord's coming. Christian vigilance has its order of precedence: there are special functions and charisms.

The eucharistic assembly is the Church vigilant, reading in the march of events the coming of the Lord, encountering the Lord of glory in human history and the history of salvation. But the vigilance that Christ demands from his own is no longer the vigilance that the ancient prophets used to call for from the people: we don't have to wait for particular times — times that are already implicitly past — but instead we have to read about what has happened, and to find its meaning. In spite of this watchfulness, though, the coming of the kingdom will be sudden and, at least partly unexpected. It will also be completely different from anything our vigilance may have envisaged in advance — for that is the hallmark of God's presence.

IX. Luke 21:25-28, 34-36
Gospel
3rd cycle

Like the two preceding gospels this passage should be replaced in the difficult context of prophecy concerning Jerusalem's fall. Using the terminology customary in Jewish apocalypse and eschatology, our Lord makes the event assume the dimensions of an ending for all things.

a) Today's reading immediately follows the description of the siege (vv. 20-24). The city's fall is seen as the result of a cosmic catastrophe, which will unhinge even the stars and plunge men into the greatest confusion (vv. 25-26). Jewish apocalypse always described the destruction of a city, or the "Day of Yahweh," in terms of cosmic catastrophe (Is 24:10-23; 13:6-10; Jr 4:23-26). Like Babylon, Samaria, Gomorrha and many another pagan city,

Jerusalem herself now undergoes the chastisement of the "Day of Yahweh." In illustrating with images of a cosmic order (more conservatively though than the parallel passage in Mt) his description of Zion's fall, Luke does not necessarily proclaim the end of the world. What he does is present the fall as a decisive stage in the establishment of Yahweh's reign in the world, in contemporary literary style.

The implication of all creation in the city's fall was a typical biblical approach. The messianic kingdom tended to be presented as a "new creation" which would reverse the fundaments of the old (Jl 3:1-5; Hg 2:6; Is 65:17). Hence Jerusalem's fall seemed to be the dawn of a new creation.

b) Having alluded to the cosmic significance of the collapse, Luke goes on to announce the *coming of the Son of Man in a cloud* (v. 27). This is obviously a reference to the mysterious personage foretold by Daniel (Dn 7:13-14) who will be the judge of nations. As he sees it, the manifestation of the Son of Man, Lord of nations, begins precisely at the moment of the temple's fall. It was considered the place of the nations' great assembly under the rule of Yahweh (Is 60); but Christ had transferred the prerogative to "he who comes" or "he who comes in the cloud" (Mt 26:61-64; 23:37-39). "Coming in the cloud" was a phrase used of someone haloed with divine glory, and the Christians had no difficulty in applying it to the risen Christ. Until the end of time he is the "one who comes" (Rv 1:7; cf. Rv 14:14), since the moment of his resurrection and in every event that helps to establish his Lordship. The time of the Church, inaugurated at the resurrection, and more actually still after the fall of Zion, constitutes then the "coming of the Son of Man."

c) When the account is finished the gospel goes on to moral applications. Luke invites his contemporaries (vv. 31-32) to see a "sign" of the proximity of the Kingdom (vv. 27-31) in the fall of Jerusalem. Proximity not of a temporal order as if the end of the world were imminent, but ontological rather. The Kingdom is in a state of becoming in each event of human history and of salvation history, and we must endeavor to discern it there. Watchfulness is a virtue precisely of the man who concerns himself with the Lordship of the Son of Man, and who watches it germinate in each person and "in all things." *

A stage in the coming of the Lord on the cloud was marked by the fall of Jerusalem, because it forced the Church to open her ranks irrevocably to the nations, and to shape a spiritual cult purified of the temple's particularism. Every stage then in the evangelization of the world, linked to all the stages in the humanization of the planet, is also a stage in this coming of the Son of Man. Each conversion of heart by which man opens himself to the action of the Spirit of the Risen One, and relies a little less upon the "flesh," is a new manifestation of the coming. Every eucharistic assembly, united "until he comes again", is the recipient of the glory and power of the Son of Man on the cloud, and is indeed the stage *par excellence* of this coming.

---

*See doctrinal theme: *vigilance,* p. 32.

B. DOCTRINE

1. The Theme of Vigilance

There do not seem to be natural roots in human psychology for the biblical doctrine of vigilance, and modern man does not differ from the ancients in this respect. Hope of fulfillment for the ancients depended on the security offered by cosmic stability and immemorial laws about individual and social life. There was no reason for vigilance. Man's task was to seek perfect harmony with the archetypes, established once for all by the gods when the cosmos began. The thirst for the absolute which troubles the hearts of men could only be assuaged by cyclic recurrence. In such a climate the event, with its novel and unforeseen aspects, is quite simply rejected; there is a constant urge to evade it, to cancel its reality.

Modern man's attitude to the event seems to be different; but really it is not. He has the same urge to cancel its reality. But he cannot now evade it. His increasing mastery over the data of nature and over man himself enables him to "possess" the event, to bring it within foreseeable limits. Here too there is no room for vigilance in the biblical sense, only for foresight. True, there is no myth of a recurring cycle to give validity nowadays to human existence. All are faced with the complex task of transforming the world and building structures which make it habitable for human beings. To surmount the great challenges nowadays to human happiness, hunger, war, injustice, there is continual need for ingenuity. But, in theory anyhow, the time will come when nothing can disturb universal security.

The Church, at the very outset of the liturgical year, recommends that this attitude of vigilance, so essential to Christianity, be deepened. The word should not be lightly used, for the issue is grave. Deprived of its biblical implications, vigilance holds no particular interest for the Christian. But when properly understood it illuminates an aspect of our faith, the permanent relevancy of which one cannot overstress.

Vigilance and the regime of faith

From the moment, in Israel, when the regime of faith appeared among men, vigilance began to have meaning. The event began to assume realistic proportions, inconceivable in pagan terms. The series of concrete happenings, individual and collective, so stamped themselves on human existence that this seemed the only valid area of investigation in the quest for fulfillment. Without doubt, confronted day by day with the march of events, Jewish man found himself more and more deeply disjointed. He was involved in a dramatic adventure, the key to which escaped him, and he had not, by himself, the resources to gain the fulfillment he sought. A corollary though of this realization of "poverty" was the extraordinarily fruitful discovery of a "Totally-Other-God," who saves by intervening at the level of the event, the dramatic adventure in which man is actually engaged. The God of Israel reveals himself as the Existing, the Living One *par excellence*. Only he can save the people he has gratuitously taken to himself. He leads them day by day. He meets them on the concrete historical plane; but can only fulfill them if they are faithful according to the terms of the Covenant he made with them in the desert. Yahweh comes; he does not cease to come. One should anticipate his comings even when they are not responses to human expectation, particularly when they are not. One should anticipate them by being vigilant, by watching lest we fall into temptation.

Not today or yesterday did Jewish man serve his apprenticeship to vigilance. Throughout her long history Israel had shown herself stiffnecked, preferring the pagan securities, even those of slavery, to the discomfort of encounter with the living God. Sin however is not the total explanation. Being under the regime of faith brought about considerable interiorization, both individual and collective; but it was only gradually that Israel reached the depth of self-emptying required by faith. Her gratuitous selection implied privileges, and her difficulty was to avoid interpreting these in terms of security. The prophets were always having to `intervene to correct the inevitable misunderstandings that arose.

The city of Jerusalem is a case in point. It is clear from the prophetic texts of the first week of Advent that the Jerusalem which pleases the heart of Yahweh, where there is perfect encounter between him and his own, where all the nations find their place, is other than terrestrial Jerusalem and its temple of stone. These were liable to fail in their mission and be destroyed. The awaited Jerusalem, in the time of fulfillment, is one where all justice will flourish, where the call which comes from God the Father and Savior will find hearts unceasingly vigilant, always ready to listen.

Intervention of the Messiah and Christian vigilance

In the gospels the theme of vigilance is far from accidental. In those texts, parables and discourses, which speak of the proximity of the Kingdom, it is always present. There is even insistence about vigilance, to the extent that in the person of Jesus proximity has become actuality. The happening which is the historical intervention in the world of Jesus of Nazareth manifests the "Lord who comes" in such fashion that all our energies must be mustered to confront it. Vigilance reaches its peak point. It summons us to a precise involvement: following Jesus, being present when the bridegroom passes and joining in the cortège. Expectation is fulfilled; but that itself is a stumbling block. It obliges man to empty himself to the point of obedience unto death. To follow Jesus is to bear his cross too. Hearts are prepared by vigilance for the comings of the Lord; but this means that the believer is plunged into the tensions which freewill will cause. He is always summoned by God, and finds no true support except in turning to the merciful Father. Vigilance means the aspect faith assumes when it has the clear vision of empty hands.

Jesus has given us the example. All through his time on earth, he lived under the sign of that vigilance he requires from his disciples. His nourishment is to do the will of the Father who sent him among men. Nor is this will made clear for him through the medium of private revelation. For him, like every man, it was a matter of discovering in the procession of days the path he must follow here below. It was not determined *a priori*, clear from the first day. Always he examines the events; but he does so with that sovereign realism which is proper to him, and whatever it costs him, he engages himself with perfect fidelity and obedience. Gradually the Passion looms on the horizon; because Israel will not agree to follow a Messiah who proposes such a demanding road, that of love without limits, of total renunciation.

So Jesus is the Vigilant One in the fullest sense. But because he is Son of God this very vigilance discloses him to the eye of faith as the Lord who comes. Aligned as he is with the will of his Father, Jesus, in the very moment of his response, reveals the plan of God and the true import of his interventions among men. With Jesus and in him the vigilance of faith affirms its true identity: it is the welcoming of God's today in human history, a welcome, it should be added, which engages all the energies of human liberty restored to its true state.

The vigilance of the Church and the temptation of the synagogue

The primitive Church was strongly insistent about vigilance: we should be in readiness for the return of the Lord. Since his Pasch is now an event of the past, his return must be imminent. It is however an object of faith and therefore unforeseeable: it will surprise like the unexpected visitation of the thief. Hence the absolute necessity of vigilance: Christians must keep vigil, live every moment virtuous lives, and strive not to fall into temptation.

We notice that the first generation of Christians retains a horizontal and temporal notion of the Lord's return, even while insisting on the aspects that only faith could discern, which subsequent experience would delineate more sharply. In the year 70 an event occurs, which has strong repercussions on the concept of the Lord's return, and consequently on the Christian notion of vigilance: the destruction, that is, of the city of Jerusalem. So prominent a place did terrestrial Jerusalem have in the religious world of the first Christians, that its destruction was unimaginable except in direct relation to the end of the world. However the return of the Lord did not coincide with this evidently divine intervention. So it is that the return of the Lord is always an actuality present in life, its immanence and its unforeseeable character emphasizing the fact that it is transcendental. So it is too that God's today in human history means the annihilation of all particularism, even when that is based on the privileges of a chosen people.

The vigilance of the Church, as she holds herself ready for the return of the Lord, is especially related to her catholicity. At every moment she must go to meet the Lord who comes, demonstrating the power of universal charity which animates her. She must watch so as not to fall into temptation, and the temptation which besets her always is that of the synagogue. It was on this point that the Council of Jerusalem, the first council of ecclesial vigilance, declared itself. The temptation of the synagogue is the temptation to particularism. Link Christianity to a people, a group of peoples, a particular culture where the Church is already spread, and we are immediately according privileges which they do not actually have to an enclave or group of people. Has not the idea been widespread in the Church that the mission to non-Christians is exclusively the business of the white races? Even today, traces of it remain.

Evangelization of the world under the sign of vigilance

Two major questions, both challenges to the Church's catholicity, are posed to the People of God in these days. Firstly, does the Church build her unity by embracing all the diversity of human beings and the tensions that diversity implies? Secondly, is the Church capable of adapting herself to a secularized world, and propagating the good news of salvation in a manner that will be relevant to it?

To answer these challenges with deeds the People of God must display exceptional vigilance. Particular churches will be more and more diversified. This is an irreversible trend, largely favored by Vatican II in response to the signs of the times. All the vigilance of our faith will be required to avoid stifling the process uselessly on the one hand, and on the other to prevent ecclesial differences from solidifying into walls of separation. Nowadays, too, efforts are being redoubled to reevaluate the content of our faith for accommodation to the modern mentality, or to demonstrate the importance of service to the world in the task of evangelization. Here again all the vigilance of faith is called for — to forward the efforts on the one hand, and on the other to ensure that the mystery of Christ is faithfully transmitted.

The kind of vigilance demanded in the evangelization of our actual world calls for daring in the first place. To be in the actual world and to witness true Catholicity, the Church everywhere needs a radical change, which has scarcely yet begun. The shockwave engendered by Vatican II still awaits the proper results; much courage and imagination will be needed to accomplish necessary reforms. Individual churches will not bear witness to Church unity unless they develop a reciprocal exchange of life and energy; unless dialogue and intercommunion govern the growth of their interior life.

Our initiation to vigilance in the eucharistic celebration

A primary function of the Christian liturgy is to rescue Christians from their torpor, to rouse them from the sleep where they always run the risk of being blanketed in security. It is now all the more necessary, because the modern world in which Christians like others are immersed certainly does not tend to develop the vigilance of faith.

Yesterday, in a Christianized world, it was possible to be content with reminding the faithful of the rules to be observed in their moral conduct. The air they breathed was, in principle at least, impregnated by the faith. Today that is not so. Every influence in the surrounding world turns people, Christians as much as anyone else, to the search for security. Everything makes them blind to the mystery of human liberty in its daily confrontation with the unforeseeable in human history. So then, it is essential that the eucharistic celebration, and above all the Liturgy of the Word, should provide the basis for permanent initiation into the vigilance of faith.

2. The Christian Sense of Time

Today, as in the past, man's natural tendency is to attempt to deny the passage of time, which is synonymous with insecurity. He wants to reject the concept of an *event*, with all its suggestions of the unexpected and unforeseeable. He is for accepting only what he can tame and master. When "traditional" man, who was powerless over nature, sought escape from the fluidity of time he took refuge in cosmic cycles where he could be a ritual participant, and where the stability of the "sacral" would supplant profane time.

Modern man reacts against the alienation involved in such procedures, and challenges time itself. No longer is there any necessity for recourse to the "sacral": it is even deleterious. Thanks to developments in science and technology, and to the mastery over nature which this has meant, man can confront time on its own ground, determined to meet its challenge of insecurity. Henceforth time and the future belong to him.

This means, inevitably, that we are faced with a serious question. Is not the emergence of faith in the history of human spiritual endeavor bound up with an estimate of time and history, for which modern man, not without reason, can have little sympathy? If there is to be a Christian view of time it must be evaluated according to the needs of modern men. Otherwise our religion is liable to meet the same fate as those of history.

The linear time of Jewish man

For Jewish man any attempt to ignore or deny time was unrealistic. Human existence is so burdened with meaninglessness and death that escape or self-deception become impossible. The event, good or bad, success or failure, is invariably unexpected, unforeseeable. Is not this, Jewish man asked himself, evidence that it is God's way *par excellence* of coming to men? Israel was in fact convinced by her historical experience that the event is the veritable epiphany of God. For him, seen as the Totally-Other, everything has meaning. But his standards are not ours. He leads his people according to his own fashion; he liberates and he chastises. He is the God who intervenes in the life of his people, the God of Abraham, Isaac and Jacob, the God of Exodus, but also the God of the Babylonian exile.

In such a view the mythical events of creation are removed from the sacral domain of Time and Space, and become history in their turn. On the first day God created. But he does not cease to create; the universe always hangs upon the creative benevolence of the all-powerful Master of our destiny. Like every man, Jewish man lives his life in search of salvation, but the salvation he awaits will come from God at some future date. God is the Savior of man, and in the salvation offered by him, the object of man's hope, man must somehow cooperate. One day the decisive intervention by Yahweh will take place, and then the "last times" will have begun. In the final salvation the present state of things will be supplanted by a new heaven and a new earth. Once for all the ambiguity of present time will be surmounted; death and suffering will be no more; the time of insecurity will have passed. The reward of those faithful to the covenant will be terrestrial happiness of a stable and enduring nature.

Christ and the inauguration of the last times

Jewish eschatology of course, from a closer viewpoint, tends to undervalue time; because the "last times" mean the end of history. Their realism in estimating the present becomes utopianism where the future is concerned. The fundamental insecurity into

which man is plunged by profane time remains in their estimate
an abnormal condition, from which he will be delivered by the
salvific intervention of God. And so time is, in this sense, under-
valued, even though it be the means *par excellence* of coming
to recognition of the Totally-Other God.

The appearance of Jesus of Nazareth meant that Jewish
eschatology was shaken to its roots. Jesus declared himself "Son
of Man"; but he did not resemble in the slightest the messianic
figure suggested by Daniel. He is the son of Mary; his origin is
known, and he participates fully in the common lot here below.
He asserts that he is the promised Messiah, that the Kingdom is
inaugurated. But there is no indication of that cosmic drama
which, according to Jewish eschatology, will definitively establish
the people of Yahweh in earthly happiness. On the contrary: the
culmination of Jesus' earthly career is an ignominious death on
the cross. What attitude could one take? Reject the concept of
salvation? No, the Jews preferred not to recognize their Messiah.

Those who did recognize him, who believed the Risen One
had vanquished death on the cross, came gradually to redefine
Jewish eschatology in a radical manner. If the Day of Yahweh,
so much longed for, was realized by the historic intervention of
Jesus, then the "last times," far from being the end of history,
rather marked its beginning in the real sense.

It is important to recognize that with Christ the prehistory of
salvation ends, and salvation history in the true sense begins. In
him is found the spiritual principle which directs salvation history; because it is in him that man finally finds the power of
active cooperation in what is gratuitously offered by God. Death
was conquered on his own territory by acceptance of the death
on the cross. Time at last gets a full valuation. The dilemma in
which it held man prisoner is fully resolved by the mysterious
joining of God and man in the person of the Savior.

The time of the Church a time of increase

Once Christ has come, a future becomes really possible. By

being linked with the First Born of the new creation, all men are called to active cooperation in the building of the Kingdom. In Christ all has been accomplished; but yet all remains to be done. The foundation has been definitively laid; our task is to build the edifice. "What has been accomplished" is always the source of "what is to be accomplished." Ever since the resurrection of Christ eschatology becomes involved with present time, and guarantees for it true fulfillment. So far from canceling history it gives history its true shape. When the Body of Christ attains perfect stature, death will be finally vanquished, and salvation history will know the time of its accomplishment.

The event, for the Christian, takes on a special significance. It is the point of encounter between the human and the divine. God and man become partners in a common history; but it is only in Jesus Christ that this extraordinary adventure becomes possible for us. In the insistent language of Saint Paul we must "put on the Lord Jesus Christ." All the moments of a Christian's life take on a character that is unique and irreversible: "salvation is now nearer than the moment when we first believed." Thus all moments are moments when we are required to "awake from our sleep."

Such a view of salvation history does not shut out consideration of the enterprise of civilization. On the contrary it includes that, in very positive fashion. Active cooperation by the adoptive son of the Father in salvation history obviously requires active cooperation in the shaping of merely secular history, with full recognition of its profane character. To exercise one's 'filial' function necessarily means correct exercise of one's 'creatural' function.

Mission the principal task of salvation history

In the history of the primitive community we may obtain an excellent insight into the Christian concept of time. The intervention of Christ in history meant that Jewish eschatology was thoroughly reversed, but it was only gradually that Christians became aware of this. At Jerusalem, after Pentecost, the apostles firmly believed that the Parousia was imminent. One condition however was necessary before the Lord could be revealed in glory: the gospel must be preached to every nation. Saint Paul above all shared this conviction. Throughout the greater portion of his missionary life he thought the evangelization of the nations was something within the power of the first Christian generation. He hoped to be still alive when the Lord returned in glory. Little by little he came to realize the true dimensions of the Church's mission: there would be work for others besides him.

After twenty centuries of Christianity the mission is still at its beginning. The world of the white man has been thoroughly penetrated by the faith; but where other centers of human habitation are concerned the surface has been no more than scratched. Everything remains to be done. Yet, in the long course of human history since the beginning, what do twenty centuries signify? Today, when we have a clearer understanding of how closely the evangelization of the world is linked to this planet's hominization, there is no reason to be surprised that the Christian view of history should be directly concerned with the process of civilization. Universal mission is a long, long task. Its dimensions indicate the dimensions of the cooperation which God expects from man in the realization of his plan for salvation.

The Eucharist, a historic stage in salvation history

In the Christian concept of time the Eucharist plays a primary role. In fact, in the deepest sense, it is the focus of encounter between eschatology and present time. In the image dear to our Eastern brethren, eucharistic celebration means bringing heaven to earth. The Risen Jesus becomes present among his own; he gives himself to them in a meal of union. The mass is the most intense anticipation imaginable, in the present, of the future. In it "all is accomplished" takes on a special meaning: it enables us to reach the utmost limits in our estimate of time. For Saint Paul it was the proclamation in act of Christ's victory over death "until he comes again." That is to say, until the time of fulfillment.

There is another reason why eucharistic celebration ought to occupy a central place in the Christian's life. It establishes a very deep awareness of his function as active cooperator in salvation history. Here, at this source, mission will be constantly renewed. It is through the Eucharist that the Christian becomes capable of shedding the instinctive prejudices man has about time. Gradually, by this means, he is led to become a true partner with God in the realization of the divine plan for the universe.

FIRST WEEK OF ADVENT

I. Isaiah 4:2-6*   Two distinct poems are combined in this read-
1st reading   ing, a song concerning the "Remnant" of Zion
Monday   gathered round the future messianic "seed"
                         (vv. 2-3), and a second piece composed
doubtless after the exile (vv. 4-6), which is concerned with the
future restoration of Jerusalem.

a) The mood of the first poem is that of Isaiah 9:5-6. A royal
infant is just born, Hezekiah (716–687; cf. 2 K 18-20) no doubt.
Isaiah describes him as a seed of the Davidic tree and sees him
as the ornament and glory of his people. But there is a precipitous turn of events and the prophet fears an imminent
catastrophe (doubtless the fall of Samaria). Not until the heavens
are serene again will the glory of the future king be manifested
to the small group who survive the disaster. Only after a purifying trial will messianic glory and prosperity become actual. To
convince his contemporaries he uses the "Remnant" image, taking
it from Amos (Am 3:12; 5:15; 9:8-10; cf. Is 6:13; 4:3; 10:19-21),
but giving it his own doctrinal bias. He stresses for instance the
holiness of the Remnant, and considers this a participation in the
very life of God (cf. Is 6:3, 13).

b) But Isaiah's prophecy was not immediately fulfilled.
Hezekiah was not the king awaited, and the threat of Assyrian
armies did not bring Jerusalem to the desired purification. Jewish
tradition then tended to project its fulfillment into the future.
They transformed essential details into messianic titles. "Seed"
denoted the future Messiah (Jr 23:5-6; Zp 3:8; Jr 33:14-16) and
the "Remnant" the faithful reunited in the people of the last
times (Jr 23:3; 31:7; 50:20; Mi 2:12-13).

c) Not content with reading the poem in a messianic light,
Isaiah's disciples added an interpretative piece (Is 4:4-6). Was

---

*See First Sunday of Advent for commentary on Is 2:1-5

not the intervening fall of Jerusalem (587) the beginning of the purification prophesied? There is no glorious king any more; but the very glory of God will confer on the *future Zion* its new adornment (v. 5). There are no more inhabitants in the city; but shall the survivors not find there one day rest and paradisal peace (vv. 5-6)? The disciples however were too optimistic in thinking that Zion's purifying trial would revive the faith of its people. Today we know the path by which *God's glory* came to men (Jn 1:14) and by what slow process it transforms all humanity (Rm 8:18-25).

This prophecy expresses Israel's religious choice with great emphasis. Under the inspiration of her prophets she deliberately opts for a religion of salvation (a concept borrowed by Greek gnosticism and the mystery-religions) by contrast with what one might call "courage-to-be" religion (Stoicism, modern thought).

Is it only coincidence that has expressed the Christian faith within the framework of a religion of salvation? The choice of such a religion safeguards the priority of God and acknowledges his initiative on behalf of mankind. Why shouldn't there be, in cultures and beliefs less receptive to the idea of salvation, much of value to be gained for the expression of the Christian faith and its being understood by the modern world?

II. Matthew 8:5-11
Gospel
Monday

This passage is taken from a section which the evangelist devotes to a series of miracles by Jesus. Previously Matthew has featured Christ as a teacher (Mt 5-7), and now he presents him as healer (Mt 8-9). The miracles are in groups of three, each being concluded by an episode of more doctrinal import.

The first group gives us the cure of three types, hitherto excluded from the Jewish liturgical assembly, whom Christ, by healing power, on the other hand includes: the leper (Mt 8:1-4), the Gentile (our passage), and the woman (Mt 8:14-15).

The cure of the centurion's servant then has to be understood against the background of a gathering of all men, of whatever origin.

In describing the miracle Matthew speaks of a centurion, of a Gentile that is, whereas John mentions a royal official (who could have been a Jew: Jn 4:46-54). The detail is revealing and indicates the standpoint of the first evangelist. Jesus has come down from the mount of beatitudes where he has set up the new assembly and immediately he makes this actual by summoning Gentiles as well as Jews.

Matthew goes even further by underlining the contrast between the attitude of the Jew (vv. 1-4) who was cured, and the Gentile. The latter it seems can bear witness to his faith more easily than the Jew who is concerned with numerous legal obligations (Lv 13-14). It is not sufficient to be cleansed by Jesus. He must present himself to the clergy and observe the legal purifications. Here we see those Judeo-Christians in the early stages of the Jerusalem community who were concerned in equal measure about the law and the gospel.

The Gentile, on the other hand, has no such worries. His faith recognizes the power of Christ's word even at a distance (Ps 106/107:20), and is thus more remarkable. There is no question even of touching the sick person; it is faith in the omnipotence of the Word, regardless of ritual observance.

Clearly enough, Matthew's narrative is designed to furnish arguments for Christians of Gentile origin who had to encounter Jewish criticism because of their disregard for the prescriptions of the law.

There was a Jewish universalism, of which Third Isaiah (cf. Is 66:18-21) is a strong witness, but too often it was merely a matter of cultural annexation, winning recognition for the legal and moral system of Jewry. All in all Jewish proselytism had been a matter of swelling the ranks of the chosen people and increasing the temple offerings (cf. Mt 23:15).

With Christ universalism gets a totally new meaning. The basis for man's response to the universal plan of divine love is no longer a moral or cultural structure, but divine sonship. Moral and religious attitudes are the immediate fruit of the filial "yes" pronounced by a man: they do not any longer produce that "yes."

The Kingdom inaugurated by him is truly universal because all men, by virtue of their adoptive sonship acquired in Christ and renewed in the Eucharist, are enabled to contribute to its building. In this perspective all men are really equal. No longer will ethnic or moral differences be the decisive factor in membership: privilege that is based on race, on culture, or on intelligence, has been done away with.

III. Isaiah 11:1-10
1st Reading

The commentary on this reading will be found at the second Sunday of Advent, p. 47.

Tuesday

How are we to explain the fact that the bible speaks so often of peace and presents the future Messiah as the prince of peace; that papal teachings have repeatedly emphasized this point, and yet the mass of the faithful remain uninfluenced? Peace is simply the thrust of all humanity towards a greater dimension of humanity. Men today realize quite well that their aspirations can only be fulfilled on an international scale; that without peace we cannot have either science, or democracy, or justice. It is thus the more difficult to understand the indifference among Christians to Church and government involvements at the nerve-centers of war and oppression. Can it be that Christians are concerned only with peace of heart and conscience, not with sociological or international peace?

One must admit that large societies do have a tendency to lull individual members and atrophy any inclinations towards taking a stand. And in a society so centralized as the Church, those at the bottom are disinterested in the stands taken by authority at the top because they do not feel a responsibility. In this area reform of structure is an urgent necessity. On the whole however Christian indifference is best explained by insufficient information, or inability to analyze the situation properly. Unless the gospel is thoroughly analyzed and made precise it will not lead a man to active involvement. Too many Christians are unaware of such insights, or reject them with all their implications. They cannot take conscientious objectors seriously, or antimilitarists. They are disturbed when priests take attitudes in this domain that they consider too "political," as if indeed any human being in our day could possibly avoid being a member of his society. It is only by means of such involvement that the gospel doctrine of peace can become really efficacious, that the Prince of peace can really inaugurate his kingdom.

IV. Luke
10:21-24
Gospel
Tuesday

Many problems for the exegete are posed regarding the authenticity, unity and doctrine of this "jubilation hymn" of Jesus. The first portion (Lk 10:21-22) is quite like Matthew's version (Mt 11:25-27); but this is not so in the second (compare Lk 10:23-24 and Mt 11:28-29). Luke appears to have been troubled by the great number of semitisms in the version Matthew transmits and preferred another conclusion taken from a totally different context.

We have then two distinct parts. Christ first gives thanks to the Father for what they are to one another (v. 21a), and for the mission he has received of revealing all to the "little ones" (vv. 21b-22). Turning to them he invites them (according to Matthew) to enter into communion with him, or (according to Luke) reveals to them their privilege in seeing what they see (vv. 23-24).

a) The biblical background of the hymn is revealing. What Christ is actually using is the hymn of Daniel 2:23, where Daniel and the three "children" are confronted by the Babylonian "sages." Because of their prayers (Dn 2:18), the mystery of the Kingdom will be "revealed" (the word, which we find again in Luke 10:21, is Daniel's) to the former exclusively.

Christ then compares the situation between his disciples and the sages of Judaism to that between the "children" and the sages of Nebuchadnezzar. He is proposing to open his kingdom to a very special category of "poor," the ignorant that is, in spite of the contempt of Jewish doctors for such people (cf. Is 29:14; 1 Co 1:19).

b) Elsewhere in Daniel (7:14) the Ancient of Days commits "everything" to the Son of man. Christ, who claims the title Son of man (Mt 24:36), relies on this text to "bless" the Ancient of Days (under the true name of Father) for having "given everything" to him, that is, a "power over all things" (Mt 28:18; Jn 5:22; 13:3; 17:2) and a "knowledge" of the Father to reveal to men (v. 22). Christ then is the King. And at the same time he is also the Revealer of the Kingdom to the little ones, who, in grouping themselves round him, can know God and constitute with his Son a community distinct from "those who do not know God" — the pagans, that is, in the first place (Jr 10:25), and then the Jewish sages (v. 21; cf. Jn 12:39-50).

c) Happy then are those "little ones" who can see what many prophets and sages seek to unravel and understand (vv. 23-24; cf. 1 P 1:11-12; Mt 13:16-17). The prophecies of Isaiah 30:19-26 (preceding reading) and 42:18-20 are fulfilled to the letter. The blind become here the "little ones" and the ignorant. But once part of the Remnant, surrounding the Son of Man, they know the Father with the very knowledge of the Son, and become wiser than the wise and learned, more perceptive than the prophets and the kings.

If the little ones and the ignorant could know what the

learned and the prophets did not, it shows that the teaching of the faith need not be rational. No wonder then that the "little ones" might know God better than the single-dimensioned rational society to whom they were the untaught masses. No wonder, moreover, that they astonished that society by not hesitating to propose a community style of living which respected each individual person!

V. Isaiah
25:6-10a
1st reading
Wednesday

Chapters 24-27 of Isaiah, a post-exilic compilation, was long thought to be made up of heterogeneous materials. However recent commentaries, and certain discoveries like the Qumran scroll of Isaiah, tend to favor its unity and date its composition in the 5th or 4th century. The most attractive hypothesis regards the ensemble as a sort of ritual comprising three liturgies of the Word. The second of these liturgies would consist of a prophetic proclamation (24: 21-23), followed by a song of acclamation (25:1-5), then a second prophetic proclamation (25:6-8) concluded by the classic finale for prophetic readings "Yahweh has said so" (cf. Is 1:20; 21:17; 22:5; 24:3; 40:5; 58:14) and accompanied by a thanksgiving (25:9-10). The whole collection proclaims and celebrates the Kingship of Yahweh. The first reading and its acclamation announce the victory of King-Yahweh over his enemies; the second with its song (our reading) describes the sumptuous repast for King-Yahweh's enthronement (vv. 6-8) and the acclamations of the crowd (vv. 9-10).

a) Very often in the East, and particularly in the bible, a banquet is part of the enthronement ritual and publicly demonstrates the king's power (Est 1:1-4; 1 K 10:5; 1 S 16:11; Dn 5 etc.). It is also a meal of alliance where only friends and allies are invited. To partake in the banquet of the king is to set up obligations on both sides, and a solidarity which nothing can undermine (1 K 2:7; 2 S 9:6-8). Such sumptuous banquets sometimes followed victory over an enemy, with purloined victuals figuring prominently on the menu.

It is such procedures (banquet of royal investiture, of alliance and of victory) which the prophet transfers to the ceremonial of *Yahweh's Kingship.* In comparison with earthly kings God is not inferior and the magnificence of his table surpasses anything that could be offered at the time (v. 6). Truly, God is worthy to be king of the future. The meal he offers is a *victory banquet:* and the enemy whose defeat is celebrated is none other than Death (vv. 7-8; cf. Rv 21:4; 1 Co 15:26). Death in this context of course is no more than a symbol. A day will come nevertheless when the eucharistic banquet, which enthrones Christ in his lordship, will be a victory too over death and an entry into immortality (Jn 6:51).

b) Finally, the banquet of royal investiture for Yahweh is a *meal of alliance* and friendship. Already reflected over the city are the glory of Yahweh and the splendor of his banquet (vv. 6, 7, 10 — theme of the mountain); but it is the wish of the king that an alliance be contracted with all the peoples of the world (vv. 6-7). The author could scarcely have conceived such a universal alliance had he not benefited by the reflections of Third-Isaiah about the role of Zion (Is 56:6-8; 66:18-21). And when we recall the conditions of ritual purity demanded at Jewish meals, which excluded all pagans, it is evident that many tabus had to be challenged in order to envisage a messianic abundance offered to all peoples.

Besides the displeasing aspects of this victory meal, let us recognize in it the laws of the eucharistic meal where God offers a share in his friendship to those around his table; where the celebration is for the victory over no enemy except death itself; and where is particularly commemorated Christ's victory over death.

VI. Matthew   This passage amounts to a summary of the
    15:29-37   good deeds of Jesus the wonder-worker. The
    Gospel   synoptic tradition preserved a great many
    Wednesday   such representative sketches characterized by
                    stock phrases ("the multitude," catalogues of
cures) which celebrate the *miracles of the Messiah*. Matthew
often reproduces them in his gospel (Mt 9:35; 14:14; 15:30-31;
19:2; 21:14) and even attributes one such celebration to Jesus
himself (Mt 11:5).

The origin of these summaries, probably prior to the compilation of the gospels, is easy to explain. After Pentecost the
apostles proclaim the decisive event of their kerygma: Christ,
put to death, has risen and has become Lord and lives by his
Spirit in the community of his faithful. This message however had
to be conveyed to particular listeners. Their concept of the
Messiah's reign would be in terms of inaugurating the "last
times," times of peace and rest (cf. previous reading), of victory
over evil and sickness (Is 29:18-19; 35:5-6; 61:1; all three
passages directly inspiring this gospel). The answer of the gospel
is to present the paschal mystery of Christ, and his elevation to
lordship, as the fulfillment of such hopes. Hence the biblical
inspiration of these summaries of the miracles of Christ.

However, gradually in primitive tradition such unduly material
interpretations of the Kingdom are superseded. Recitals of
miracles will continue, but with the purpose of revealing the
person of Jesus himself and arousing the necessary faith in
his word.

Among the later stages of synoptic thinking on the miracles of
Christ, especially noteworthy is that which changes miracle into
dialogue between God and man. In testing the faith of his inter-
locutors, Christ rejects the idea of a miracle which would be
nothing but a display of divine power: he means it to be an
occasion for dialogue, meeting and alliance. Another stage pre-

sents miracles as signs not of the power of Jesus, but of his humiliation as the suffering Servant (Mt 8:17). So a miracle here no longer signifies Christ's power but rather his solidarity with the poorest. We must take this view into consideration when commenting on the gospel of the day.

VII. Isaiah   The passage belongs to the liturgical ensemble,
    26:1-6   Is 24-27, like Wednesday's. It seems to be a
  1st reading   description of the entrance procession (cf.
   Thursday   v. 2) for the third liturgy. The theme in any
                 case is similar to that of the whole collection,
the victory of the symbolic city of Zion over the symbolic city of Evil (vv. 5-6, cf. Lk 1-52).

a) The theme of *struggle between two cities* is ubiquitous in the bible, from the building of Babel (Gn 11) down to the final and decisive conflict between terrestrial Babylon and the heavenly Jerusalem (Rv 18-21). In Isaiah 26 the warring cities have no geographic reality or any indication of identity.

There is deep doctrinal significance in this literary device. Following Isaiah's poem "Jerusalem" and "Babylon" will continue to have histories, but independently of the concrete lot of the Palestinian and Mesopotamian capitals. Paradoxically, Christ will be able to proclaim the fall of geographic Jerusalem (Mt 24) without implying an end to its history, for that will be continued by the Church. Already in this poem as successor to geographic Zion a spiritual community is announced, which is composed of citizens with origins in Babylon as well as Jerusalem (Is 56:6-8; 66:18-21).

b) So the prophet demands from his contemporaries an account of their citizenship. Does their culture and ethos reflect the light of the spiritual Jerusalem, or the civilization of Babylon, where man is but an instrument (Rv 18:9-19)? All that is Babylonian in the world will have an end (vv. 5-6), and the victory of the "poor," the victims of that culture (v. 6), is inevitable.

c) The theme of *Yahweh, the Rock* of the new city is also discernible in the reading. *Historical Jerusalem* was built on a rock (Is 30:29, the "stone" which is laid bare in the present mosque); but the solidity of this foundation (Ps 125:1-2) would not suffice to make it impregnable. There is an ancient image in Jewish tradition which compares God's fidelity to a rock (Dt 32:4). So would the book of Psalms and that of Isaiah celebrate the new Jerusalem, founded on God's fidelity, on Yahweh-the-Rock, a much more solid foundation than the rock of Zion (Is 28:16; 30:29; Pss 17/18:3, 32; 60/61:4 etc.). The Yahweh-the-Rock theme then is messianic insofar as it reflects divine fidelity and the solidity of the alliance on which the new structure will rest.

Curiously enough scripture, though invariably opposed to the concept of cities, has always seen eschatological fulfillment against the background of a city. Babylon was always attacked, as the *megalopolis par excellence*, but we are always hearing of a new Jerusalem.

In our day, faced as we are with the likelihood that twenty years hence two-thirds of humanity will live in cities of more than 100,000, the scriptural standpoint has perhaps a particular relevance. There is sufficient distance and detachment to gain a proper critical perspective of the city, but salvation is seen nevertheless in terms of the city, a city that will be organized by God. Two comments seem appropriate.

The first is that Babylon is always present in certain contemporary cities. Cities for example that favor middle class expansion at the expense of the less privileged. Or capitals that drain the life blood of a nation for their own growth, and shape a whole people into their stereotype. Or again cities manipulated by unscrupulous power interests where goods and services are altogether utilitarian, where the agencies of culture and relaxation become instruments of corruption. Today your Christian is a citizen of one or other such Babylon. This faith, if it is more than a merely sociological faith, should make him realize that urbanization means more than assembling materials and builders. It means making such agglomerations places of human encounter, of brotherly communion, where a man can satisfy the elementary needs for silence, for congenial living quarters, for work, for communication, for leisure and culture. If we work towards these ends we are transforming Babylon into the new Jerusalem. We are demonstrating our realization that the eternal Jerusalem must be reached by means of terrestrial cities.

In the second place we must realize that in order to reach Jerusalem the problem of Babylon must be solved. To solve it, to provide the love that will transform our Babylons into cities of communion, urban experimentation will never be sufficient. The love must derive its essence and energy from communion with Jesus Christ. The Christian's business then is to make this original contribution to the development of modern cities.

World history, in biblical terms, begins in a garden (Gn 2), and passes to a desert (Ex 14). It is however to be consummated in a city (Rv 21). We do not prepare ourselves for citizenship of the heavenly Jerusalem by shunning involvement with the modern city.

VIII. Matthew From the time of its primitive redaction, in
7:21, 24-27 the pre-gospel stage, chapter 7 of the Sermon
Gospel on the Mount comprised three warnings (vv.
Thursday 1-2, 15, and 21), each followed by an illus-
tration (7:3-5; 16-20 and 24-27 respectively).
The warning of verse 21 ("put into practice") is illustrated by the parable of the two houses (vv. 24-27). Verses 22-23, not found in Luke's version (Lk 6:46-49), are a pointless overloading of the original text and are taken from another context.

The homogeneity of the piece depends upon the words "to do"

or "put into practice." In verse 21 it is necessary "to do" the will
of the Father, in verses 24 and 26 to "put into practice" "the
words I have just spoken to you." Likewise the principle
enunciated in verse 21 distinguishes "saying" and "doing" (theme
of the parable of the two sons, Mt 21:28-30), while the parable
of the two houses (vv. 24-27) stresses the opposition between
"understanding" and "doing." Such contrasts seem to indicate
that the structure of verse 21 "it is not . . . but it is" (cf. Mt
5:20; 18:3), and the expression "Father who is in heaven" (Mt
10:32-33; 12:50; 15:13, etc.) are a reworking of the text by
Matthew himself.

The parable of the two houses is an excellent example of the
catechetical preoccupations of Matthew. He tends to cull from
Jesus' words everything with a practical application to living.
Here we have the mentality of the primitive community, which
reacted strongly against any suggestion of formalism in the
Kingdom, and against a faith devoid of works (Jm 1:22-25;
Mt 5:17). This practical, moralizing tendency explains the subsequent insertion of verses 22-23. To the teaching of Christ
(Lk 13:26-27) Matthew gives a particular emphasis, no doubt
with certain members of the primitive community in mind. These
abounded in charisms, but lacked the most elementary moral
"practice" (we recall the situation in Corinth, 1 Co 12-13). He
is reacting against the legal formalism of certain Jewish groups
and the gnostic speculations of certain pagan ones. There can be
no Christian religion without involvement. For him the image of
the *rock* stresses the concrete aspect of commitment.

Christians are never weaned from the gospel. It is always there
when they want it, and in its name they can speak of justice, of
hunger, of peace. They do however lack the concrete analytic
knowledge that enables people trained in the Marxist system to
become seriously and actively involved. Among the people of

God there are many prophetic voices raised in the name of the gospel (v. 22), but they shun political involvement because they are not analytically trained and their excuse is that the Church as such has nothing to do with politics. They do the Kingdom no service (v. 24). They do not build upon the rock, or understand how solid is our foundation on God our rock.

IX. Isaiah
29:17-24
1st reading
Friday

There were certainly two stages in the compilation of this prophecy.

a) In the first, Isaiah forecasts an early setback for those politicians who wished to involve Samaria and Judah in the anti-Assyrian coalition led by Egypt (725). The poor and the humble will survive the disaster and constitute the nucleus of the future people. Here, as in Isaiah 14:32, the *Remnant and the poor* are identified: they are regarded as the victims of contemporary social and political conditions (Is 3:14-15; 10:1-2; 11:4; 32:7). Isaiah's poor tend to rely on God while the rich trust their own resources; and the social and political domains are coloured by his religious conception. The "poor" will constitute a new spiritual society, distinct from the national community of Israel (vv. 19-20).

b) In a second piece, certainly postexilic (v. 17), the contrast between the lot of the political counselors and that of the poor is described in another figure. A proud Lebanon is reduced to a simple orchard and an orchard raised to the rank of forest. Isaiah's poor become the deaf and blind miraculously healed (v. 18), and the political counselors become the unjust accusers of the poor before the tribunals (v. 21). Imagery has been modified, but the idea is the same. The future *Remnant* will gather together those who trust in Yahweh, and the poor will have first place because they open themselves to God's intervention.

X. Matthew
9:27-31
Gospel
Friday

The cure of the two blind men is actually related twice by Matthew (9:27-31 and 20:29-34), and the interpretation we give the episode will depend on the account we follow, primitive tradition or the evangelist.

a) The accounts have some resemblances. In both the blind men hail not alone a wonderworker but the Son of David himself. We find ourselves in the climate of messianic expectation that must have been dominant in Palestine just then. Not only do the unfortunate men want to be cured; they see in their cure the fulfillment of prophecies (especially Is 29:18, today's first reading), and a guarantee that the "last times" are inaugurated.

b) Matthew 9:29-31 stresses the misgiving of Jesus lest the cure be interpreted in terms of naive popular messianism, as a sign of the coming of the new David. This could arouse an enthusiasm which would have nothing in common with the faith required by Isaiah for membership of the messianic people (Mk 1:42-45).

The principal difference in the narratives concerns precisely Christ's question regarding the *faith* of the blind man. A little earlier (9:22) Matthew has stressed the part of faith in salvation, with a view to the great discourse in chapter 10 on the manner in which preachers of the gospel should act.

Jesus puts the faith of the two men who importune him to the test. At first he continues his way without heeding their outcry, and then questions them at the end of it. Is the real object of their faith his person and his power (v. 28)? The faith he demands concerns the messianic character of his action, and the exercise of this faith in at least one of the healings foretold in Isaiah 29:18 and 35:5 indicates that it is the faith understood by the prophet, that is, a strong adherence to the new religious community which is composed essentially of the poor gathered round a spiritual Messiah and free from the political leanings of ancient Israel.

The theme of the blind enables us to link the day's two readings. In the first the theme clarifies the composition of the messianic people; in the second what is insisted upon in the healing is the necessary attitude for membership of the Remnant, faith in the divine power vested in Jesus Christ.

The eucharistic assembly is a profession of faith by the "poor in spirit," that is by those participating in a human activity, of which Christ alone can reveal the meaning and which finds its fulfillment in him.

XI. Isaiah   The Isaian authorship of this oracle is very
30:19-21, 23-26 much debated; it is difficult to form an
1st reading   opinion. On the hypothesis that it has been
Saturday   largely glossed from a Second-Isaian source
                 we may perhaps presume that the primitive
material is genuinely Isaian.

a) The people of Jerusalem will encounter a period of distress and anguish (v. 20) but it will not last long. Like a blind man suddenly seeing, or a deaf one suddenly hearing,* they will see their God and hear his voice of encouragement on the *road to conversion* (vv. 20-21). Conversion is seen as the abandonment of the dumb idols ridiculed by Second-Isaiah (Is 40:12-21; 41: 6-7; 44:9-20), and entry into paradisal happiness (vv. 23-26), described also in Second-Isaian terms (Is 41:17-20; 43:16-21).

b) Placed as it is immediately after the testament of Isaiah which lists all his grievances (Is 30:8-18), the oracle seems to be a corrective giving *reasons for hope.* Very harsh terms are used to describe the coming catastrophe, but the author dreams of a kingdom free of every kind of evil, famine, sickness, military violence, social injustice. Here Isaiah is the most human and universal prophet of hope. But he does lay down conditions for approach to this Kingdom: belief in the first place that God

---

*Second-Isaiah gives blindness and deafness a symbolic significance (Is 42: 18-20); but the symbolism was already indicated in First-Isaiah (Is 6:9-10).

alone can build it, then sufficient poverty to realize that man cannot gain such happiness by his own resources (cf. the idolatry of v. 22).

From this reading we remember especially the profound association between man's return to moral balance through conversion and nature's return to its original harmony and abundance. The bible teaches that there is a deep communion between man and nature, sometimes to the naive extent of asserting that a fault committed by man immediately affects nature, but the teaching that man cannot be saved without the cosmos is basic, and right. Not only is the risen Lord in communion with the members of humanity; his power also irradiates nature, preparing it for the transfiguration to come (Rm 8).

This helps us to understand why the Advent liturgy is so urgent in its call for conversion and its yearning for the transformation of nature. It firmly conjoins the effort of the spiritual man who seeks for conversion and the research of the scientist who tries to dominate nature.

XII. Matthew 9:35 The mission discourse, of which today's gospel **and 10:1, 6-8** gives us the setting and provides the intro-
Gospel   duction, has been preserved in different tra-
Saturday   ditions. In Mark 6:7-11 we have a very brief account, that which is taken up in Luke 9:3-5 and associated with the mission of the Twelve. However, in Luke 10:2-16, we have a long version of the same discourse, associated with the mission of the seventy-two disciples. There Luke follows his usual practice of avoiding any over-preoccupation with the functions of the Twelve.

Matthew chooses to combine the two accounts and actually adds other items drawn for instance from the eschatological discourse. This procedure gives a new dimension to the original purpose of Christ. We are given a small treatise on general missiology rather the concrete occasion of Christ sending the Twelve throughout Galilee.

a) The discourse opens with the theme of *harvest* (cf. Mt 9:37-38; Lk 10:2; Jn 4:35-38). Like the fishermen whom he summoned to be fishers of men, Jesus invites the harvesters of grain to become spiritual harvesters.

This harvest image suggests the conclusion by God of human history and the inauguration by his judgment of the Kingdom of the last times (v. 7; cf. Am 9:13-15; Ps 125/126:5-6; Jl 4:13; Jr 5:17; Mt 13:28-39; Rv 14:15-16). The harvest has a dimension of judgment: the wheat is separated from the tares. Consequently it is not surprising that the harvesters are exposed to persecution; they will be lambs in the midst of wolves (Mt 10:16).

b) A more important consideration is Christ's own concept of himself as "rabbi" in his own country. Unlike the other rabbis who surround themselves with disciples in a school or at the gate of a town, he wants to be an itinerant rabbi. He will not wait for disciples to come to him, but will go to encounter them in their own life situation. He does not then propose to be like the temple clergy who accept money and sacrificial victims from the faithful without any concern for their salvation. Nor will he follow the example of the Pharisees who confine their attentions to the elite. His mission is to the "lost sheep" of Israel, lost and forgotten (v. 35). His disciples will not, like those of other rabbis, engage in discussions with him. He wants them to share his missionary wanderings and devote their attention to the abandoned sheep (vv. 36 and 10:1).

This is a totally new departure in rabbinic practice. At once the mission of Jesus becomes one of "pity" (v. 36) and mercy. It is directed to the poor, the sick, the sinners (vv. 7-8), "sheep without shepherds" (v. 36), whom priests, Pharisees and rabbis do not deign to notice.

c) Matthew differs from the other synoptics in giving us the names of the twelve apostles, not at the time of calling (Mk

3:16-19; Lk 6:14-16) but at the time of mission. He is more concerned about their mission than their calling, and by mentioning the apostolic group at the beginning of the missionary discourse he seems concerned to establish a connection between *apostolic collegiality* and *mission,* something that is also emphasized in Acts 2:14, Mark 1:36 and Luke 9:32.

d) Nevertheless the mission is to the sheep of *Israel* only: Jesus explicitly excludes Gentiles and Samaritans (vv. 5-6). Doubtless he is very conscious that as yet his messianism must be reserved for the chosen people. He reflects the contemporary mentality which placed the call to the Kingdom of Gentiles in the eschatological future, a gratuitous act of God. That he regarded the gathering of the nations as a matter for eschatological initiative by his Father is demonstrated by the fact that throughout the public life he did not concern himself with them (Lk 13:23-32; Mk 7:24-30). He is observing an economy of salvation that is "primarily for the Jews" (Rm 1:16), that Luke observes very scrupulously in the Acts. He describes the expansion of the Good News from Jerusalem and Judaea. Before messianism (and apostolic mission) could be extended to universal dimensions (Jn 12:20-23, 32) the purifying events of death and resurrection had to intervene.

It is evident that there has been a considerable progression in missionary awareness on the part of the Church and the apostles. Texts such as Matthew 10, for all that a theology of mission is being elaborated, remain as yet confined within the limits of Israel. Persecution will have to intervene before the apostles leave Jerusalem and go among the Diaspora. It remains true however that the Church is essentially missionary, that orientation towards the non-Christian world is part of her vocation. The eucharistic assembly is only meaningful when the assembled members are turned in that direction.

SECOND SUNDAY OF ADVENT

A. THE WORD

I. Isaiah 11:1-10 These verses are extracts from a prophecy of
1st reading   First-Isaiah concerning the future King of
1st cycle   Israel. It is not certain that verse 10 belonged
to the primitive poem; possibly it is part of
another passage (Is 11:10-16). The liturgy, however, attaches it
to the preceding poem in order to emphasize the theme of the
davidic tree.

a) It is customary in biblical literature to represent the ups
and downs of the royal dynasties by the image of a *tree*, at
times sturdy and flourishing, at times uprooted and reduced to
a mere shoot (v. 1; cf. Ez 27; Jg 9:7-16). Isaiah then may be
offering a solution which shows continuity in the dynasty of
David before it flourishes anew. (vv. 1 and 10). In any event,
the future King must pass through trial; he personally assumes
all the characteristics of the remnant.

b) The King, emerging from the test, will be invested by the
Spirit of God, who will give him six gifts, presented two by
two, one concerning obligations to God, the other obligations
to men (the Vulgate will add a seventh virtue: piety, doubling
the "Fear of Yahweh"; and initiating the later catalogue of seven
gifts). These virtues are those of his ancestors. The royal offspring is nourished with the same sap as the ancestral tree: the
intelligence and wisdom of Solomon (1 K 3:14-15), the strength
of David, the fear of the patriarchs (Gn 15:1-7; 18:27; 28:17).

These extraordinary qualities of the future King will therefore
be a gift of the Spirit of God. For Isaiah, the Spirit of God is
first and foremost the mysterious reality of the wind, faithful
servant of the designs of God, expression of his violent anger
against the enemies of his people (Is 17:12-14; 27:6-9; 30:27-30;
33:11). The force of the "breath of Yahweh" will be revealed

47

above all in the new Exodus which will gather together the dispersed "Remnant" (Is 11:15-16; 4:4; cf. 41:16). However Isaiah has already begun to spiritualize this mysterious force. He sees there the work of the Spirit of God which opposes all that is flesh (Is 31:3; cf. Is 40:3-8). This force will establish the ideal Messiah as it established King David (1 S 16:13; 2 S 23:2). The intervention of the Spirit will place the King in the context of the new Exodus and will confer on him those prerogatives which enable him to accomplish the salvific plan of God.

c) The King adds one important personal virtue to those of his ancestors: *justice* (vv. 3-5), guaranteeing the people their rights (Ps 71/72, which serves as the gradual verse to this reading), and realizing the ideal of social justice formulated by Isaiah himself (Is 1:15-17, 21-25). The evolution of this notion of justice in the course of time is worth noting. Isaiah is not content with a simple distribution of goods according to need, or with simple retribution according to right; this justice must be manifest among the weakest, the poorest especially. It is rather the image of God's justice, which transcends the distributive justice of men, and seeks pardon and justification for the weakest. It is doubtless for this reason that justice is an element of the knowledge of God (v. 9), since its mystery involves the very plan of God.

Isaiah's naive hopes in the young King Hezekiah rendered great service to messianism by insisting on the human character of the future Messiah. What he is saying in effect is that the Spirit of God, which had performed so many wonders in wind and storm and in a thousand other extraordinary ways at the time of the Exodus, is now contained and limited by human possibilities. No longer will God save mankind through the miraculous or sacred but through the liberty of one of mankind's own members. More than that: atavism and heredity no longer predominate in the character of this man; it matters little what he has from his father or great-grandfather. What matter are the answers to precise questions which will be put to him: social justice, peace among nations, those eternal problems which face mankind. Christ makes his davidic sonship relative when he declares himself, not through the quality of the royal blood in his veins, but by sharing this blood, on God's behalf, with all those who suffer with him for a better humanity. This is the blood he offers at communion in the Eucharist to all who live the same hope.

II. Isaiah
40:1-5, 9-11
1st reading
2nd cycle

The Jews of the 6th century, both those who remained in Palestine and those deported to Babylon, looked to the past with nostalgia and discerned in the ancient historical or prophetic traditions some sign of their coming liberation. A prophet appeared on the scene about the year 540, who proclaimed new prophecies, a sort of "resistance" literature. Aware of the campaigns led by Cyrus, King of the Medes, against the Babylonians, he gives hope and encouragement to his compatriots. But in order not to draw the attention of the Babylonians, he describes the future liberation in cryptic terms, borrowed for the most part from the vocabulary of Exodus.

Today's reading reproduces two of the three poems of this prophet, (vv. 3-5 and 6-8). It is worth noting that each begins and ends with a classical formula which alludes to the word of God (a voice . . . ; for the mouth of Yahweh has spoken . . . ; the word of our God remains forever). In these formulas, new to the scriptures, we see the beginnings of an attempt to spiritualize. No longer will God be physically manifested as in the vision of Is 6 or Ez 1-3: he will be a "Word," received and understood by the prophets.

a) The first prophecy is addressed especially to the "hearts" of the citizens of Jerusalem (v. 2), that is, in terms of Jewish anthropology, to their spirit, their faith.

The word of God commands the leaders of the exiled communities to seek out a *way* for Yahweh across the desert. Second-Isaiah alludes perhaps to the obligation laid on Jewish peasants of assisting Persian engineers in building a road through the desert east of the Jordan. He encourages them not to interfere with the work because this route can become for Yahweh the counterpart of the "Sacred Way" built by Babylon for the procession of the God Mardok. The latter had been accomplished by enormous feats of engineering (cf. v. 4). In any case, it is God's glory revealed to all mankind, that it will one day escort to Jerusalem (v. 5). The processions of Mardok on the Sacred way inaugurated the New Year of which he was the sacred King. However, the procession of Yahweh up to his temple consecrates not only the New Year, but the last days and the dominion of Yahweh over all creation (v. 5; cf. Pss 96/97; 98/99).

b) In the Greek version the messenger of *joy* has the title "evangelist," and Jesus when he asserts that he evangelizes the poor (Mt 11:5; cf. Mt 4:24) will claim that title. He will see his messianic ministry as one of salvation and joy (cf. Is 40:9), where John the Baptist and his followers only think of judgment and violence (Is 40:10, cited in Lk 7:18-23). It was possible for a reader to be misled by the poetic vocabulary of Second Isaiah, to see the coming of the Lord in its plentitude in the restoration of the historic Jerusalem. One needed to remember that the vision of First Isaiah was of a more spiritual city, one founded on the person of the Messiah and the faith of men from all the nations.

c) The Baptist uses verse 10, which describes the *coming of the Lord in force and power*, to indicate the Lord Jesus Christ (Lk 7:18-23). Frequently Second-Isaiah had portrayed the coming of the Lord as that of a warrior-conqueror (cf. Is 51:9-10); but such imagery was designed to suggest not so much Israel's ancient struggles with other nations as the triumph of God's unicity amid civilizations given to dualism and idolatry. Because God is one, no evil force can interfere with the accomplishment of his plan.

d) Verse 11 returns to the idea of a coming of the Lord in gentleness. It gives us the image of the *good pastor* who gathers the lambs, allows the ewes to rest (Ez 34:23-24; Lk 15:4-5), and guides the flock along the path of the Exodus. The prophet is always ready to evoke the Exodus theme (Is 40:3; 43:16-21; 41:17-20 and above all 49:9-11) when he describes the return from exile. He is affirming the unicity of history, which depends on the unicity of God, the guide who leaves his mark on all events, past and future.*

III. Baruch 5:1-9   The Book of Baruch is a collection of various
    1st reading   elements: penitential (1:15-3:8) or sapiential
    3rd cycle   (3:9-4:4) prophetic (4:5-5:9) or epistolary
    (6:1-72). This anthology, probably no older than the 1st or 2nd centuries, is a rather faithful reflection of the mentality of the Jewish communities of the Diaspora (which would explain its absence in the Palestinian Canon).

The Jews of the Diaspora cared little about formulating original prophecies or elaborating new doctrine, and so contented themselves most of the time with borrowing from the ancient prophets.** Baruch 5:5-9 in fact constitutes a sort of digest of Second-Isaiah. Verse 5 is inspired by Isaiah 51:17; 40:9; 60:1-4. Verse 6 restates Isaiah 49:22; 60:4-9. Verse 7 borrows from Isaiah 40:3-4 (likewise taken up in today's three gospels) and 49:11. Verse 8 borrows its vocabulary from Isaiah 41:19 and 55:12-13. Finally, the conclusion is inspired by Isaiah 40:11; 42:16; 52:12; 58:8; 62:10-11.

---

*See doctrinal theme: *the way* p. 73.
**Psalm 11, of Solomon, presents a text similar to Baruch.

Although the passage is scarcely original on the literary level, nonetheless it reveals to us the essential points which motivated the exiled Jews, as well as the biblical themes which best expressed their expectations.

a) The Jew of the Diaspora, member of the kingdom of God, must live his membership in dispersion, under the yoke of strange laws (Ba 4:15). His only desire is to live his membership in the Kingdom fully and unequivocally. In his eyes, *Jerusalem* symbolizes the ideal city where the dispersed will reassemble as a homogeneous people, distinct from all others (vv. 5-6). This will take place as soon as events and the will of God permit. This return to Jerusalem is presented as a *new Exodus*, guided by God himself with the cooperation of nature, which is placed at the disposal of the people for their needs (vv. 7-9).

b) This new gathering of the people will be the work of God himself and not the result of man's efforts. The Jew of the Diaspora has the presentiment that only a miracle can put an end to his exile: a miracle of *mercy*, since God must forget the infidelity of his people (cf. Ba 4:5-13); a miracle of Justice, since God will separate the Jews once for all from other nations (v. 9).

The Christian in turn is by vocation a member of the Diaspora. This is certainly true in a world which extends beyond Christian limits. The Eucharist is for him, assembled there with his brothers, the realization of the ideal which Baruch projected for Jerusalem. Thanks to that assembly, he is conscious of his membership in a unique people, and he already lives there his heavenly citizenship. However the disciple of Christ does not wholly share the hopes of the disciple of Baruch. The choice is no longer between Zion and a foreign world, since his membership of the new Jerusalem depends on the manner in which he is part of the world. The justice of God is no longer to be revealed in a judgment which will separate him, a member of the

Kingdom, from other nations, but in a separation of the just from the wicked, whatever their national allegiance.

IV. Romans 15:4-9 In the primitive communities the fact that
2nd reading   Judaeo-Christians lived side by side with
1st cycle   Gentile-Christians presented certain difficul-
                   ties. The former certainly were more adapted
to Judaeo-Christian tradition, and it is not difficult to imagine a certain snobbishness on the part of Christians of Jewish background toward those of pagan origin, the "strong" and the "weak" of Rm 14:1–15:6. Paul will not allow this counter-witness: he recalls the example of Christ (vv. 7-9)* and bases his arguments on the scriptures (vv. 10-12). Verse 13, where the Apostle blesses the efforts of the Christian, is by way of general conclusion to the preceding chapters, not to this particular passage.

a) The solution to this conflict between two mentalities is found in the attitude of Christ who *welcomed* all. New structures must be found to welcome all. Christ placed himself at the service of the Jews, not because they had some sort of right to this (Paul does not bring in here the law and its observance), but because God is faithful to his promises (v. 8).

One might expect some declaration by Paul to the effect that Christ made himself the servant of the Gentiles as well. However, Jesus during his public ministry had few opportunities to manifest himself to non-Jews (Mt 15:24). Nevertheless, they benefit from the divine mercy because the existing structures of the Body of Christ permit them to enjoy full integration into that Body (v. 9).

b) Certain *scriptural illustrations* strengthen this line of argument. Paul would normally have recalled the principal promises

---

*Christ in Luke 10:21 is likewise against the opposition between the wise and the ignorant.

made to the Patriarchs of the chosen people, but his readers of Jewish origin already knew them all by heart. Accordingly he unites four scriptural passages which were perhaps less known and which deal with the gathering of the nations in cult: (Ps 17/18:50; Dt 32:43; Ps 116/117:1 and Is 11:10). Three of them recall that Yahweh's cult is accessible to all the pagans and that his glory, once confined to the Temple precincts, is now offered to all nations, which opens up to them the benefits of the messianic promise.

Israel therefore no longer has the monopoly of ancient privileges (the glory, the name, the cult, the messianic dynasty). How could she now, absorbed in the Church, maintain over the Gentiles an authority and primacy which belong to a former age?

The Christian as well has the tendency to consider his membership in the people of God as a privilege which separates him from others. But it is primarily a source of responsibility toward those whom he must welcome. Today more than ever the world poses the problem of coexistence among men, of ideological blocs, of races and social classes. Christianity is often confused with those groups from whom concessions are required in order to bring about the reality of coexistence: the white races, Middle Classes, Western man. The Eucharist, however, gives Christians the opportunity to prove their sense of universality and their refusal of any distinction between the "weak" and the "strong," for there in the Eucharist the Lord offers himself "for you . . . for all."

V. 2 Peter 3:8-14   This passage, composed at least 50 years after
  2nd reading   the resurrection, comes precisely at the end
  2nd cycle   of the period of Revelation. The preaching of
the apostles had been centered around the
promise of the Second-Coming of Christ. Certain of the faithful
began to have doubts about the Lord since he had not come.

Had he not been unfaithful to his promise? What was the use of remaining faithful to the demands of the gospel (2 P 2:15, 21; 3:13)? As a witness of the Transfiguration, an event which prefigured the return of Christ (1:16-21), the author is in a better position to bear witness against all the inventions of false teachers (2:1-22). Further, he is able to reply to their objections. The end of the world is as inescapable as the deluge (3:5-7); God has not the same notion of time as do men, and so the delay is apparent only (3:8).

a) The liturgical reading brings out a new reason for the delay of the Parousia: God is *patient* and waits for the greatest possible number of sinners to be converted (v. 9). The second letter of Peter thus traces the broad lines of a *theology of delay.* God, in choosing to save humanity through the incarnation, finds himself automatically forced to take man into account, his growth that is and sometimes tortuous ways, the hesitations brought about by human liberty. God will not save man without man, nor will he cure him without faith, or give him sonship without conversion. In this encounter, God takes the necessary time to convince his partner and lead him to share his life (cf. Ws 11:23-26; Ez 18:23). This law of incarnation is an important lesson which the Church runs the risk of forgetting, whenever she sacramentalizes without the necessary initiation, or transforms her mission of dialogue and mediation into a monologue which faintly suggests monophysitism.

b) The theme of repentance as well appears in this passage. In Judaism and in the preaching of John the Baptist, the Jews had to take this step *before* the coming of the Kingdom. The Acts, St. John and St. Paul preach on the contrary a permanent repentance associated with the Kingdom, which is the privilege of those who belong to it. 2 Peter 3:9 manifestly returns to the Jewish concept and that of the Baptist. Further, the eschatology in this passage is by no means Christological (as is Revelation), nor is it inspired by the resurrection of Christ (as in 1 Co 15). It is the Jewish concept of the relationship between God the Creator and the world that is operative. How could the author defend such a retrograde outlook after the entire pauline development? His position is understandable if not justifiable. Inasmuch as the resurrection of Christ was still within the memory of everyone and his return held to be imminent, these two events could have been understood as one, as two complementary facets of the one Day. As the intervening period grew prolonged, the two events became distinct, and the life of the Lord was no longer seen as a simple promise (cf. 2 P 3:2, where the Lord is compared to the ordinary prophets). Everything was awaited in his return, and the same anxiety which the Jews evinced began to develop, because the life of Christ was not yet considered as the beginning of the eschatological era.

c) The Day of the Lord will come as a *thief*, unexpected (v. 10a). This was a classical comparison in the primitive communities (1 Th 5:2; Rv 3:3; 16:15; Mt 24:36-44), and served as an argument *ad hominem*. Already in Mt 24:36-44 it is addressed to the heedless who do not believe in the Master's return. To his friends, however, the Lord will come as a friend (Rv 3:20).

d) The return of the Lord is nevertheless accompanied by cosmic upheaval and the destruction of all creation by *fire* (vv. 10 and 12). Peter is dependent on Judaeo-Christian traditions which interpret certain passages such as Isaiah 24-27; 34-35; 65-66 in apocalyptic fashion (Book of Enoch, the Sybilline Books). This genre need not be taken literally. Peter does not announce annihilation; for his heaven and earth are overwhelmed by the deluge only to appear again (vv. 5-7). Likewise, the "end of the world" will destroy by fire only in order to make room for the "new heaven" and "new earth" (v. 13). The argument might appear somewhat weak, based as it is on the very localized episode of the flood. However it is an essential argument when the deluge and Parousia are used to emphasize the incessant mutation of the cosmos through the constant rhythm of death and rebirth (Is 65:17; 66:22).

e) The *moral conclusions* drawn by Peter from the fact of our belonging to a world destined for the change and transformation of the parousia, are identical with those of Paul. Holiness of life and prayer constitute our communion with God, and assure us that amid elements which "will dissolve" or "melt in the flames" (v. 13) there is a solid and serene security. They also put us in a state of "expectation" (v. 12, 13) for the coming of the Lord, an active expectation which may hasten his coming. God awaits man's response, since man must effectively prepare for the Day of the Lord. His holiness is not only the object of the last judgment, but is this judgment itself in preparation. His prayer does not envisage the Lord's coming as a precipitous event, but sees it already in the events of human history.

The Eucharist is celebrated "until he comes," since it places the faithful in eschatological tension, and also constitutes the return of the Lord to his work in time and space, and in each individual man. Participation in the Eucharist, with the idea that the Lord's coming is a reflection of human history and renders man's efforts meaningless by its suddenness, is a falsification of the real meaning. The Eucharist is made from the bread and love of men. It is a falsification too of the real significance of the Lord's coming. It would be impossible to "hasten" that coming if one had no grasp of it, and the only way to achieve a grasp is through a daily witness of holiness of life.

Furthermore the Eucharist is the sacrament of God's patience, and the source of our tolerance too. God is "slow in coming" simply because he loves the other in all his otherness, even his rejection and his sin. It takes time to know the other, to understand the distinctive nature of the stone which it is his business to contribute in building the Body of Christ. The patience of Jesus in waiting for the other actually transcended death and Christian tolerance should be nourished by that example.

VI. Philippians After his opening address (vv. 1-2) in this
1:4-6 and 8-11 epistle, which was written either in 56 at
2nd reading Ephesus or in 62 at Rome, Paul makes a
3rd cycle solemn thanksgiving (vv. 3-11). It follows the
traditional pattern of Jewish thanksgivings: a
blessing (vv. 3-8) and an epiclesis (vv. 9-11).

a) The reason for the thanksgiving is the generosity the
Philippians have shown by participating in Paul's apostolate. It
is a guarantee for the future (v. 6). Since God has begun to
pour out *his grace* on the community in such a striking fashion
there can be no doubt about the future. If God has begun to
manifest his love his grace will not be wanting.

b) The theme of the epiclesis is the *increase in charity* among
the Philippians. He means charity in the general sense, love of
God and brethren, in a word the whole Christian life. Increase
is demonstrated by the fruits that have followed. Among these is
knowledge (epignosis), not some sort of speculation but an experimental and loving knowledge of the mystery of God (cf.
Col 2:2; 3:9-10; Ep 1:17; 4:13; Rm 3:20); and *comprehension*,
a delicacy of conscience as it were, which enables a man to
discern the better thing and quickly adopt the proper attitude
for the high moments of life.

c) Knowledge of this kind and genuine fulfillment in the
Christian sense enables us to appear pure (or whole) on the
day of the Lord, without shortcomings (or reproach), and
clothed in justice (vv. 10-11). Jewish phraseology like this
could designate merely legalist justice were it not that Paul gives
it special nuances. One must be "filled" with this justice, which
"comes through Jesus Christ." The word "filled" in Saint Paul
always indicates the action of the Spirit, who is at work even now
until the day of the Lord (Rm 15:13-14). The justice that comes
through Jesus Christ is divine justification brought to men by
the mediation of the Savior (Rm 5:9).

The God whose day we await is so present in the generosity, charity and delicate feeling of life's daily round, that the day-to-day pattern of Christian life can be regarded as a continuous "Day of Yahweh."

VII. Matthew   In this Sunday's liturgy we read in succession
3:1-12   the three synoptic versions of the mission of
Gospel   John the Baptist. The commentary will deal
1st cycle   first with the elements common to all three
gospels and will then attend to particular items.

Points common to the entire synoptic tradition are: the name of John the Baptist, his preaching in the desert, the conversion and confession of sins demanded of the candidates for baptism, the baptism itself in the waters of the Jordan, and finally the citation of Isaiah 40:3, which was considered a fairly apt resume of the ministry of John.

These details are described as primitive not because they are common to the three synoptics. All the texts are strongly influenced by the earliest tradition, which was originally concerned only with the baptism of John and the crowd which gathered around him.

1. The Synoptic Message

a) The synoptics are in accord in presenting the preaching of John beginning with Isaiah 40:3. This text evoked a new Exodus (Is 40:3; cf. Is 43:16-19) by which God could call back into his Kingdom those who had escaped from exile. But the synoptics agree in modifying the quotation of Isaiah and instead of saying: "voice that cries: in the desert prepare the way," they write: "voice that cries in the desert: prepare the way." Thus John appears to be the voice of God, or the friend of the bridegroom, calling his fiancee into the desert to spend their honeymoon there.

The Christian tradition unites the theme of the new Exodus,

objective and historical, to that of an espousal more nostalgic (a lost ideal) and intimate. It corrects the unilateral intervention of God in Is 40:3 into a dialogue and a loving encounter of two freedoms.

b) Was John conscious of the theme of the "royal way" contained in Isaiah 40:3? He would seem to have been more intent on emphasizing the moral theme of *conversion* (v. 2), the "renewal of the whole being" (*metanoia*), a change of direction or orientation. The return of God to his people depends on the return of the people to God, to Yahweh. John remains faithful to the insights of the prophets: God will not manifest himself any longer to a particular people, as on Sinai, but to all who are converted. He "will return" to those who "return to him" (Jr 3:22-4:1; Dt 30:1-5; Ml 3:7; Jl 2:12-14; Ps 79/80: 4, 8, 15). God "repents" of the wrath he was to show to those who are now themselves "repentant" (Jr 18:7-8). This is the theology of the remnant, evoked particularly by Isaiah 2:1-5 where God makes known that he will only come to a people refined by conversion.*

In preaching conversion or repentance, John initiates a type of instruction which will resound throughout the New Testament in the preaching of Christ (Mk 1:15; Lk 13:3-6), in the kerygma of the apostles after the resurrection (Lk 24:47; Ac 2:28), and finally in the proclamation of Paul (Ac 26:20). The manifestation of God in the world is not an unforeseen intervention but an encounter between two free agencies.

The Hebrew word "conversion" signifies that a man realizes that he has taken the wrong path and returns to God with a desire for salvation (Jr 17:5-11; Is 2:6-22; Jr 31:16-22). It is not a question of simple remorse but a positive commitment to the way shown him by God. John is precise on the subject: the imminence of the kingdom (v. 2) dispenses from a return to the past, and obliges us to positive conversion (Lk 3:10-17).

c) Baptism in the Jordan is the culmination of John's preaching and the conversion of the faithful. Whether or not this rite

*See the doctrinal theme: *conversion*, p. 67.

recalled the passage through the Red Sea, or the Jordan, at the time of the Exodus is difficult to say. It was in any case a common enough practice in the religions of the time, and in Judaism itself, occurs in the baths of purification at Qumran, as well as in the ablutions of the Temple, or even in the baptism of proselytes. These baths were self administered, and authorization was given to repeat them during the course of a lifetime (except in the case of the baptism of proselytes). The baptism of John is something different. It was given only once, at the hands of a "baptizer," and involved, beyond legal and ritualistic purification, personal conversion.

The baptism of holiness was not something one procured oneself; it was received from the hands of God's prophet (cf. Mt 3:11) simultaneously with his message concerning the kingdom and conversion, in fulfillment of prophecies such as in Ezechial 36:25.

The uniqueness of the baptism of John is symbolic of the eschatological era now inaugurated, where these rites take on a value and significance they did not previously possess.

2. The Particular Characteristics of Matthew's Narrative

a) Matthew, more than the other evangelists, is aware of the connection established by the Baptist between conversion and the proximity of the kingdom (v. 2) (Ac 2:38; 3:19; 10:43, etc.). However, the "conversion" proposed by Saint John, following the Old Testament prophets (see also 2 P 3:9) is linked with the proximate coming of a terrible Judge. This contrasts with the conversion proposed by New Testament missionaries, which is a joining of self to the death of Christ, and by that very fact entry into the glory of the kingdom. The call to conversion is always associated with a discourse on the death and resurrection of the Lord (Ac 2:38; 3:26; 5:30-31; 17:30-32). Conversion is not only a preliminary condition, it is a permanent attitude.

b) John's life-style, his clothing (cf. Mt 11:8-9; 2 K 1:8) and his food (v. 4) must have strongly impressed both Matthew and Mark (Mk 1:6). The skin worn by John, traditional clothing of the prophets and especially Elijah (2 K 1:8; 2:8, 13), and suggests the identification of John and the *new Elijah* announced in Malachi 3:23.

Jewish apocalyptic literature interpreted the disappearance of Elijah as an instantaneous return of the prophet to God, who revealed his will to him and charged him to reveal it to mankind before the end of time. The gospel tradition saw the accomplishment of this mission, heretofore reserved to Elijah, in the ministry of Jesus (compare Lk 4:23-30 and 1 K 17:7-16; Lk 7:11-17 and 1 K 17:17-24; Mt 4:1-5 and 1 K 19:1-8; Lk 9:54-55 and 2 K 1:9-16; Ac 1:1-11 and 2 K 2:1-18; Mt 16:13-15). However, there was another school of thought which saw this in the ministry of the Baptist (Mt 17:10-11; Jn 1:21; Lk 1:17 in reference to Ml 3:23).

Belief in the return of a new Elijah is not of such great import to the Christian today. However, Matthew, and to an even greater extent Mark, by placing the Baptist in the line of Elijah and the prophets, make conversion a human step, a response to the divine initiative to which the prophet bears witness. Conversion is response to the Word of God, and the rite of baptism is an encounter between two free agencies.

It seems then that the essential message of John the Baptist in Matthew is a call to conversion to a Kingdom that will be "select." The eucharistic celebration presumes this continuous conversion. Men are gathered together who bring all the riches of their own experience and culture. Their hopes, the secular progress they have made, are all accepted. But, once associated with the mystery of Christ's death and resurrection, a conversion becomes necessary that will liberate them from egoism and dispose them for a fidelity to the Father that resembles that of Christ on the cross. There is however an important distinction. The conversion demanded by the Baptist was to an angry God.

In the Eucharist we are asked to turn to a God who loves man, who, even to the point of death, has taken the time to understand man at the levels of his greatest alienation, sin and rejection.

VIII. Mark 1:1-8   This narrative contains the themes common
   Gospel   to the three synoptics (analyzed above, p. 59
   2nd cycle   regarding Mt 3:1-12) and also makes use
                 of two themes proper to Mark.

a) Mark introduces into the text from Isaiah 40:3 a reference to the theme of the messenger of Malachi 3:1 (cf. Ex 23:20 and Mt 11:9).

Malachi reproached the Temple priesthood for the formalism of its cult and the invalidity of its sacrifice. God will come as a Judge to establish a new cult, more worthy in his eyes, however he will be preceded by a messenger whom the prophet identifies as Elijah (Ml 3:23). The allusion of Mark to Malachi 3:1 confirms the identification established by the other synoptics between John the Baptist and Elijah. The role of the messenger announced by Malachi becomes specifically liturgical, since there was question of purifying the levitical priesthood. John, himself born into a priestly caste, proposes — to the great scandal of the priests and levites (Jn 1:19-27) — a purity more profound than that of the ablutions, which might be obtained only by the remission of sin. He proposes a priesthood joined with the prophetic office such as that demanded in Ml 2:7 and finally realized in the apostles. In placing the ministry of the Baptist within the perspective of Malachi 3, Mark makes John the precursor of the kingdom of God itself. The prophecy of Malachi describes a future shaped by Yahweh himself and not by some descendant of David. John the Baptist appears then as a minister of God, not as the herald of an earthly king, even the Messiah king.

b) Mark's gospel is distinguished from the other synoptics in affirming that John came "proclaiming a baptism" (v. 4; cf. Lk 3:3; Ac 10: 37; 13:24). This link between the baptismal rite and prophecy prefigures the bond which Christians will establish between Word and Rite (Ep 5:26). This is no longer a simply human gesture: it is essential to the realization of the plan of God. In John 1:19-25, the Baptist blends into a single reality the rite of baptism and the voice which cries in the desert. The baptismal rite is, therefore, a prophetic gesture charged with the will of Yahweh and with the faith and conversion of those who have "ears to hear."

c) Mark is the only evangelist to begin his gospel directly with the preaching of the Baptist, the "messenger" of the kingdom. Matthew and Luke had this intent originally; but later prefaced the narrative with two preliminary chapters on the infancy of Jesus. Mark's intention is to associate Jesus Christ directly with Old Testament messianism. He accomplishes this by means of an allusion to the "Good News" of Second-Isaiah (encompassing the themes of return from exile and of Consolation). He gives a certain nuance however to this allusion calling for conversion, repentance and a return to the desert, the traditional crucible where the people of God were *put to the test* and shaped.

We no longer await a messenger from Yahweh to purify the temple because it has become the very person of Jesus Christ, unique High-Priest of the new alliance. However, the priestly people, united to Christ in the eucharistic celebration, have yet to complete their own purification and conversion. The Eucharist constantly purifies the heart of those who celebrate it. The remission of sins, at first attached to the baptism of John, is now offered to the assembly in the cup of salvation, in the measure that the rite becomes again an incessant prophetic appeal, and a message that calls effectively for conversion. In this way, John

the Baptist is truly, the eyes of Mark, the procurser of the new
spiritual liturgy.

IX. Luke 3:1-6   Besides the themes common to all three
    Gospel   synoptics (see below, p. 59), this gospel
    3rd cycle   makes use of themes proper to Saint Luke.

a) Luke, in dating precisely the ministry of John (vv. 1-2),
makes the event central in human history, and thereby gives a
universal emphasis to the coming of the Lord and his messenger.
This intention is confirmed by verse 6, which prolongs the
classical citation of Isaiah 40:3 to include verse 5, thus emphasizing the fact that "all flesh will see the salvation of God."
Luke is a universalist: salvation is offered to all, man and
woman, rich and poor. Samaritans and Romans will accept it
even before the priests and levites.

b) Luke is also the evangelist of *goodness* and *mildness*. In
prolonging the citation he alludes perhaps to the tortuous routes
which must be made "straight." The qualification is really too
juridical: the Hebrew meaning is rather a certain "agreeableness
of heart" capable of rendering our ways more pleasing to God
(cf. Dt 6:18). This tempers a bit the terrible side of conversion
to an intolerant God in the text of Matthew 3:10-12.

The eucharistic celebration reveals the salvation of God to all
flesh. The blood of Christ is offered there for the "many" and
communion already assembles men of all languages, races and
cultures until that day when the barriers which separate them
will crumble in the fire of God's glory.

However, Christians still risk confusing the universal Church
with the historical and limited image she now presents. Surely,
even there where she is a local entity, the Church has the mission to show herself open to all, but the parochialism of many
of her members often hurts this mission. The Christian must be

thankful for anything which works the other way, the present-day ecumenical movement for instance, spreading the Church to other continents, being open to other cultures.

Behind the numerous references to Isaiah 40:3 in the synoptics and in John 1:23 we can discern the primitive Christian ideas about the meaning of baptism. It is invariably seen as something objective, a road through trial opened by God for his people to the land of blessedness. The synoptics discern here also the renewal of espousals between God and his people, with all that is implied by espousal, communion, mutual affection, knowledge and discovery. In Mark, in addition, baptism means the opportunity to share in a new and purified sacrifice. In Luke there is a missionary nuance: baptism is conferred so that all flesh may see the salvation of God.

But for all, baptism is the encounter between two free agencies: God who calls, man who is converted; God who remits sin, man who confesses his sin. The ritual ceremony, when there is a ceremony, is always built around this essential dialogue of conversion and acceptance.

B. DOCTRINE

1. The Theme of Conversion

Modern man seems scarcely attuned to the theme of conversion, especially when this means conversion towards God. Faced as he is with so many serious challenges, modern man seems conscious of his responsibilities, and even declares himself prepared to mobilize all the forces at his command to meet them. The task is immense, and the first demand made on man today is that he avoid seeking the easy way out. In this sense a daily conversion is required. The conversion implies first of all a conversion of man to himself, to his own truth. Conversion to God, implying as it does a fundamental humility and total renouncement of self, leaves man more often than not untouched, or even in a state of revolt. Some would say that such conversion throws man back on his own weakness, rendering him often ineffectual, and furthermore that it alienates him from his own resources by diverting him from his real tasks.

This state of mind is shared by numerous Christians who live close to the world of our time. Conversion, whenever referred to, is more often than not reduced to a simple moral virtue. Today's Christian in no way seeks to avoid the real problems. The problems of his contemporaries are his problems; he must be conscious of his contribution to the plan of God in finding solutions. The God of Jesus Christ expects man to play his part in the work of creation, which means that all Christians should deliver the best of themselves and their talents to humanity's problems. But what is the role of conversion to God in this process?

It is unnecessary to emphasize the importance of this question. If Christians lose their sense of conversion to God, the very Christianity which they profess will present to men simply the image of another humanism among many, and will see itself deprived of its own proper religious depth. This is precisely what is at stake in the reflections we shall make.

The necessity for conversion in Israel

In all traditional religions the approach to the divine lays bare a feeling of guilt in man, which varies in intensity. As if in some way man were turning away from the world of the sacral, of which he feels himself a part. Certain sins have been committed, rules transgressed, and it is indispensable that he have recourse to penitential rites in order to reestablish himself on the road to salvation. Isaiah, at the point of departure in his spiritual journey, sees the necessity for conversion in terms which parallel what is happening round him. Penitential rites occupy an important place here as well. However, as Yahweh concludes the alliance with his people, a new element appears. The religion of faith has a historical dimension: it sees the event as the point of encounter between God and man. This means a change in the guilt sentiment: sin, which turns us away from Yahweh, is above all a historical fault — Israel has resisted the shepherding guidance of her God. It is no longer simply a question of transgressing cultic ancestral rites and regulations; Israel sins in refusing to welcome Yahweh's interventions in the events of her history.

Under the influence of the prophets the call to conversion undergoes a process of interiorization. In the first place moral lapse begins to be emphasized instead of ritual fault; the failure lies in not imitating the goodness and mercy of God. Penitential rites themselves are altered in significance and retain validity only to the extent that they indicate desire for moral conversion. Then little by little a deeper dimension of conversion begins to emerge, the proper religious dimension. Yahweh leads his people through unforeseeable historical events; but the people become insecure, and in their pride refuse to play the role given them by God. The need for conversion becomes a need for radical poverty or humility before the interventions of God, the Totally-

Other, who alone is capable of saving mankind. Constantly man must turn away from his illusory ways and use the ways of God. But man's sin is such that repentance itself is a grace that must be begged of Yahweh.

With the Precursor, John the Baptist, the theme of conversion takes on a particular urgency; the decisive intervention of God is in fact very near. God will visit his people; and conversion is required not simply because observance of the law demands that, but because it is absolutely essential for encounter with the living God.

Jesus of Nazareth and the call to conversion

The theme of conversion is quite central in the preaching Christ: his continuity with the Old Testament is evident in this matter. There are however certain characteristics to be noted which bring the specifically Christian view of conversion into sharper focus. First of all conversion now must be understood as essentially religious in nature. The fundamental option for the Kingdom means a total stripping of ourselves and the renunciation of all forms of pride. The royal road to be followed is the path which is ever open to the guidance of the Spirit, and this implies an obedience unto death, if necessary the death of the cross. The man who wishes to follow Jesus must be emptied; he must lose himself in some way. Then it is important to realize that this conversion is possible for every man, no matter what his social or spiritual condition, no matter what degree of virtue he may have attained. Conversion indeed is proposed to all men, because all are sinners and Jesus himself declared that he came only for sinners. We find ourselves then in a climate where all men are included, and it is typical of Jesus that his message of conversion is not firmly linked with any particular penitential practice.

Nor does the universal aspect stop there. Jesus calls man to a radical openness and invites him to practice the new commandment without imposing limits on his love, because now the love of God and the love of men are identical. The bond between religious conversion and universal fraternal love is very strong indeed. The new commandment is a religious commandment and the man who is converted to God is liberated from the sin of pride to the point of practicing the new commandment. He is restored to the true human condition. Far from being alienating, this conversion enables man to mobilize all his forces, all the resources of his creative freedom. The new commandment touches man at the focal point of his relationship with God, and inevitably it overflows into various other relevant human projects.

The people of God a converted people

All who are converted to the God of Jesus Christ form a new people, the Church, which is the Body of Christ. This people is not simply the sum of its members; all are joined to it. It is impossible then to be converted to the God of Jesus Christ without taking on the bonds of universal brotherhood set up in the person of Christ, the unique mediator. In him, who delivered himself up for men, the people of the new and eternal alliance has a potential scale of existence, embracing humanity in its entirety. All men are called to this people, and will find their place there, according to the measure in which their call to conversion fitted them for fellowship with all other men, of whatever race, social condition, or spiritual identity.

The theme of conversion provides a good insight into the nature of the Church, since the ecclesial bond is constituted by something which is of its very nature religious. The rite of baptism, which joins a man to the people of God and binds him to Christ in his paschal mystery, must express a real conversion to God, a renunciation of Satan by renouncing pride in all its forms. In this sense, the Church as a people of converts cannot be considered identical with any single people on earth, since the cohesion of their national structures is of a different nature altogether. The Church on the contrary is called to build her unity on love. A man turns to God in conversion in order to share in the realization of a plan of love which embraces all mankind. Christian conversion will always be insistent on the urgent nature of mission. Finally, the affirmation that the Church is a people of converts reminds us that the Church is called to render a service to the world for which there is no substitute. The genuine conversion to God and liberation from sin to be found in her constitute the main reservoir from which the best human efforts flow most naturally.

The good news of salvation and the call to conversion

Within our own times fortunately we have come to see that the evangelization of a people need not necessarily mean interference with its spiritual pilgrimage, but on the contrary its fulfillment. However we sometimes do lose sight of the fact that it implies a call to conversion, which is the sole means of giving life to our link with Christ.

The nature of this conversion we should thoroughly understand. It is a fact that the word has unfortunate historical associations. How many times in the history of the Church has the conversion of a people, or of individuals, meant cultural uprooting! The call to conversion to the God of Jesus Christ is obviously not a summons to rejection of one's culture. It is a call which, when woven into the spiritual dynamism of a people, fuses spirit and heart, and invites the people to a total stripping of self, to a radical humility before God and his plan of universal love. It leads us to break with this or that particular form or structure, in order to embrace a universal form of love. For any people acceptance of the good news of salvation means decentralization from the self; it means voluntary rejection of previous securities that were illusory, and recognition of the fact that true fulfillment becomes possible by following the way of the cross.

For the missionary, the call to conversion which he proclaims concerns his own self in a particular way. He can only summon a people to this deemphasis of self by giving example, by witnessing to it in his own person. In other words, if the word of conversion is to find effective response in his bearers, the missionary must exhibit real fidelity to the new commandment. It is only the witness of unhesitating love that will sustain the summons to conversion to the God of Jesus Christ. The person bearing such witness may indeed cause scandal, as Jesus did, but for those exposed to it his witness will have weight and command decision.

Today, as it did always, the evangelization of the world requires a call to conversion. We must however show that conversion to the God of love, and conversion to the truth of the human condition, are intimately associated. We must see conversion to the God of Jesus Christ as the ultimate source of true human progress. If Christians join with all other men today in the struggle to shape human destiny, they must demonstrate that the deepest truths concerning man are those which concern God.

The Eucharist of the converted

At the sacred time of eucharistic celebration the call to conversion should always be evident. The essential proclamation in the Mass, which must always be manifest, is that of the death of the Lord; this is the act *par excellence* by which Jesus of Nazareth turns towards the Father with complete readiness and perfect obedience. It is the act through which the world received salvation once for all. When Christians assemble for the Eucharist the Church expects from them one thing above all: that they demonstrate their conversion by taking their place in the furrow opened for them by Jesus, by putting on Christ, by allowing him to work within them.

Under such conditions we can easily see the eucharistic celebration as a fraternal banquet. Christians who have been initiated into Christ and into his death on the cross are now introduced to the fraternal bonds proper to that Kingdom, which, in Jesus Christ, means universal love actualized. The love is given so that all men can make it operative in their everyday lives. Christians can only realize all this when the assembly, stirred to action by the Church, is itself a sign of the brother-hood of the Kingdom.

The liturgy of the Word is a challenge to the assembly's faith to choose the road of conversion and cling to it; and we should never leave the celebration of Mass without eliciting new incentives to conversion. There is great need today that the preached word be relevant to the concrete situations and responsibilities faced by modern man. Otherwise the conversion called for by the Word will not exercise influence at the one level where influence is of paramount importance.

2. The Theme of the Way

Modern man, to a much greater extent than his forebears, is really conscious of the task he has before him, of the road he must travel. Task and journey are of collective dimension today, of interplanetary scope. Nature is no longer the stable framework within which men and nations develop in search of their own well-being. On the contrary, nature now appears as a complex entity and points towards a job to be accomplished, history to be made. The whole enterprise will prove arduous. The obstacles which line the path humanity must travel are many and these give a dramatic character to the whole business. We have only to think of the terrible challenge presented by the facts of starvation, under-development and the seemingly ever-present state of war in the world. But modern man believes himself equipped to handle such obstacles. He wishes to reassure himself of the necessary means, and for many of our contemporaries recourse to God is superfluous if not indeed harmful.

The search for the "ways" of God in Israel

The people of Abraham lived the greatest moments in their religious history while yet "on the road." Abraham himself became a nomad in response to the call of God. It was a long journey across the desert at the time of the Exodus, which finally brought the people out of a land of enslavement into the promised land. At the time of Jerusalem's destruction, the elite of Israel took the road into exile.

This road was for Israel a valuable religious experience, for it placed the Jew in a state of insecurity — this was especially true of the wandering in the desert or the road to exile. This insecurity provided an excellent reason for recognizing God as totally other, the master of our destiny, Yahweh who retains the complete initiative in the work of salvation. It is he who sets forth the route to follow, who leads his people where he will and who finally opens up the passage from death to life.

However committed to their paschal journey they may have been, the people resist with all the force of pagan impulse; they constantly deviate from God's path and follow more willingly a wandering destiny. Throughout the bible God speaks out to them through the prophetic word: "My ways are not your ways" (Is 55:8). However, his fidelity is unwavering: Yahweh never ceases to return to his people and calls them to return to him. The paschal road is the road of conversion.

Christ, the true way

Jesus came to accomplish the will of his Father. This will became flesh in a journey which passed through death and demanded in Jesus an obedience even to the cross. The paschal journey which the Father willed for his Son is precisely the way which Jesus, in full liberty, traveled with an absolute fidelity. When Jesus said, "I am the way," he expressed above all the perfect coincidence in himself of the path of God and the path of mankind.

Why this perfect harmony in Jesus? The answer is not to be found in his incomparable moral qualities, but in his condition as man-God. The obedience of Jesus unto death could never be the result of mere human resource: only the eternal Son of the

Father could effect such an obedience in a man. There is perfect
harmony in Jesus between the path of God and that of men.
Since Christ's human condition is the faithful reflection of his
divine condition as Son — it is his humanity which is fully engaged in the eternal yes of the Son.

This is the reason why Jesus could call himself the way in
an absolute sense. Because he is the man-God, he is the revelation of God's way at the precise moment he constructs the
human journey which leads to the Father and saves mankind.
His paschal journey brings to a meeting point the perfect
Revelation of the Father and the perfect Religion of man.

Further, as Jesus turns towards men, the invitation he addresses
them is identical for all: "Come, follow me." The only means
for man freely to join himself again to the will of God is to
follow the path of Christ, to live his life and follow his way.

The nearness of Christ in the Church

The Church, as the Body of Christ, is the agent of the paschal
journey of her Head. She becomes herself the "Way." Through
the lives of her members and through sacerdotal intervention
she ·is at once the revelation of the divine initiative, and the
discovery of the actual way which will lead men to the Father.
Her mediations allow the individual, at the cost of the necessary
conversion, to bring his personal itinerary into line with the way
of Christ.

The position of the Christian in relation to the Head places
him in "proximity" to his Lord. This closeness is not of a chronological nature but ontological. This means that in the Church the
members receive the spiritual equipment necessary to be capable
of placing their feet on the path of Christ. This, however, does
not remove the fact of sin, which always places a certain distance
between them and Christ.

The nearness which the Lord offers to his members is determined by their fidelity. This fills the believer with joy but it
presupposes as well a constant "conversion" and always implies

a call to repentance. Without this penitential effort, the Lord's nearness ceases to be a reality for the Christian.

On the other hand, the shaping of man's paschal journey by Christ and the members of his body has immediate bearing on the enterprise of civilization, by restoring to it its own dynamism. Better than anyone else, the Christian knows that he has a task to accomplish here below, a historical work to perform. Genuine faith when lived is no alienation. Quite the contrary, it is the source of restoration. Each time the Christian returns to God that which has come from him, he discovers himself better equipped to confront the many obstacles which call real human effort into question.

Mission, as the manifestation of the paschal journey

The role of mission is to perform for all men what Jesus did for Israel. Jesus did not create the materials he used in the construction of the way to the Father; he borrowed them from the spiritual quest of Israel. What he did create was the way itself, removing thereby the uncertainty and indetermination which characterized all previous efforts.

The Church must do the same when she proclaims the good news to nations that have never heard the message. To go out on mission is, then, to plant the roots of the mystery of Christ in the spiritual tradition of a people to whom it is as yet unknown. From this planting, which must be done with due regard for adaptation, should result a confrontation in depth. At the very heart of the search of this people and its groping to find its own way, there will emerge gradually the path to be followed, if the people is to take its place in the Family of the Father through the mediation of Christ. This paschal way belongs to Christ; but the materials from which it is fashioned are furnished by the peoples for whom it is destined.

In the light of this, it would be superfluous to emphasize the tremendous responsibility borne today by the young churches of Africa and Asia: they must translate into reality the new outlines of the paschal way for all mankind. This task can only be fulfilled properly if new ties are developed between themselves and the churches of the West. This exchange of life and energies must be an exchange where each of the partners is conscious that he has as much to receive from the other as he has to give.

The Eucharist, viaticum of those who build the paschal way

He who would follow in the footsteps of Christ must be initiated into his mystery. The Eucharist is the privileged occasion of such initiation. Since Christ is at its center, the Christian finds in the Eucharist the veritable stages of the paschal road of mankind — he refreshes and restores himself there in the sharing of the Lord's Table. Nowhere else is the nearness of the Lord felt so keenly. There, too, he should henceforth hear with the greatest clarity the call to joy and conversion.

SECOND WEEK OF ADVENT

I. Isaiah 35:1-10 Although inserted in the first part of the book
1st reading of Isaiah, this poem is by a disciple, perhaps
Monday Second-Isaiah.

The theme of the poem is *the return to Paradise*. The coming
of the Savior will change the desert into paradise (v. 1-2, 6-7;
cf. Is 41:17-20; 43:20; 48:21); all sicknesses will be healed (v.
5-6), even fatigue will disappear (v. 3).

These few verses then announce the coming repeal of the
curses that followed the fall of Adam. Hardships of labor (Gn
3:19), suffering (Gn 3:16), the thistles and brambles of the
desert (Gn 3:18) will be nothing more than a sad memory.

The theme of the return to Paradise, which appears in the
narratives of the conquest of the Promised Land (Dt 8:7-10)
and especially in those of the restoration of the country after the
exile (Is 43:18-21), will lose its marvelous character in the New
Testament. Nevertheless the return to Paradise remains a reality,
for the new Adam had reentered Paradise by his absolute
obedience to his human condition, including death, and his total
fidelity to the Father. The many paradises which man tries to
build by overcoming war, hunger, and the bondage of labor are
merely steps that lead the Christian to the Paradise prepared
by God.

II. Luke 5:17-26 This whole passage must have had a very
Gospel checkered textual history. It seems to be a
Monday combination of two different traditions: the
first (vv. 17-19, 24b-26) recounting the cure
of a paralytic in the presence of an admiring crowd; the second
(vv. 20-24a) describing a discussion between Jesus and the

scribes about the power of forgiveness granted to the Son of man.

a) The combination could have come about because the cure of the paralytic was regarded by the primitive community as evidence that the *forgiveness of sin,* after the pattern of Isaiah 33:23-24 where paralytics and sinners are associated in the same salvation, had now become a feature of the times. The evangelist might well have been led, by such a doctrinal interpretation, to recall the discussion indicated that Jesus was the Son of man foretold by Daniel 7:13-14, but he had come to forgive and justify rather than condemn.

The combination of the two items gave origin to a new idea: forgiveness of sin depends on the faith of the sinner and that of the surrounding people (v. 20, as in Lk 7:48-50; Ac 10:43; 13:48; 26:18).

b) The discussion about forgiveness had certainly taken place at a stage when Jesus' thaumaturgic powers were being explained as characteristic rather of the Son of man (Mt 26:64; 24:30; 13:41; 19:28; 12:8) than the Messiah. The powers of the former were better understood and were semidivine.

The phrase "on earth" in verse 24 only becomes understandable when seen as a contrast to the future glory of the Son of man, when he comes on the clouds (Dn 7:13-14). What Jesus is affirming here is that in his earthly mission too he is already invested with power over sin, a power that he will exercise in its fullness when he occupies the seat of judgment. Furthermore his power is discretionary. Because God, who alone can forgive and judge, has delegated the power to him it can be used both to pardon and to judge.

Accordingly the manifestation of the sovereign judge on the last day is being initiated here below by the exercise of forgiveness and mercy. The faith required, if one is to benefit from these gestures of the Son of man, is a recognition here and now of God's judgment on the world.

Men today, to the extent to which they have lost the sense of God, have had their sense of sin atrophied. Consequently they do not understand a Messiah who forgives and dies so that sins may be pardoned. The Christian cannot be a witness to God's pardon, or its necessity, unless his own concept of sin is purified. He must rid himself of overly materialist notions and recover the concept of free offering or rejection. He must see forgiveness not as a one-sided paternalistic gesture, but as a common enterprise of love for the advancement of peace and social justice throughout all domains of human life.

Christians spread all over the world have the task of proclaiming and extending this pardon to all men. In the Eucharist they maintain relationship with the merciful initiative of the Father, who manifests his pardon in the breaking of the bread that is consecrated by his only-begotten Son's victory over sin and death.

III. Isaiah 40:1-10 The commentary on this reading will be
1st reading   found at the second Sunday of Advent, p. 49.
Tuesday

IV. Matthew   Of all the "parables of mercy" recorded in
18:12-14   Luke 15, this is the only one reported by
Gospel   Matthew.
Tuesday

Because of their strict laws on purification and ablution before meals, the Pharisees had automatically excluded from sacred repasts a whole group of sinners and publicans. To such ostracism Christ opposes the mercy of God, who always seeks to save sinners. He himself is therefore faithful to the will of his Father (v. 14) when he pushes this search for the sinner to the utmost limit. This intention of Christ is at once evident in the parable of the lost sheep. Matthew may be more reserved than Luke, as he omits the direct comparison between the joy of the shepherd who has found his sheep, and that of God. Neither does he say that the sinner is loved more than the others; the joy of recovery should not be confused with love for all men.

Modern man feels uneasy when faced with the classical theme of mercy. The word itself, in most languages, suggests something sentimental and paternalistic; but most of all, it gives an impression of religious alienation, as if the Christian, by turning to God's mercy, were evading at the same time his true responsibilities.

Yet the biblical notion of mercy is much deeper. The term belongs to the most profound vocabulary of faith. The love involved indicates faithfulness to one's commitment as well as affection of the heart. In a word, it denotes a total attitude of being.

Experience of man's miserable and sinful condition has colored the notion of God's mercy, suggesting merely God's attitude when faced with man's sin. Yet it is much more than just blotting out the past. The mercy of God is nothing naive: it is an invitation to man to practice mercy himself, in turn, towards others, especially pagans (Si 27:30-28:7).

On this point, Jesus follows the Old Testament. He shows the mercy of God in its full breadth, linking it with the practice of human mercy, so that it may be a joint undertaking by God and man, an active response by man to God's initiative. His mercy is boundless, open to sinners and the excommunicated.

Christians should be conscious, as a spiritual experience of God's mercy towards them. He takes them as they are, and at no moment of their lives is a rupture with God consummated. God is always there, he is even searching for them always. Consequently one can always have recourse to his fatherly benevolence. It should be realized however that the sinner is only truly repentant, when divine mercy moves him not alone to conversion but to the exercise of mercy towards other unhappy human beings. Similarly the Church as a whole will not have a proper understanding of the divine mercy to which she owes her origin, until the day when she removes those obstacles that divide her as an institution from the poor and the sinners among men, without in any way hurting their dignity.

The Eucharist is the memorial of Christ's death; it reminds us that one person only has been merciful to the full measure of divine mercy. Sharing his table, we become sharers in this mercy of the man-God. Our recourse to divine mercy in the Eucharist is no longer an escapist gesture; it becomes witness in a demanding way.

V. Isaiah
40:25-31
1st reading
Wednesday

Here we find the final two verses of a poem on the majesty of God (vv. 25-26) and another poem on hope (vv. 27-31). In the eyes of Second Isaiah, it is indeed the former that justifies the latter.

a) The author had written the poem on the *majesty of God* to comfort the exiles who were confronted by the elaborate cult of gods in Babylon: they must not think Yahweh inferior to Marduk. If the prophet records the greatness of Yahweh mostly as revealed in creation, it is because Babylonian legends celebrated the triumph of Marduk over the evil forces of chaos. At this time, Jewish cosmogonies often borrowed items from those legends to attribute them to Yahweh (victory over chaos and the waters, over the monster, etc.: cf Gn 1; Ps 103/104; etc.).

But there was a weakness in Marduk: it is only after a council of the gods that he undertook creation and the battle against evil. Yahweh, on the other hand, never took advice from anyone; his transcendence remains intact, and Jewish monotheism feels reassured.

b) In over-emphasizing the majesty of God, the prophet ran the risk of alienating the people from Yahweh. Men would appear mere grasshoppers when faced with this God, and how could their history be of interest to someone so distant (v. 27)?

Second-Isaiah answers by insisting that this transcendent God is actually near to man and wishes to bestow upon him some of his own strength (v. 29). To those weary exiles, he reveals the fountains of life which gush in the depths of their own hearts, and give them the *courage* to live and strength to overcome weariness in the midst of anguish and despair.

VI. Matthew   This passage, proper to Matthew, comes after
11:28-30   the jubilant hymn of Christ, where he blesses
Gospel   his Father for revealing the mysteries to
Wednesday   "mere children" rather than the learned (vv.
                   25-27). A commentary on the hymn according to Luke's version (Lk 10:21-24) appears earlier.

Though concerned with the problem of the poor and weak, Luke did not retain the typically Jewish piety and vocabulary for these verses. But they are certainly authentic.

a) In the preceding verses, Christ had opposed ignorant and simple people to the learned and clever, and "mere children" to the doctors of the Law. He wanted to show that the humble, though without knowledge of competence, were blessed with a divine "revelation" which compensated for their ignorance.

The ignorant are thus introduced into the community of the *poor of Yahweh*, and promised a share in the Kingdom.

"Those who labor and are overburdened" (v. 28) seem to be the "children" and ignorant of the preceding verses. Indeed, the yoke and burden point, in Judaism, to the observances of the Law (Si 51:26; Jr 2:20; 5:5), which the scribes had loaded with innummerable prescriptions (Mt 23:4). The simple people tried hard to observe them all, being unable to distinguish the essential from the relative. Christ is therefore not calling the sufferers in general, but rather the simple people, who are enslaved by the burdensome prescriptions of legalism.

b) Christ is calling the simple in the same way that the wise recruited their disciples (v. 29). We are reminded of Is 55:1;

Pr 9:5, or Si 24:19, all sapiential texts. But the yoke he imposes is easy to bear (1 Jn 5:3-4; Jr 6:6) because Jesus is himself part of the community of poor announced by Zephaniah 3:12-13 and gathering the "gentle and humble in heart." The new master of Wisdom is himself *Poor*, a member of the messianic remnant. He is such "in heart" because he has freely agreed to be such.

There will always be heavy yokes and burdens in the world: man is so anguished that he accepts religious prescriptions, rites and dogmas in hope of finding there some assurance and security. This explains why changes or simplifications in religion cause so many people dismay and turns them back to their fundamental anguish. Quite often man only rejects religious burdens to be crushed by even heavier yokes, those of political fanaticism or the religion of science.

In announcing an "easy yoke," Jesus is not proclaiming a religion less legalistic, ritualistic or dogmatic than the others. He is not preaching a new religion, but the discovery of a new reality that frees from religion. In revealing that we are accepted as we are, with our troubles and anguishes, he brings us peace, and makes our courage meaningful. Good does not now appear to us as the fruit of our religion, but we know that we are in him, because he has seized us, notwithstanding our weakness and sin, or the fragmentary and ugly character of our persons and of the world. Of course, we cannot find this reality, but can be sure that it has found us, as it found Jesus Christ and determined all his life.

In turn, the Church repeats the call of Jesus: "Come." But she has no right to call to a Christianity burdened with religious legalism. Her mission is to call man to this new reality, of which she is only a sign and witness, and which is truly manifested only in Jesus. This is important in dialogues between Christians and atheists. In interpreting Jesus' message, the Church does not aim at making Christians of atheists. She proclaims Jesus who transcends religion or absence of religion, Christianity or atheism.

For him religion is but a witness of this transcendence, and calls man to a deeper level of life, where one feels accepted by the Other.

VII. Isaiah   The Book of the Consolation of Israel (Is
   41:13-20   40:55) provides basis for an apologetic of
   1st reading   monotheism in face of false gods, for a the-
   Thursday   ology of redemption through the *Suffering
   Servant,* and for a typology of the eschato-
logical future (Is 40:3-5; 41:17-19; 43:16-20; 48:21; 49:9-11; 51:10; 52:5, 12; 55:12-13). Our reading comes from this final ensemble.

a) The miraculous character of verses 18-19 should be a surprise to no one; the Exodus was for Israel the era of miracles *par excellence*. Second-Isaiah demonstrates to his contemporaries that the Exodus is renewed in every moment of the history of salvation: the hurried character of the flight (Is 52:11-12), the protective cloud (Is 52:12b), the passage through the Sea (Is 43:16), the water gushing from the rock (Is 48:21), the metamorphosis of the desert into a paradise (Is 43:19-21), the creation of a roadway which is not only geographical but a way to the Covenant and holiness (Is 35:8).

b) These marvels which occurred at the time of the Exodus proclaim the reality of the One God (v. 20). In the dualistic religion of the Medes, the elements of good and evil confront each other without assurance about the outcome. In Jewish monotheism, God leads the evolution of the world and no force is capable of opposing him. It is only necessary to know God and his plan of salvation to understand the history of the world and to be assured that its evolution is towards good.

For Isaiah, history has meaning because Someone knows where it is leading. God communicates his knowledge to men by defining their route through miracles stamped by his hand. Modern man, be he Christian or atheist, pretends to lead his own history to a productive end through his own work. However, the Christian knows that he thus accomplishes the designs of God in history.

VIII. Matthew   Jesus pronounces his eulogy on the Baptist
11:11-15   (vv. 11, 13-14) to which Matthew adds a
Gospel   verse about violence (v. 12).
Thursday

a) *The praise of John the Baptist* (vv. 11, 13 and 14) is curiously linked to certain declarations (vv. 12 and 15) which have no connection with him. Luke could have avoided this juxtaposition of texts (cf. Lk 7:24-30), but in another passage (Lk 16:16) he leaves us under the impression that this is an ancient collection of texts.

We shall not return here to the affirmation of the Baptist's greatness and "leastness" (v. 11). Matthew, however, provides us with a tentative explanation. John is great because in him is shown the realization of the prophecies and the Law (v. 13); he is least because he is only a precursor, a new Elijah (v. 14; cf. Ml 3:23; Mt 17:10-13): he is, therefore, still in the domain of prophecy, not of fulfillment.

b) Verse 12, on the violence of those who take the kingdom by force, is ambiguous. The praise of the Baptist might be based on his violence of character, or his asceticism; or again, the eschatological nature of his message might be the ideal way which leads to the kingdom. This is probably the most logical interpretation. However, there could well be a reference to the endeavors of certain zealots, who sought to reconquer the kingdom by force of arms, turning away from the prophecies which announced its coming in terms of meekness and humility. This interpretation would go well with the lesson of the preceding verses (Mt 11:2-10 or Lk 7:18-22).

IX. Isaiah
48:17-19
1st reading
Friday

For the first — and almost only — time, Second-Isaiah allows some expression of doubt to appear. He considers the possibility of failure for the promises made to Abraham (v. 19.).

Up to this point the prophet had consistently related the present failures of Israel to her infidelity. But are things ever to change? He seems to hesitate: God now speaks in the present tense (v. 17), and the people seem unwilling to follow him? Even among the restored people, infidelity makes inroads and casts doubt on the fulfillment of the promises.

X. Matthew
11:16-19
Gospel
Friday

Matthew combines a short parable (vv. 16-17) and a discourse (vv. 18-19), apparently regarding the teaching as identical.

a) The parable of the children who would not play was very likely originally a popular proverb used by Christ to depict his "generation." A group of children chide their playmates for not dancing to festive tunes or mourning to funeral dirges. The parable thus accentuates the "obstinacy" of the present generation which is given over to fads and with whom no communication seems possible.

b) The discourse contained in verses 18-19 is more precise. The contemporaries of Christ were incapable of reading the signs of the kingdom: John came as an ascetic (Mt 3:7-10) preaching conversion and he was not heard. The "Son of Man" came to preside at the messianic banquet of the poor (cf. Is 25:6) and was misunderstood. In attributing to himself the messianic title "Son of Man" (Dn 7:13), Christ asks his audience to *see finally in these events* the coming of the definitive kingdom.

The discourse should be interpreted in an eschatological sense.

It is not an answer to the question whether or not Jesus' manner
of life is preferable to that of the Baptist. The context confirms
this interpretation: Israel's cities will be punished for not having
understood the signs of the kingdom and failing to grasp the
meaning of the miracles performed amongst them (Mt 11:20-24.)

c) In juxtaposing the parable and the discourse, and adding
to the latter the conclusion, "Yet wisdom has been proved right
by her children," * Christ conveys to his hearers the message
that his generation was incapable of reading the signs of salvation in spite of its pretended wisdom. Only the "children of the
wisdom of God," perhaps the "little ones" as opposed to the
"wise" in Lk 10:21-22 or to the whimsical children of the village
square (v. 17), will be able to read the "signs of the times."

XI. Sirach 48:1-4, The praise of Elias is one of the most re-
9-11   markable and important of Ben Sira's series
1st reading   of eulogies on outstanding figures in Jewish
Saturday   history.

a) The figure of Elias is indicated immediately by *fire* (v. 1).
It is the element by which man is united to God, the instrument by which sacrifices are offered (Lv 1:7; 6:6), by which
God's will is manifested on earth (Ex 40:38; 13:21-24; 3:2;
19:18; Nb 14:14; Pss 77/28:14, 21; 103/104; 2-4). Deuteronomy
often associates fire with the Word of God (Dt 4:12; 15:33,
36; 5:4). Consequently, because God is a "devouring fire" (Dt
4:24; 9:3) it is to be expected that he who bears the divine will
have a countenance of fire. And, finally, the last times of the
Day of Yahweh will come by fire (Jl 2:3-5; Dn 10:6; Pss 17/18:
9, 13-14; 28/29:7; 96/97:3).

Elias was unmistakeably the fire prophet. He had drawn upon
the earth a fiery drought (1 K 17:2), a thunderbolt upon Carmel

* The version of Luke 7:35, which forms a better link with the ensemble of
the context than that of Mt 11:19. The expression "child of wisdom"
gives it a primitive ring (Hebraicism).

(1 K 18), or on the armies of Achab (2 K 1:10-12). Finally, he had ascended to the heavenly court in a chariot of fire (2 K 2:1-14).

b) There is a remarkable correspondence between Elias' divine fire and the role of fire for *Moses.* We recall Yahweh's appearance to Moses in the burning bush (Ex 3:1-6), the fire that invests Sinai as he receives the law (Ex 19:18), the chastisement by fire of his adversaries (Lv 10:2; Nb 16:7-35). Nor is the parallel between the two confined to mastery over fire. Ben Sira (v. 7) recalls that Elias was a pilgrim to Sinai and crouched in the very cave of Moses to receive once more the will of God. In verse 9 furthermore he refers to the prophet's death, mysterious like that of Moses. And in verse 10 he borrows from Malachi 3:22-24 a characteristic applied by that prophet to Elias to suggest his Mosaic qualities. "Turning the hearts of fathers towards their sons and of sons towards their fathers" means turning the newer Jewish generations towards observance of the Mosaic law. The business of Elias is to preserve the Mosaic heritage.

This explains the simultaneous appearance of Elias and Moses beside the transfigured Christ (Mt 17:1-13): the Word of the law, vindicated by the Word of the Prophet, finds fulfillment in the Word made flesh in Jesus.

c) In fact Ben Sira is the first biblical author to bring up the topic of Elias' proximate return as *precursor of the Messiah* (vv. 10-11). The mysterious nature of his disappearance gave origin to a belief that he would come back at the beginning of the messianic era to complete his work. He would anoint the Messiah (cf. v. 9; 1 K 19:15-18) and exercise the power of life and death, as he had done already in the case of Sarepta's child (v. 5; cf. 1 K 17:17-24). As he seemed thus to escape the law of death, he becomes witness to an era when death will be conquered, when all men will be enabled "to possess life" (v. 11).

Primitive Christian tradition was thoroughly convinced about

Elias' return, but there was considerable hesitancy about identifying with him either the person of John the Baptist, or even Jesus himself. Matthew 3:1-4, 11:14; Luke 1:17 associate the Baptist with Elias, while Luke 4:23-30, 7:11-17; Matthew 4:1-5, Luke 9:54-55; Acts 1:1-11 find traits of the prophet in Jesus. Could it be that this function of Elias has really been entrusted to the Church and its witnesses in the world? They are signs of the presence among men of a God who gives meaning to human history.

XII. Matthew   The transfiguration of the Lord witnessed by
17:10-13   the apostles was only momentary, as Christ
Gospel   could not really attain his glory until after
Saturday   his death (v. 9). But the link between death
and glory had escaped the disciples, and so
Christ led the conversation to the subject of his coming death.

Is John the Baptist the new Elijah (v. 10)? Jesus gives an affirmative answer, and refers the apostles to Ml 3:23-24 (v. 11). He then goes on to say that John has not been recognized and was put to death (v. 12). The isolation and suffering of the new Elijah prepared the work of the Messiah; the Son of Man will suffer in similar fashion (Mt 21:33-42; 23:34-36).

The death of John the Baptist (Mt 14:3-12) gives Christ an opportunity to mention his own suffering and to make it acceptable to the apostles, who were a little too enthusiastic about his transfiguration. In this way, the martyrdom of John the Baptist prepares the way of the Lord.

If the Son of Man belongs to the line of suffering prophets, his disciple will also have to take this way, as he is not greater than his master (Jn 15:20). He must therefore bear witness to a glory that comes through suffering and death. Nor could it be otherwise, since in the Eucharist the Christian shares the memory of the passion and resurrection of the Lord.

THIRD SUNDAY OF ADVENT

A. THE WORD

I. Isaiah
35:1-6a, 10
1st reading
1st cycle

The commentary on this reading will be found at Monday of the second week of Advent, above, p. 78.

II. Isaiah
61:1-2, 10-11
1st reading
2nd cycle

Chapters 60 and 62 of Isaiah are attributed to Second-Isaiah, yet exegetes tend to ascribe chapter 61 to a later disciple. After describing his vocation as prophet (vv. 1-3), the author analyzes his message (vv. 4-11).

In a style which foreshadows the beatitudes, v. 7, the second half of which appears in the reading, makes use of antinomy: to a double share of shame is opposed a double share of happiness; to disgrace, an everlasting *joy*, characteristics of the eternal alliance between God and his people. God's alliance with Moses was not eternal because of the threat of punishment and exile which hung over it (Dt 30:15-30). The effect of the new alliance will be universal; all nations will marvel at the new people which is a sign of God's blessing (vv. 9 and 11 should probably be grouped together).

Verse 10 may be taken as a conclusion. Upon hearing the prophecy, the people sing their Magnificat (which is indeed used as Responsory to the reading). They are clothed with salvation from God as with a cloak of joy.*

The eternal alliance does not consist merely in an indefinite stay in the promised land, but in actual sharing of the life of God and unceasing dependence on his unfailing love. Neither

*See the doctrinal theme: *joy*, p. 104.

91

will it be the exclusive prerogative of one people; it will be open to all nations. Memorial of the sacrifice of the Lord, the Eucharist seals the new alliance and reveals the Savior as open to all men (*novi et aeterni testamenti**; *pro multis*). In so doing, it enriches our life with a dual dimension of unfailing attachment to God and of openness to all.

III. Zephaniah   Zephaniah proclaims his message just before
3:14-18a   the reign of Josiah. The moral corruption of
1st reading   the country is the worst known for a long
3rd cycle   time, and the threat of Assyria has been
                        growing over the years. The message of
Zephaniah is rather pessimistic: the Day of the Lord will not be delayed; with it will come the punishment of Judah and of the nations; only a small remnant will be saved. Yet, as his book ends, Zephaniah has some glimpses of hope: King Josiah appears as a great reformer, and Assyria seems to be temporarily releasing its grip. Under the circumstances, in two short poems (3:14-15 and 16-17) which serve as conclusion to his message the prophet can foresee better days for Jerusalem.

The main theme of these poems is a call to *joy* directed to *Jerusalem*. The prophet announces a great feast where there will be nothing but dancing and joy and exultation. The reason for this festivity is twofold: on the one hand, the enemy is moving away from the borders, (v. 15) and on the other, the people are renewed through the alliance reestablished under Josiah (v. 17). Both these events manifest the Lord; he it is who saves the people from war, and who, in his love, gives his alliance a renewed vigor.

This reading is particularly interesting as background to the

---

*Note that the word "aeterni" is not found in the gospel narratives of the Last Supper; it has been inserted in the Canon under the influence of Is 61:8 and Heb 13:20.

narrative of the annunciation by Saint Luke. The phrases "re-joice," "fear not," "the Lord is with you" (or in you) appearing in vv. 14, 16 and 17, not to mention the dance (v. 17) or leap that John the Baptist will perform in his mother's womb, are taken up almost word for word in the message of the angel to Mary. As such, the festival is no longer situated in a city, but in a human person, object of God's love, in whom pardon is granted for the first time (cf. Lk 1:26-45).

IV. James 5:7-10 Having already addressed the rich, James
    2nd reading now turns to his "brethren" (v. 7), the poor.
    1st cycle He exhorts them to be patient, until the Lord
        comes (vv. 8-11) and not to swear (v. 12).

James wants the poor to be *patient*. He does not urge any revolution because in his eyes the economic system of the rich is corrupt and about to crumble. This catastrophe will be a coming of the Lord (v. 8) since it will condemn the unjust and enable the poor to recover happiness and freedom. James may be pointing specifically to the catastrophe of the year 70 (fall of Jerusalem), as signs of it are already evident at the time he writes.

Just as the future (i.e. the coming of the Lord) brings re-assurance for the poor, so too does the past, because of numerous examples of courage and patience in adversity (v. 10). James is here using a classical argument of Jewish and Christian litera-ture: the praise of the Fathers is destined to strengthen the faith of contemporaries (Si 40-40; Heb 11; Mt 5:12; 23, 34; etc.).

Patience* is not resignation. It is the fruit of love, the willing-ness to discover the other person and help him in every way to liberate himself from alienating influences, money included. This takes time. The patience which James requires from the poor

*See the doctrinal theme: *patience*, p. 110.

brethren, consists does it not, in using for the rich the time limit that love sets to loving? Love should be given the opportunity to act, before the self-destructive force that has seized the powerful and rich can complete its task.

V. 1 Thess.	St. Paul brings his letter to the Church in
5:16-24	Thessalonika to its conclusion with a series of
2nd reading	recommendations. After certain counsels con-
2nd cycle	cerning relations between superiors and in-
	feriors (1 Th 5:12-14), and some remarks of

a disciplinary nature (1 Th 5:14-15), the Apostle makes a number of more particular recommendations (1 Th 5:16-18) and gives his opinion on the use of charisms (1 Th 5:19-22). He concludes this list of counsels with a final invocation (1 Th 5:23-24).

a) Paul wishes the Christian to live in *joy* (cf. Rm 3:5; 2 Co. 12:10; Ph 4:4-5), in *prayer* and in *thanksgiving* (Rm 12:12; Col 4:2). The Christian's life on earth is the same as that of others; but in his inmost depths he enjoys certitude of salvation, his view of history enables him to see in everything the events of salvation. It is not then in fleeing his condition that he bears witness to salvation, but in considering it a stage in the coming of the Savior.

b) The five sentences which determine the use of charisms already indicate the broad lines of doctrine in 1 Corinthians 14. The manifestations of the Spirit must not be stifled, but they must be properly evaluated according to a criterion which Paul discloses to the Corinthians: the building up of the community.

c) This passage was chosen for the Advent liturgy for its final invocation (vv. 23-24): God is a God of peace, of material well-being that is (the sense of peace in the Old Testament) and of spiritual well-being also (the plentitude of divine life given in Jesus Christ). He wishes that the whole man, body, spirit and soul, attain this well-being through holiness,* little by little, until the Parousia of the Lord.

It is not necessary to attribute capital importance to the "trichotomy" of St. Paul (v. 23). He often allows himself to get carried away by a certain rhetoric, not strictly anthropological. *Spirit* and *soul* seem to designate the same reality, but from slightly different points of view.

Paul demands that the Christian be beyond reproach not only on the day of judgment but throughout his entire life, in integrity of soul and body. This integrity is the proof of God's action. Man lives without reproach thanks to God who enables him to do so through the mediation of his glorified son.

Paul invites the Christian to measure his moral performance according to the Parousia not so much because its accompanying judgment will evaluate the actions of a man's life. The reason is, above all, because a Christian's attitude in daily life is the real sign of the coming of the Lord: the glory of God was made manifest in the life — and death — of Christ. It is no longer a question of escaping a life of exile, but of living that life as a sign of the Lord's coming.

The Eucharist, which is communion in the Risen Christ, is a stage on life's journey, until he comes.

VI. **Philippians 4:4-7** *2nd reading 3rd cycle* It is difficult to determine whether the reading is the actual conclusion of the letter or a separate note sent by Paul to the Philippians.

At any rate, the passage is under the sign of *joy*. Paul is encouraged by his trust in God, by the help received from the Christians of Philippi, and by some vague promise of freedom (Ph 2:24). But he mainly rejoices at the progress of the work of God in the Church (theme of the

---

*A theme dear to the heart of Isaiah (cf. Is 6:3; 4:2-6).

whole letter: cf. 1:4, 18, 25; 2:16-18, 28-29; 3:1 — duplicating today's reading; 3:20; 4:1).

a) This *joy* is expressed "in the Lord" (v. 4), because it is the result of his works. It originates in the nearness of the Messiah (Is 9:2-5), and so is a characteristic of messianic times (Is 35:1). Saint Luke has often stressed the joy of those who benefited from the messianic redemption (Lk 1:14, 44, 47; 5:34; 10:20; etc.).

b) Nevertheless, the *nearness* of the Lord (v. 5) is not considered in a temporal sense: it is not only the "day of the Lord" that is near, but the Lord himself: he is near to all who fear him, who pray and obey (religious meaning of nearness, as in Ps 84/85:10; 118/119:151; 144/145:18; Is 55:6).

The nearness of the Lord no longer depends on events more or less distant; it is a constant manner of presence in the Christian's life, until the fulfillment of the Parousia. The Christian who experiences this nearness is no longer subject to the feverish and vain expectation of false eschatologies; he lives calmly in prayer (v. 6), peace (v. 7) and joy (v. 4).

c) This nearness of God to the Christian's activity creates in him an openness to everything good and sincere that is done by his brothers, and a solidarity with it (v. 8). He does not shut himself in some moral structure of his own. On the contrary, he knows how to adopt as his own the virtues proper to any generation, the distinctive *elan* of any mentality, the particular excellence of any system of thought. The optimism that should be the fruit of a certainty that we live with God means taking an optimistic view of all that is good in circles not our own. In fact however many Christians are so defensive about God's nearness in their own lives, so fanatical, that they are blind to goodness and truth in other areas.

Openness to others is always the result of a joyous personal communion with God, that is balanced and relaxed.

VII. Matthew This gospel is made up of two distinct parts:
  11:2-11   the narrative of the deputation of the disciples
  Gospel   of John the Baptist (v. 2-6), and the praise
  1st cycle   of the latter by Christ himself (v. 7-10).

a) The Baptist's disciples are deputed to ascertain whether
Jesus really is "he who is to come." This expression must be
understood in the sense given by John the Baptist. It is borrowed
from Is 40:10 (a passage which the Precursor knows well, since
he quotes v. 3 in Mt 3:3), in which the coming of the Messiah
is described as being accompanied with *force* and violence. And
John is convinced that the Messiah he announces will be exceptionally violent (Mt 3:11). For it is indeed against the background of the terrible day of Yahweh that the Messiah is to
appear.

But Christ fails this expectation by revealing that his messianic
works are all works of peace and salvation. Instead of judging
and condemning, he heals and liberates. This mission has been
foretold by the scriptures and is in keeping with messianic hope
(cf. Is 61:1; 35:5-8). However, two different messianic concep-
tions divided the chosen people at that time: some expected the
last days to be days of power and violence; others, days of
liberation and happiness. But his opposition to John's disciples,
Christ reveals a style of life which baffles them and which will
be a scandel so long as the mystery of the Man-God on the
cross is not understood. Such indeed is the significance of v. 8
(cf. Mt 13:54-57; 16:20-23; 26:31-33 and especially 1 Co 1:17;
2:5). If, while recognizing that Christ fulfills this or that prophecy, some were nevertheless scandalized because of him, the
reason was that something unusual happened at his coming —
something which no prophecy could have foretold: the mystery
of the Man-God.

b) The Old Testament text to which Jesus directs the attention of the Baptist (principally Is 61:1) is awkwardly detached
from a promise, that is nevertheless a frequent prophetic theme:

"proclaiming freedom for prisoners." The Baptist, who knows the scriptures well, is in fact in prison. Thus the answer of Jesus does not in any way apply to him personally. Here we have the second *scandal*. He who seeks Jesus Christ must realize that the "signs" of the Son will not be for himself but for others. When he looks on the healed body of another the prisoner will find the fulfillment of his own hope.

c) Neither could John the Baptist have foreseen this unexpected feature of Christ's personality. In order to prove it, Jesus praises the Baptist.

To prepare his audience for the idea that John is a prophet, Jesus employs a series of images: contrast between well-dressed people and the man wearing a garment of camel's hair (Mt 3:4; 2 K 1:8), between the prophet who does not shake and the fragile reed (Jr 1:17-19). But John is more than a *prophet*. He is the greatest of the prophets. By quoting Ml 3:1 and Ex 23:20, Jesus defines the Precursor's role as that of a servant leading the people of God into the long-promised land. And yet (v. 11) John is the least personage in the Kingdom. This remark is all-important for understanding the true significance of the gospel. John is the greatest of the Old Testament, but, as such, still bound to too human and too specifically Jewish and interpretation of prophecies. That is why he is the smallest in the kingdom. He lacks insight into the wholly unexpected dimension which Christ, the Man-God, brings.

The two parts of the Gospel are therefore complementary. It is not enough to realize that Christ and his forerunner fulfill the scriptures, nor to describe them according to ancient prophecies. If a man stops there and does not pierce the mystery of Christ's personality, he remains the least in the Kingdom. Christ is not only the last of a lineage of spiritual poor of whom John is the penultimate link (v. 8-9). He is "ontologically" poor by his human and divine obedience to the Father, and his poverty unto the cross is but the earthly echo of his eternal condition of absolute dependence as Son on the Father.

Following Christ, men can attain this poverty of the children of God, this complete dependence on the Father. The Eucharist which they celebrate invites them to follow the initiative of the Father, and equips them for the adventure.

VIII. John 1:6-8; 19-28
Gospel
2nd cycle

A moderate, though realistic exegesis can distinguish in Jn 1:19-36 a basic narrative which would run as follows:

19 The Jews sent priests and Levites to question John. 24 Now among these were some Pharisees 25 They put this question to him: 19c Who are you? 20 He not only declared, but he declared quite openly: I am not the Christ. 21 Well then, they asked, are you Elijah? — I am not, he said — Are you the Prophet? — He answered: No. 22a So they said to him: 25 Then why are you baptizing, if you are not the Christ, and not Elijah, and not the Prophet? 26a John replied: 26c There stands among you one unknown to you.

The synoptic additions are found in v. 23 which introduces the quotation of Isaiah 40:3 (cf. Mt 3:3), in v. 27 which introduces the theme of the sandal (cf. Mt 3:11), in v. 28, the origin of which is uncertain, and in parts of verses which allude to baptism of water opposing it to the baptism of the Spirit (e.g. v. 26). We refer the reader to the commentary below on Luke 3:10-18 for an analysis of themes common to John and the synoptics.

a) The Jewish leaders send some priests and levites — specialists in ritual ablutions — to ask John on what grounds he is introducing a new rite of ablution (v. 19). But the conversation soon turns to the *personality of John* (who are you? is a frequent question in the 4th gospel: Jn 6:42; 7:11-12, 40-42; 9:36; 10:24).

By declaring himself neither the Messiah, nor Elijah,* nor the "prophet" whose coming after centuries without prophecy, was to end God's silence (Ez 7:26; Is 2:1-3; Lm 2:9; Ps 73/74:9; 1 M 9:27; Dt 18:18), John leads the discussion to *Christ's personality* (v. 26), more important than his, but much underrated.

This dialogue is according to the usual procedure of the fourth evangelist. He will start off with a fact (often ritualistic: the water in the well: Jn 4; the multiplication of the loaves: Jn 6; or, here, the baptism of John), continue with a discussion between the unbelieving Jews and Jesus (here John), and finally bring up the matter of the human and divine personality of Christ.

b) John was baptizing at Bethany, or better Betabara (v. 28), meaning "place of passage", which could be an allusion to the crossing of the Jordan by the Hebrews before their entry into the promised land (Jos 3-4). If so, we would have an interesting typology of the baptism of John. But the detail seems foreign to the intention of the fourth gospel, and does not deserve much attention.

There is some one among us who may remain unknown if we only see in him the hero of human messianism, the theoretician of brotherhood or of some earthly happiness, the extraordinary wonder-worker. The secret of Jesus' personality and his faithfulness to the Father, even unto death, will not elude the eyes of a clear faith.

IX. Luke 3:10-18 The final two gospels of this Sunday have
    Gospel many points in common. We shall comment
    3rd cycle on both together, because Luke gives us here
    only material common to all the synoptics.

a) The opposition between baptism of water and baptism in "the Spirit and fire" is the most important common aspect (Jn

---

*Whereas, for Mark & Matthew, both quoting Ml 3:23-24, John is really Elijah.

1:26, 33; cf. Mk 1:8 and Ac 1:5). John the Baptist probably did not intend to oppose his rite to that reserved for the Messiah. In those days, "baptism" was not necessarily a rite (Mk 10:38-39; Lk 12:49-50; Ac 1:5).

His allusion to baptism in the "Spirit and fire" points to the judgment of the nations by God. All will have to go through it, but those who have received the ritual baptism of John will bear a mark that will preserve them from extermination (Ez 9:4-11; Rv 7:3; 9:4).

It seems that John may not have spoken of baptism in "spirit and fire," but in "wind and fire." In Hebrew, the same word "ruah" denotes both spirit and wind, and John may well have had the latter in mind. He presents the judge as a thresher (cf. Is 41:16), who entrusts his wheat to the wind (Mt 3:12; Lk 3:17), to separate the grain from the chaff which is destined to fire. The book of Isaiah often presents the judgment of God as the unfurling of tempest and flames (Is 29:5-6; 30:27-28; 33: 11-14; 66:15; cf. Am 1:14). The evangelist is perhaps referring to certain contemporaneous apocalypses which foresaw judgment as a river of fire, engulfing the world like the earlier deluge (Dn 7:10; 2 Ch 3:5-7). Men will be "plunged" into this river of fire unless they agree to be "plunged" in the water as a sign of conversion.

The contrast between baptism in water and baptism in wind and fire indicates that only conversion (cf. Mt 3:11) can preserve the faithful from catastrophe.

b) In fact, Christ has brought a really spiritual wind and fire (Lk 12:49; Ac 2:2-3). The early Christians recalled the words of the Baptist and substituted "spirit" for "wind," as etymology allowed. In so doing, they opposed John's baptism to Christian baptism (Ac 19:1-7), and gave a new meaning to the Precursor's declaration by making it an announcement of Christian baptism and an avowal of its superiority. What better argument could be found than a declaration of their master to confound the straggling disciples of John!

The early Christians not only introduced a new element to the words of the Baptist; they also inserted into the very narrative of the fourth gospel (or at least the sources used by John) the notion that the Baptist was baptizing only in water (Jn 1:26a: I baptize with water; 31: with water; 33 with water . . . ; the man . . . is going to baptize with the Holy Spirit). The controversy concerning baptismal rites therefore emphasizes the close link between Christian baptism and the coming of redemption and judgment, maybe less spectacular than that expected by the Precursor, but more efficacious.

c) The Baptist's audience seems to have reacted immediately to his kerygma. They inquire *what they should do* (vv. 10, 12, 14). Luke's emphasis on this question, so often asked in the context of Christian catechumenate (as in Ac 2:37; 16:30; 22:10; and see Lk 18:18), suggests that it was a ritual question. The man who wished to be converted indicated thus his readiness, to be proven by catechumenate, to adopt a new life style.

In fact John determines precise behavior as a sign of conversion for three classes of people whom he encounters. Selfishness must not be the criterion of behavior: one must not seek to enrich oneself unjustly through a profession or trade. These evidences of conversion are indeed elementary: we are still far from the sermon on the mount. But perhaps a decision to remove "self" from the central position in one's living is already a good indication of a turning towards the Kingdom?

d) A second detail that is common to all today's gospels is that of *loosening the sandal* (it is found also in Ac 13:24-25, and was probably inserted in Jn 1:27 in an account where there was no mention of it). This act of humility Christian tradition understood as the gesture of a servant who looses the sandals of his master after a journey. It demonstrates the distance that divides the Precursor from Jesus, and puts his message and his rite in their proper place. In controversy about the two baptisms it was an important point.

Matthew 3:11 however speaks not of "loosening the fastening

of sandals," but of "taking off the sandals." Perhaps there is an allusion to a penitential gesture required of the faithful by John, as in the case of David (2 Sm 15:30) or Micah (Mi 1:8; cf. Ez 24:17-23). This would be an assertion on the Baptist's part that he could not impose conversion on Jesus (cf. Mt 3:13-17).

B. DOCTRINE

1. The Theme of Joy

Joy is one of the scripture's principal themes, both in the Old and New Testaments. The bible message is fundamentally optimistic: God wills the well-being of all men, their success and growth; he desires them to be crowned with abundance and plenitude. Joy for man means the sense of fulfillment already present, or of fulfillment yet to come.

The world scarcely knows this complete joy which presupposes a profound unity in man's being on the level of his destiny as willed by God. Without doubt, there are joys proper to modern man, such as the joy over success in the mastery of nature's mysteries. However this is reserved for the few and remains vague for the majority. Modern man generally seeks joy in evasion, in fantasies and pleasures, embracing thereby a superficial and meaningless existence.

Christians should know that the good news of salvation is a message of joy. In a world rich in potential but likewise given over to contradiction and absurdity, or so some think, they must communicate to those around them the joy which they live, an extraordinarily realistic joy, which expresses certitude founded on the victory of Christ: that, through all the difficulties and contradictions, man is in the process of building his own future. The world is not absurd, because God is in love with it, and the living principle of his victory has been given us once for all in the event of Jesus Christ.

Christian joy, however, is not simply any joy, and it is therefore necessary here to study its meaning in depth and bring out particular qualities.

The covenant: source of joy in Israel

The story of joy in the bible follows step by step the gradual deepening of faith. The most spontaneous joys are those which flow from possession of the basic securities of everyday existence, which were considered Yahweh's blessings: the joy of harvest and vintage, the joy of completion in a work well done, or of an earned repose, the joy of the fraternal meal, the joy which the faithful and fruitful wife brings to her husband, the boisterous joys of the great days, which become an intimate joy of the heart. The feast day, with its varied forms of cultural celebration, forms the backdrop par excellence against which these joys were felt and expressed. There Yahweh invites Israel to rejoice in his presence with the same joy he himself experiences in seeing the works of his own creation. The joy of Israel is to praise her God for the marvels of that creation.

However, the progressive discovery of faith is that the God of the alliance intervenes in history, and that these interventions, often unforeseen, do not always bring with them the security men naturally seek. Joy deepens as it is no longer linked with the possession of some object. Yahweh reserves true joy for those who become poor in his sight and who await all things from their God in fidelity to his law. Nothing can tarnish this joy, not even suffering or trial which, on the contrary, are now able to make it fruitful. The joy of Yahweh is the strength of those who seek him.

Further, faith induces the poor of Yahweh to set their sights on the future. God intervenes in history and this is a cause for joy in the poor. However, the day will come when the divine intervention will bring final salvation in its train, and then the joy of God's poor will more than answer all their expectations. Heaven and earth will cry out for joy. Joy will reign in Jerusalem, which will see within her gates the reuniting of all the dispersed and exiled. For the people of God there will be only joy.

Jesus of Nazareth and messianic joy

The intervention of Jesus in history, as the gospels have narrated it, took place in a climate of joy and exultation. The infancy narrative of St. Luke is significant in this regard. At the time of the visitation, the Precursor leaps for joy in the womb of his mother, and the Virgin Mary exults before God, who has filled the hungry with good things and sends away the rich with empty hands. The same holds true at the birth of Jesus in the stable at Bethlehem. The heavens themselves resound with joy as the good news is announced to the shepherds.

It is certain that Jesus' public life, even to that last ascent to Jerusalem, was marked with moments when the crowds who followed him expressed their joy and enthusiasm, even to the point of recognizing him as the messiah. It is just as certain that Jesus excited reactions of messianic joy in those around him: if he is the bridegroom, the disciples should not fast in his presence.

However, several considerations lead us to deepen our concept of messianic joy in a particular way that demonstrates how ambiguous were the spontaneous reactions of the crowds. First of all, messianic joy is confined to the poor and to sinners who have repented, for these alone perceive the nature of the salvation wrought by Jesus and of the joy it has produced in their hearts. Secondly, this joy has its source in the Messiah himself: Jesus bestows a joy which is his own and which has led him to the total gift of self and perfect obedience to the Father. But only those receive this joy who in their turn observe the new commandment of love without limitation. "If you keep my commandments, you will remain in my love, just as I have kept my Father's commandments and remain in his love. I have told you this so that my own joy may be in you, and your joy be complete" (Jn 15:10-11).

The joy of the gospel is a joy which comes from above, but which at the same time, must rise up from the very heart of man: it is a divine-human love. Jesus is the final source of this joy. It is a paschal joy since it is necessarily linked to that ultimate act of obedience to the Father in which Jesus gave his life for all men.

The joy of the spirit in the people of God

The joy of the Church is the joy of the Spirit. The sending-forth of the Spirit which constitutes the Church attests to the fact that the salvation of the world has been definitely accomplished in the death and resurrection of Christ. This mission seals the alliance between God and humanity: between the God who has never tired of communicating his love to men, and the humanity that has found in Jesus of Nazareth its own perfect complement. The sending forth of the Spirit which brings joy to the hearts of men was accomplished jointly by the Father and by Him who has Risen. The Spirit could only enter the picture after that life-journey in which the man-God made himself obedient even to the death of the cross. Jesus had to traverse the trial of his passion in order that one day the sorrow of his disciples be transformed into joy.

The people of God give thanks unceasingly for this gift of the Spirit, their feelings of joy being transformed into feelings of gratitude because the salvation which they received is primarily a gift. This dimension of their joy is essential: Christians know that the success of the human adventure radically depends on the providential mercy of the Father. "This is the love I mean: not our love for God, but God's love for us" (I Jn 4:10). The Magnificat of the Virgin Mary expresses marvelously the fundamental tone of Christian joy.

However, let us make no mistake here. Thanksgiving in this context is by no means the passive attitude of one who simply recognized that everything has come to him from above. It manifests the joy of partnership. At the very moment when the sharing of the Spirit is given him, the Christian sees himself called to contribute his share to the building up of the temple of God. The members of the body of Christ can only know the joy of the last days by following the path opened up for them by Jesus. The Christian must himself follow the same journey of obedience unto death, and, if necessary, even to the death of the cross. Christian joy necessarily entails this element of active cooperation.

Further, the joy of the Spirit which the Church knows in her earthly existence is the joy proper to the period of construction. It has yet to become the joy of perfect accomplishment which man will know when he is brought to fulfillment on the last day. The New Testament expresses this in declaring that here below we possess only the "pledge" of the Spirit.

The witness of constant joy

Each time that St. Paul described his missionary life he insists on the many difficulties and obstacles that he encountered, but he does so in order to make the point that these are for him a source of joy. The passion of Christ always appears on the horizon of the Pauline ministry and in every circumstance Paul seeks to identify himself with the obedience of his Savior. The Apostle of the nations knows that this conformity alone can bring his work to fruition and render fruitful the role he must play in the service of the Kingdom, where he is called to model his life on that of Christ. The proclamation of the good news of salvation is indissolubly linked to the life of witness. If salvation brings with it joy and exultation, it is necessary that those who proclaim the Good News be joyous themselves (2 Cor 6:10), whatever the trials and tribulations of their ministry.

Joy in the trial — which might even reach martyrdom itself — this is the sign *par excellence* of the authentic Christian. This joy is not the outcome of some form of fanaticism. It alone renders possible a secret accomplishment; it unveils the vital fact that the royal way of the cross leads to the only life that can bring man to fulfillment. Joy under fire is not spontaneous joy. It can only be the result of gradually more perfect obedience to the Father. It expresses the practical conviction that the way of perfect obedience truly brings man to completion. The important fact for the Christian is not that he is often joyful but that he is always joyful. Christian joy, especially that of the missionary, has to be constant, and it is precisely in this constancy that it reveals that which is most proper to itself.

Another dimension of the joy that should radiate from the face of the missionary should be emphasized: his necessary relevance. By this I mean that the secret accomplishment of which the missionary's joy is the messenger, must be a response, unhoped for but actual, a response to the most profound expectations of modern man. From this point of view, the missionaries of today must manifest more and more their conviction that salvation in Jesus Christ directly concerns the concrete success of the human adventure, for which all men bear responsibility. A much stronger tie should be evident between the growth of the missionary endeavor and the construction of the world undertaken by men. The witness of constant joy should be incarnated in the Church serving the world.

The joy of eucharistic sharing

The eucharistic celebration is one of the privileged occasions where true joy ought in some manner to be communicated and experienced. The desire of the Church in calling together all the faithful around the two tables of Bread and Word is to make them live in anticipation of the salvation belonging to the Kingdom, and to experience the all-inclusive brotherhood which will accompany its arrival. In this sense the eucharistic banquet is objectively a source of joy.

It goes without saying, however, that the eucharistic celebration does not automatically have this effect. To do so, it is above all necessary that the Mass truly become a celebration. Christians who come together in assembly must see themselves as involved at a deep personal level. This supposes particularly that the proclaimed Word effectively relate to the life and responsibilities of those who hear it. It is further necessary that the assembly itself reflect the catholicity of the Church: Christians called together for the celebration must discover that in their diversity they are made brothers by the grace of Christ which overcomes all barriers which separate men from each other. This is a very important point, and if care is not taken here, the eucharistic celebration can end up being no more than a source of merely human joy, a simple meeting among men who are already brothers by racial affinity, social milieu or common interest. The celebration would only be, in this case, a sacralizing of pre-existing relationships, by adding to them a deep dimension of affectivity. Such a celebration is certainly capable of setting in motion a fraternal experience of the Kingdom; but this is insufficient, and pastors must profit from every occasion to open their eucharistic communities to the riches of human diversity. The joy thus experienced might be less spor.taneous but how much more real!

2. The Theme of Patience

The frequent recurrence of the theme of patience in the Advent liturgy makes it a characteristic of the season. It appears on the countenance of love. Modern man, who seeks instantaneous and tangible results, almost automatically, has little time for patience. When he sets himself to work through a long-term project he counts on having partial results at least fairly soon. So in the spiritual and moral domains his tendency is to attempt the accomplishment of everything at once: the idea of necessary new-beginnings is resisted. Christianity, founded as it is on love, encourages us to react against such impetuous tendencies. The matter deserves deeper consideration.

Viewed thus, the theme of patience neatly complements the theme of conversion. Some today are quick to identify the Church of the "converted" with a Church of the "pure," which, according to them, would be so much more effective than a Church of sinners. But the truth is that such a Church would be ineffective because it would soon become intolerant.

The Old Covenant a period of divine patience

Israel's infidelity to the obligations of the covenant provoked the wrath of God, and the prophets were constantly reading signs of God's anger into the reverses which the chosen people seemed to encounter. The very nations served Yahweh as instruments of vengeance. However the prophets never contented themselves with a mere recital of such facts. God's anger was not the final item in his self-revelation to men: pardon was always implied. Yahweh, rich in kindness and fidelity, is always ready to repent of his threats, provided Israel sets herself on the path of conversion. Divine patience with sinners will even embrace pagans. The story of Jonah shows how the mercy of Yahweh is open to all who repent. It is true that Israel did not immediately draw all the conclusions from this divine revelation. The select Israel, the poor of Yahweh, become impatient. They freely call down the vengeance of God on their enemies; and indeed there are many of these, from pagan neighbors to mediocre fellow citizens. They are annoyed when divine wrath is slow to manifest itself.

The patience of Jesus an incarnation of divine patience

Jesus inaugurates the Kingdom of the last days. But far from appearing in glory, as a judge dividing the just from the unjust, he comes as a universal shepherd. His coming is principally for sinners, and he calls on all men to acknowledge that they are such. No one is excluded from the Kingdom; everyone is called and everyone can enter. Throughout his entire life Jesus is the incarnation of divine patience in his attitude to sinners; no sin is capable of wrenching man away from the merciful power of the Father; God's will to forgive is without limit.

The secret of this patience is love. Jesus loves the Father with the very love by which he himself is loved, because he is the son. When he turns towards men he loves them with the same love with which the Father loves them, a love universal by its very nature. It is worthwhile to notice how patience became in Christ one of the most fundamental expressions of self.

Love invites us to dialogue, to perfect reciprocity. Loving men for Jesus means inviting them, with an infinite respect for what they are, to build in partnership with him a free response. This response, because for each individual it is unique, demands time. It grows little by little, and the period of its shaping constitutes a veritable spiritual adventure, where advances go hand in hand with moments of backsliding, the giving of self with withdrawal into self. The love with which Jesus loves men might be described as patient, since this implies actual, integral respect for another even in his very otherness. But there is more. For Jesus, to love men is to love them even in their sinfulness, even in their refusal of the plan of God. The greatest proof of love is laying down one's life for the beloved; it is man's sinfulness which led Jesus to the cross. Even though the sins of men have struck him down, his love remains, is deepened, and is finally victorious. Furthermore, it is in his passion and death that the patience of Jesus is fully manifested. At the supreme moment, when it seemed that the divine plan was jeopardized by the attitude of men, his love is altogether merciful: "Father, forgive them, they know not what they do."

His patience causes scandal, because it bears witness to a love of God and man which is totally based on a stripping of the self. Undertaking the bonds of love proposed to men by Jesus means acceptance of the demand for radical humility. Man tends to fear such total self-denial, because it gives him the feeling of losing everything. When he revealed the mystery of divine patience in his own life and death, Jesus was calling on us to leave everything in order to gain everything.

The all-embracing patience of love in the Church

Because she is the Body of Christ, the Church's mission is to incarnate his patience among men. Her task is not to act as judge, sorting the just from the unjust, but to show all men the true countenance of love. Her patience then, springing from love, challenges her members above all to complete reverence for the neighbor, be he believer or unbeliever. She does not seek the annexation of peoples; she seeks to make them really free partners in the love of Christ. Through her every man is called to make his own irreplaceable contribution in the building of the Body of Christ, to be an individual cooperator in realizing salvation history. Patience must govern the manifestation of our total reverence for others, because time is a necessary element in the total process. We require time to recognize a neighbor and accept him for what he is, called by God, with God as his final goal. We require time to strip away the self, in order to be capable of accepting others exactly as they are. Our difficulty in distinguishing the truth from our personal expression of the truth has been so often demonstrated. The Christian is not free from the temptation to be intolerant.

It is also true, and this corresponds to what has been already said about Jesus, that the love of which the Church is witness leads inevitably to suffering. Man does aspire to universal brotherhood, but he has no natural inclination towards the type of love that will surmount the walls of separation. This means the sort of bond that brings with it seeming insecurity, because he is asked to place his whole security in God alone. The Church indeed, in the ultimate estimate, has been more accepted by men than was Jesus himself. The world will not hesitate to use her when it is expedient, and whenever she has offered resistance to such use persecution has followed. Yet it is precisely thus that her true nature is revealed, when she endures apparent defeat with patience, and shows that, once for all, love has in fact defeated death and sin.

Mission and the delays that beset the Kingdom

Mission is the real proving ground where the patience that springs from love is learned. When we agree to be "sent forth" we are in fact accepting fraternal love on a universal scale. Because mission is the privileged work of love, and the demands of love reveal its true nature. Whenever mission fails to manifest love and brings about its own degradation, it becomes automatically a mere work of propaganda. The will to annex will predominate.

In fact and by right, mission is an extraordinarily complex and lengthy enterprise. Transmitting the mystery of Christ from one already Christianized culture to an area where the gospel has not been preached involves fraternal encounter in total dimension, particularly in the collective aspect. Only little by little do missionaries learn to share the life of the people to whom they wish to bring the gospel. Likewise only little by little, under the impulse of the Spirit, do the people come to encounter Christ. For the long process there must be total involvement on both sides.

There is however another, more profound, reason why mission is a work of patience. Being as it is a call to universal communion in the denial of self, it will always in the last analysis be a stumbling block to men. Patience under difficulty requires that the Church conform to the image of her Head, and this applies especially to those responsible for the mission. Jesus came to fulfill the destiny of Israel and was nailed to a cross. The same fate awaits the Church when she tries to fulfill the spiritual destiny of any people.

Eucharist the effective sign of Christ's patience

No one can claim a share in the patience of Christ without nourishing himself on the Word and the Bread. The reason is simple: Christ's patience is no mere moral virtue, but the incarnate expression of the love with which he loved men to the end. In sharing the eucharistic Bread and being renewed interiorly, we gain entry into the great Thanksgiving of Christ, who delivered himself over to a love of oblation in the crucifixion. The Eucharist is accordingly a pledge of final victory over death. Hearing the Word is no less necessary; for by its forceful penetration it gradually forms us in the image of the patient Christ.

THIRD WEEK OF ADVENT

I. Numbers
24:2-7, 15-17
1st reading
Monday

Invited to curse Israel (Nb 22) Balaam, a soothsayer from the Euphrates, on the contrary blessed it because he was faithful to the word of God. He utters four oracles on mounting levels of intensity, which sketch the immensity of the chosen people and marvel at the grandeur of its future vocation (Nb 23:7-10, 18-24; 24:3-9, 15-19). Today's reading brings us the main verses of the third oracle and one verse from the fourth. These prophecies derived from ancient Yahwist traditions (9th century), where the fact that a pagan soothsayer talked in the name of Yahweh caused no misgiving. The more recent priestly documents were hostile to the memory of Balaam, probably to show that Israel owed nothing to a pagan (Nb 31:8, 16; 22:14). Later tradition followed this pessimistic portrayal (2 P 2:15-16; Jude 11).

These views cannot be shared. As a great prophet and an excellent poet. Balaam was among the very first to outline the future of Israel.

a) The third oracle (Nb 24:2-9) blesses the *fruitfulness of Israel*. Balaam compares the tents of the Hebrews pitched in the valley of Moab to a paradisal garden (v. 6). The Hebrew text of v. 7a follows this image and sees Israel as fertilized by masses of water! But the Septuagint version alludes to a hero who arises from Israel and will one day reign over countless peoples. The Greek text thus gives a messianic nuance to an oracle that in fact merely promised happiness to Israel. The king in v. 7 is probably God himself (cf. Nb 23:21), and Agag is a title traditionally reserved for the king of Amalek (1 S 15:9-33).

b) The fourth oracle refers directly to a *messianic king*. The sceptre (v. 17) is obviously a royal emblem (Gn 49:10), as is also probably the star (Is 14:12; cf. Mt 2:1-2), the appearance of a star being considered by the magi as a sign of royal birth. The Septuagint further emphasized the messianic character of the poem by replacing "sceptre" with "man." This prophecy of Balaam undoubtedly refers to the davidic dynasty.

Though not strictly messianic, the oracle is one of Israel's most ancient royal poems: where royalism is beginning to merge into the figure-type that will finally be the Messiah himself.

This text is the first to place the hopes of the chosen people on the royal line. That this recognition of the messianic calling of the chosen people was made by a pagan is a matter of pride for Israel. But it also underlines a responsibility which in the course of its history the Jewish people may have seemed to abdicate.

II. Matthew   As the levites, specialists in ritual matters,
21:23-27   had questioned John the Baptist on his title to
Gospel   introduce a new rite (Jn 1:19), so now the
Monday   chief priests and elders ask on what authority
                     Jesus teaches and disturbs the customs of
the temple (Mt 21:1-22).

Jesus' authority comes from the Father. John stresses this repeatedly (Jn 5:19-47; 7:16-19; 8:18-19), where the synoptics, being without the vocabulary or theology required to express the idea, tend to insist on the secrecy Jesus kept concerning his origin (Mt 9:30; 17:9). In order to remain anonymous, he confronts the high priests and elders with this query concerning the authority of John the Baptist: do his rite and his message come from God or from men? Their perplexity (vv. 25-26) frees him from the necessity of replying, and so due to their insufficient knowledge the secret can be maintained.

This discussion concerning the authority of John the Baptist and of Christ presupposes some relationship between the two. Both are indeed signs that the rulers of Israel fail to understand (Mt 11:16-19). The Baptist is the forerunner of the Messiah in that he has lived in advance the mystery of rejection and suffering (cf. Mt 17:9-13) which will be the lot of Christ.

The world has the right to determine by what authority the Church claims to witness. By introducing the Christian to the life of the Father, the Eucharist enables him to reveal the authority by which he is sent. This should not however make him authoritarian. He does not don the authority of God as if it were a garment of prestige and power. His "authority" is based on knowledge of a God who is in the service of man, and solicitous that no one should be lost *en route*.

III. Zephaniah
3:1-2, 9-13
1st reading
Tuesday

Zephaniah is writing a century after Isaiah (around 640). The downfall of the kingdom of the North is by then only a dim memory, but Judah, which had miraculously escaped the invasion of Sennacherib (Is 37:30-38), is now in decay, both economically and politically. Zephaniah is the first to see in this miserable condition a possible relation to God: "poor" in the eyes of Assur, should the people not also be "poor" in the eyes of God (Zp 2:3)?

Such a spiritual poverty would also enable Judah to escape the judgment of the nations and of the people, as announced by the prophet in God's name (Zp 1:14-18). Unlike many other prophets, Zephaniah points out the positive aspect of "the day of Yahweh": this disaster will affect only the proud, those who did not keep spiritual poverty in their hearts.

After the disaster, some men will be found both among pagans and Jews, who are spiritual enough to merit survival. Such is the topic of the two poems (vv. 9-10 and 11-13) read today.

a) As Isaiah had done in Is 19:18-25, Zephaniah announces

the conversion of Egypt and Ethiopia, (The Land of "Cush"), although his *universalism* is not as deep as his predecessor's: God will give the nations clean lips (Is 6:7), enabling them to offer a sacrifice of praise pleasing to God; but they will have to perform their cult in Jerusalem (v. 10). This influx of pagans in the temple will not bring confusion to the Jews (v. 11). They will be purified by the purge of the proud and arrogant, who consider Mount Zion and its temple as an exclusive prerogative (Jr 7:1-15).

Universalism will only become a reality if Israel and its temple, destined to welcome the nations, purify themselves of all exclusivism and pride (v. 11b; cf. Mt 21:12-13). It is the first time that a prophet subordinates the gathering of the nations to the purification of the Jewish people. Any mission which relies on the humiliation of others is bound to fail: true mission must begin with the conversion of the missionary.

b) The condition essential for conversion, in the case of those to whom his mission is directed, is defined by Zephaniah as *poverty* (v. 12). It is expressed in the social vocabulary of the day, but in terms transposed to the religious level: *ani* (poor) and *dal* (humble) (cf. Zp 2:3).

It is remarkable that the notions of poverty and universalism are here brought together. If the Jewish people wishes to retain the temple and possess Yahweh, its material poverty will be of no avail, and the universal plan of salvation becomes impossible. The poverty of the missionary consists in not "possessing" his God or the privileges of his religion.

Christians concerned with the problems of evangelization are uneasy about the riches of the Church. All do not have the vocation to voluntary renunciation in the same degree, but every one must respond to the missionary need for poverty, lest the Church become the sort of instrument of glamour and power which elicits the condemnation of Zephaniah 3:11b.

IV. Matthew   The parable of the two sons is found in
   21:28-32   Matthew's gospel only. An early reduction
   Gospel   ended with v. 31 (I tell you). In that primi-
   Tuesday   tive form, the parable simply demonstrated
                     to the adversaries of Christ why the gospel
was finally directed to sinners; the just had refused it.

But before being recorded in the three synoptics, traditions
were often grouped together fairly arbitrarily, by combining
key-words for instance. Thus to the parable of the two sons,
which ends with an allusion to tax collectors and prostitutes
(v. 31) was added an independent saying (Lk 7:29-30 reports
it as a separate saying) which also mentions tax collectors. The
second conclusion makes the parable an allegory on the history
of salvation.

Matthew reworked v. 32 (note the insertion of righteousness,
the change to 2nd person, the mention of the Baptist) and
placed vv. 28-32 after a passage (vv. 23-27) concerning John
the Baptist.

We shall first discuss the primitive parable, and then the particular interpretation of v. 32.

a) The parable of the two sons justifies the *direction taken by
the gospel in addressing those who are despised,* a new category
of poor. Christ is indeed directing it to the chief priests and the
elders (Mt 21:23), just as he directs similar parables to the
Pharisees (the Pharisee and the publican: Lk 18:9; the two
debtors: Lk 7:40; the lost drachma: Lk 15:2). Here he wants to
convince all those who are scandalized at his love for sinners
that they are closer to salvation, if they repent, than people who
consider themselves righteous (cf. Mt 9:10-13). Sinners have
opposed the will of God, but they have also repented, like the
prodigal son; while the others declare themselves to be at the
service of God, but do not really accept his plan of love for
all men!

Consequently the parable is addressed to people who, in the
very name of righteousness, shut themselves out from the good

news. It shows the love of God for the despised ones, who are still capable of repenting and obeying with more love than the proud and self-sufficient. It is therefore a good apology for Christ's attitude towards sinners.

b) The addition of v. 32 turns the parable into an *allegory on the history of salvation*. Like the men sent to the tenants of the vineyard (Mt 21:33-38) or those invited to the wedding feast (Mt 22:1-9), John the Baptist in his prophetic mission encounters refusal and disdain from his audience, and is thus led to address another category of persons (compare Mt 21:32 with Mt 21:41 and 22:8-10). This explains why the Church does not confine herself to the chosen people. Matthew was particularly prone to allegorization of the parables, when demonstrating the new character of the church of Christ as opposed to the structures and limitations of ancient Israel. The figure of John the Baptist is here purely incidental. He was just one of the people sent by God to men, but possibly the one who understood most clearly that the nation would be stripped of its privileges for the benefit of "others."

The people of the last days are in continuous growth; always being increased by the conversion of those who without claiming any personal righteousness welcome the Sent One *par excellence*.

V. Isaiah 45:6b-8; This short poem may be considered as the
18:21b-25   conclusion to the second oracle dedicated by
1st reading   Second-Isaiah to the person of Cyrus, king
Wednesday   of the Persians. His destruction of Babylon
permitted the Hebrews, around 538, to return
home (Ezr 5:14). Already a first oracle concerning Cyrus (Is 41:1-7) has emphasized his mission of liberation. However, the new oracle goes much further in attributing to him the title of "anointed" (v. 1), heretofore reserved to the kings of Israel and to the Messiah (Ps 2; 1 S 9:26-30; Ex 30:22). In recounting the

vocation of Cyrus in the very terms the great prophets used to describe their own calling (Jr 1), the text tends to make a messianic figure of the Persian.

a) It is not surprising, then, that the conclusion of the poem proclaims an impending messianic renewal. This is presented as a new era of peace within the framework of a *renewal of nature itself*, (for, in the scriptural view, mankind can only find happiness if all creation shares the benefits: cf. Rm 8). The earth was barren during the period of exile (v. 8); but the victory of Israel and of Cyrus will be reflected in nature itself, as a fertilizing dew (Ps 84/85: 11-12) which causes an unexpected seed to germinate: the messianic seed itself (Is 4:2; Jr 23:5; 33:15; Za 3:8; 6:12).

b) This optimistic vision of nature is only possible in the context of the monotheism propounded by Second-Isaiah. Yahweh is the sole author of nature: heaven and earth, light and darkness (v. 7) are all of divine origin. His work to save his people in the plan of history has repercussions in the plan of creation, because he is the guide of both.

Springing from our earth, the Christ-Messiah effectively united the evolution of the cosmos to the redemption of men. For this reason, the Christian who collaborates in man's gradual mastery of nature knows that he is thereby witnessing to salvation.

VI. Luke 7:19-23   John is imprisoned but his prophetic ministry
Gospel   has prepared the way of the Lord (Mt 3:11;
Wednesday   Ml 3:1). However, a certain doubt persists.
Is this Jesus, whose miracles have been reported to him, indeed the Christ whom all await?

a) Judaism had always held that the *coming of the Lord* would take place in great power and would coincide with a terrible judgment of the nations (Is 40:10; 51:9). John depicts the era of the Lord as a period of fire and destruction (Mt 3:11-12). However, the deeds and actions of the Lord are, on the contrary, full of discretion and mildness. In answer to the questions posed by the disciples of John (vv. 19-20b), Christ gives a list of miracles (v. 21, proper to Luke; in Mt 11:4 Jesus refers to his interrogators to already accomplished miracles). The revelation of his works of *mildness and salvation* runs counter to the expectation of a powerful (in the sense of force) coming (v. 22). Christ, in replying with scriptural citations (Is 26:19; 29:18-19; 35:5-6; 61:1) to the scriptural allusions of John, follows a normal rabbinic procedure. The answer to John's question is given in the confrontation; it appears in verse 23 where the Lord disassociates his coming from the judgment. Christ thus modifies the Jewish conception of eschatology by distinguishing the moment of the "coming" in patience and mildness from the time of fulfillment and from the judgment. The history of the Church occupies the period between the two events.

b) This new conception of human history and of God's patience *scandalized* those who were expecting the advent of the avenging power of God (v. 23). But this scandal is a mere echo of one more profound, which will resound throughout the entire New Testament: the very mystery of the personhood of the Man-God (Mt 16:20-23; 26:31-33). The scandal provoked when he cured instead of condemning faintly indicates that which will arise from the human-divine personality of the Lord.

c) St. Luke gives his account a particular slant by adding verses 20 and 21. Here he speaks of the "two" disciples of John (cf. Dt 19:15), emphasizes words like "sent" (vv. 20 and 22) "called" (v. 19), and tells what the disciples "saw and heard" (v. 22).

This is his way of indicating the characteristics of the Christian *disciple*. Judaism had the regulation about "two" witnesses, and invariably the disciples of rabbis departed on their missions in pairs. Luke is happy to point out that in the case of Jesus' disciples it was the same (Lk 10:1; cf. 19:29; 23:32, 55; 24:13; 7:19). Being in twos was a way of authenticating, according to Jewish law (Dt 19:15), the truth of what one had to offer.

Discipleship depended first upon a "call" and a "mission," and the mission consisted in relating what one had seen and heard. (Same theme in Lk 1:1-2; in Lk 4:22 where the witness follows the list of miracles in verses 18-19; and above all in Lk 5:1-12, where the call of the first disciples follows a list of miracles.) For Luke then the disciple is one who has seen the historical Jesus and affirms this before the Christian community. In this way he proves the "apostolic" character of all Christian faith and the link between the historical Christ and the Christ of the Church.

The Christian, united to the Father in the very eucharistic sacrifice of the cross, is convinced that his own attitudes of gentleness and goodness reflect the coming of the Lord into the world, and he renounces any claim of witness to God by force or the triumphalism of institutions.

VII. Isaiah   This reading unites two distinct poems in
54:1-10   honor of Jerusalem (vv. 1-3 and 4-10). Once
1st reading   again, Second-Isaiah calls our attention to the
Thursday   restoration of the historical city, with an acute
poetic sense, but with less doctrinal depth
than Isaiah himself.

a) The first poem sings of the *fecundity of the New Jerusalem.* Deserted by her children during the exile, she remained barren but will once again, like the wives of the patriarchs, bear fruit. She will expand and take possession of the lands of the nations (v. 3) and establish there her own people. We are a long way from the universalism envisaged by First-Isaiah, from the spiritual

Jerusalem, city of all believers (Is 2:1-4; 4:2-5)! The relations established by Second-Isaiah between Jerusalem and the nations are on the contrary marked by revenge and exclusivism. The hope for a material restoration of the city stifled within him all genuine universalist sentiment.

b) The second part of the poem takes up again the theme of Jerusalem's betrothal to God. Three strophes, each terminated by the formula "says your God" (vv. 6, 8, 10) annul the letters of dismissal sent to the adulterous spouse through the mediation of the ancient prophets (Ho 1; 11:1-6; Jr 3:1-5; Ez 16), and restore to her the title of "youthful spouse."

The second strophe stresses the love of God above all, a love which not even sin can arrest, in that it becomes mercy and pity, justifying the sinner. The third concentrates on the new covenant, indefectible just like the love of God. Here Second-Isaiah develops an important doctrinal theme: the new Jerusalem will derive stability not from its justice, but from the unchanging love of God. The whole new covenant indeed depends upon God's promise to convert humanity, and render man just and free through grace (Ga 4:21-31).

The conception of the new alliance fortunately transcends the narrow framework of the prophet's thought concerning the future Jerusalem, and enables us to see in the Church the fruits of the alliance. Giving witness to this covenant means that we have been given that justice which comes not from ourselves but from God. We bear witness that the initiative of salvation comes from the love of God and is not spontaneous: that this covenant is finally sealed by the fidelity of the Son to his Father, which the Eucharist both proposes and celebrates.

VIII. Luke	This passage immediately follows the Gospel
7:24-30	of Wednesday. There Christ defined the mis-
Gospel	sion of John the Baptist and set forth the aims
Thursday	of his own (Lk 7:18-23). He brings his lis-
	teners first of all to a consideration of the

prophetic character of John the Baptist (vv. 24-27) and then instructs them in the understanding of the place of John's message in the economy of salvation.

a) In order to prepare his audience for the revelation that John was indeed in the line of great *prophets* in Israel, Christ evokes the contrasting image of those who were finely clad and this man clothed in animal skins (Mt 3:4; 2 K 1, 8). The contrast is continued by opposing the prophet's steadfast character (Jr 1:17-19) to the fragility of a reed.

Jesus, quoting from Malachi 3:1, defines John's prophetic role as that of a precursor who will prepare people and cult for the necessary renewal. Jesus also makes John the "greatest" of Old Testament prophets (vv. 26-28a), the last link in a chain which leads toward and demonstrates the object of ancient prophecies (Jn 1:29-34).

Obedience to the divine plan means believing in and being baptized by John the Baptist with the baptism which he proclaims (vv. 29-30). Those who oppose him and who have not responded to his call are strangers to Christ as well. On the other hand, the sinners and publicans converted by the Baptist are to be numbered among the disciples of Jesus. John has already prepared the way for the separation introduced by the person of Christ between the ancient people and the new people (Lk 1:17, 76-77). This was the greatness of his prophetic mission.

b) But John is the "least" (v. 28b) in the Kingdom! The ancient prophecies and even his own did not succeed in penetrating the mystery of the personhood of the Man-God. This lack of knowledge causes John's testimony to be less powerful in the end (Jn 5:31-36). The severe judgment demonstrates how Christ both fulfilled and transcended the prophecies he nonetheless used to reveal his personhood, the mystery of his life and death, his messianic character, and his role as head of the new community of believers (Lk 24:25-27). However, the scriptural arguments used by Christ and the apostles are themselves somewhat blunted by the fact that the Man-God in the very mystery of his own person, transcends everything perceived by the prophets. Christ reveals something unexpected: his relationship with the Father, his own personal mystery. The prophecies taught man a sense of history directed by God towards his Messiah. This, however, is a gratuitous gift of God and its mystery escapes all the laws of historical evolution. A certain hiatus separates Jesus from the prophets, even in the fulfilment of their prophecies. This causes the hesitation of John the Baptist himself (Lk 7:18-23) and the scandal of those who hold too closely to the letter of the scriptures (Lk 20:41-44).

John is the greatest in the Kingdom because he has most deeply penetrated the sense of history and its accomplishment in Jesus Christ; but at the same time he is least in the Kingdom, because he remains unaware of the human-divine personality of Christ and of the scandal it will cause.

The Christian goes no further in his own understanding of the mystery than did John the Baptist, when, content with the obvious message concerning Christ, he fails to penetrate the mystery of total fidelity to the Father and to the human condition. In him alone does the human will conform itself perfectly to the will of God, and the operation of the man becomes, through this personal identification, the very action of the Son of God. The role of the Eucharist is forever to recall this fact.

IX. Isaiah **56:1-3a, 6-8** *1st reading* *Friday*	Here begins the third part of the book of Isaiah, postdating the exile by a century. The prophet specifies the conditions under which pagans can be admitted to the cult of the temple.

Third-Isaiah once again broached the question of universalism. First-Isaiah had foreseen a gathering of all nations in a spiritual

Jerusalem, uplifted and not founded on Mount Zion, but on the person of the Messiah. Faith alone would give the right of citizenship (Is 4:2-6; 26:1-6; 28:5-6, 16-17). Isaiah had also foreseen the conversion of pagans and the establishment of a cult independent of the temple (Is 19:18-22).

Second-Isaiah considerably narrowed the horizon by reviving hopes in the restoration of the historical Jerusalem. His view of universalism meant an apology and total submission by the nations to Israel (Is 33:17-24; 51:9-11; 52:1-2).

Third-Isaiah sees the failure of the restoration of Jerusalem, and understands that the Jewish domination over the major nations of the epoch is an illusion. Yet he remains faithful to the dominant role of the holy city and its temple, while opening the gates more widely to the pagans. The uncleanliness of the foreigner and the eunuch does not mean excommunication. Whoever clings to the clauses of the covenant, particularly to the laws such as the sabbath (vv. 2, 4), may share in the liturgical assemblies, and offer valid sacrifices (v. 7). The conditions of assembly are essentially religious: God will not gather the outcasts of Israel, but many others with them (v. 8).

Although the vision of Third-Isaiah is more open than that of his predecessor, it is still far inferior to that of Isaiah himself.

Christ stressed the failure of this prophecy in a temple of tightly-closed gates and rigid taboos (Mt 21:12-17). But are our eucharistic assemblies really much more open? Do they truly deserve to be signs of the universal gathering that we endeavor to realize in our daily lives? Can they rightfully claim to be of interest to men of different classes or different cultures?

X. John 5:33-36 Christ justifies the cure of the paralytic on the
    Gospel Sabbath by revealing his relationship with
    Friday the Father. This enrages his strictly mono-
    theistic hearers (Jn 5:17-18). Jesus insisted

on the unity of life and action existing between the Father and the Son (Jn 5:19-30). He completes his defense with successive reference to the testimony of John the Baptist (Jn 5:33-35), of the Father in heaven (Jn 5:36-38) and of the scriptures (Jn 5:39-40). He thus observes the Law which required the depositions of two or three witnesses to authenticate a declaration (v. 31; cf. Dt 17:6; 19:15; Nb 35:30). The gospel of today reports the witness given by John and the beginning of the Father's testimony.

This passage is strongly marked by the Jewish-Christian polemic of the 1st century. The Christians finally realized that the testimony of the Old Testament prophets and of John the Baptist would not convince the Jews of Jesus' divine sonship. Matthew's constant recourse to the scriptures to find in the life of Christ the fulfillment of the prophecies was not sufficient to lead Israel to the Faith. To be sure, the prophecies point to Christ, but their witness proved unable to penetrate the mystery of the God-Man. John the Baptist himself is not as great as the least (member) of the Kingdom (Lk 7:28). Another witness must be found to corroborate the work and mystery of Christ. The fourth gospel, especially John 5:33-38, attempted to find it (cf. Jn 8:18).

a) Jesus sends his questioners to the *testimony* which they themselves solicited from *John the Baptist* (Jn 1:19-34) where John affirms the superiority of Jesus and declares that he was present at his messianic investiture (v. 33). Jesus emphasizes, however, the limited character of this witness. John is only a man (v. 34) and his word, even his prophetic word, does not illuminate the mystery of Christ which is from God from whom he has received everything (the same reservation is expressed in John 1:6-8 and 15).

b) Just as the *lamp* is not the light (Jn 1:8) because it must be lit and its fuel is limited, so John is not Jesus and his influence is momentary (v. 35). The image of the lamp whose light and heat we enjoy, is a reminiscence of psalm 131/132:

16-17 where it designates the permanence of the royal line of David up to the Messiah (1 K 11:36; 15:4; 2 K 8:19).

c) Christ finally comes to the only testimony which enjoys full authority: that of his Father, as contained in the "works my Father has given me to carry out" (v. 36). The verb "given" is characteristic of the thought of St. John: the Father gives the Son to men (Jn 3:16-17; 6:32) and the Spirit to the disciples (Jn 14:16). He gives his own teaching to the Son (Jn 17:8; 12:49), as well as his works (Jn 5:36; 17:4) and the power to give himself (Jn 5:21-22, 27; 17:2-3). Finally, he gives him the cup of his passion (Jn 18:11).

Jesus spends his life giving of that which he has received: the Word (Jn 17:8, 14), the new law (Jn 13:34), Life (Jn 10:28; 17:2), the living water (Jn 4:10-14), nourishment (Jn 6:27), his own flesh (Jn 6:51).

Christ is the "light" because the Father has "given" him the light. John is only a lamp, because God did not confide the Word to John with the same authority. As important as he is, his mandate is limited by comparison with that given by the Father to his Son.

Thus John brings a new style of apologetic to the attention of his readers. The scriptural proofs and the witness of the Baptist are insufficient to demand adherence. They are too extrinsic to define the sense of Christ's mission in the world and to guarantee the authenticity of his reference to God.

This reference to the Father is only experienced in the work he performs for the benefit of men; it is in giving to them that the gift of God is perceived.

FOURTH SUNDAY OF ADVENT

A. THE WORD

I. Isaiah 7:10-14
1st reading
1st cycle

During the reign of Ahaz (736-716), the kings of Aram and Israel banded together in hopes of placing a king of their choice on the throne in Jerusalem. This new king would be sympathetic to their designs and not of the line of David (Is 7:1-6; 2 K 16:5-9). Isaiah sets out to meet Ahaz (in 735 ?) and calm his fears. Ahaz must remain constant in his faith in the promise of Yahweh, then the dynasty of David will stand firm (Is 7:9b). Isaiah probably foresaw the failure of his mission and so takes with him a son with the symbolic name: "A-remnant-will-return" (Is 7:3).

a) It is his *faith* that separates the believer from the infidel and he who believes will constitute the "remnant" of Israel. This faith will manifest itself as a response to a sign. However, Ahaz, in rejecting every sign from heaven, even that of the Immanuel, places himself among the ranks of the nonbelieving. In verse 11, Yahweh is still the God of Ahaz ("your God"). However, in verse 13, he is the God of Isaiah only ("my God") and of those who believe. The Immanuel will be the antithesis of Ahaz since he will choose good and reject evil (v. 15). He will have learned this attitude by living a nomad's life in the desert (theme of milk and honey, verse 15a; cf. Dt 8:3-4).

This is the essential message of the passage. The Immanuel is above all a sign; faith in this sign will constitute the "remnant" of believers and will be their guarantee of deliverance. Here we are back to an essential feature in the whole prophecy of Isaiah. The future people will be determined qualitatively, that is, in faith, and no longer quantitatively, on some basis of national privilege (cf. Is 28:16-17).

b) But who are Immanuel and his mother? There is no certitude that the "young maiden" of verse 14 is in reality a virgin who will bring forth a child during her virginity. The provenance of the word *almah* here could be court literature, denoting simply a woman of royal lineage.

On the other hand, it is not possible to separate the Immanuel altogether from the historical context of the epoch of Ahaz and Isaiah (cf. the "behold" (Vulgate) of verses 14 and 16). There is every indication that Isaiah had the imminent birth of a royal infant in mind (probably Hezekiah as in Is 11:1-8).

It is important to remember too that Jewish *messianism* always expressed an ideal which, until the time of the exile, was attached to a concrete individual. The thought of Isaiah concerning the ideal Messiah is clear, but here he probably attaches it to Hezekiah. Not before the later interpreters of Isaiah will the idea of the Messiah take shape as an eschatological king. Micah 5:2 has already taken a step in this direction and the Septuagint version will go yet further in its definite statement that a virgin will bring forth this child. Finally, Matthew 1: 22-23 will transcend the messianic prophecy of Isaiah and see its fulfillment in the fact that the young maiden will be virginal even in giving birth.

The Immanuel is a sign to the faithful and his role is accomplished perfectly in Jesus Christ. He is the first man who will choose very clearly the good to be done and reject the evil. He is the first to lead the life of a man in total communion with the Father. His eucharistic presence is the new "sign" given to the faith of those who, contrary to Ahaz, have committed themselves to the Father.

II. 2 Samuel   The prophecy of Nathan has long been re-
7:1-5, 8b-11, 16   garded as a tradition based on a primitive
1st reading   text which underwent various interpolations
2nd cycle   through the centuries. New elements would
attempt to give the text a more exclusively

royalist-national dimension (vv. 10-11a) or point up the responsibility of Israel's kings in the weakening of the covenant (vv. 14-15). They also contain the first broad lines of a certain messianism (v. 16). This interpretation seems artificial today and scholars are returning to a more integral and unified approach.

a) Actually, the primitive tradition sought to answer the problem of David concerning *the future of his line and that of his people*. David was not really the king of a unified nation. His various and successive anointings in the South (2 S 2:1-4), in the North (2 S 5:1-3) and finally in Jerusalem (2 S 5:6-10) demonstrate clearly that his kingdom was made up of bits and pieces, and there was, in fact, no guarantee that it would survive his death. Nathan speaks to his first concern: David must recognize that God has protected him through all the happenings of his life (v. 8-9), why should it be otherwise for his successor (v. 12)? The failure of Saul's enterprise did not necessarily affect David's.

The second cause of anxiety was the future of the people, who had lived through chaos during the entire period of the Judges and gained little stability during the reign of Saul. Further complicating matters, the factions North-South, royalist and anti-royalist, could set up civil strife. Nathan attempts to calm David's anxiety with a prophecy (vv. 10-11a): the people will regain their stability.

b) No other answer could really be expected from a court-prophet like Nathan, whose predictions form a simple message of circumstance. The *messianic* orientation given his prophecies was furnished by the influence of Deuteronomy on verses 14 and 15, which promise the longevity of the davidic line whatever the royal conduct. This idea of continuity is taken up again in verse 16 which announces the strengthening "forever" of the dynasty. The psalmists, such as Ps 88/89: 30-38 (gradual psalm attached to this reading and 131/132:11-12, will use this theme, which is clearly more profound than the original prophecy of Nathan. Taken by itself, the text of 2 Samuel cannot be considered messianic. However, one has only to see it in the total context of Jewish thought to discern an important basis for the hope of a davidic Messiah.

c) The choice of verses in the liturgical reading does not do justice to the theme of the *house*.

In order to stabilize his dynasty and at the same time create a center for his people, David contemplates the building of a house to shelter the Ark of the Covenant (vv. 1-3); but Yahweh replies that it is he who will build a house for David (v. 11b). This does not mean that God rejects the temple outright, but signifies that the future of the people and of the davidic line will rest more on the Covenant entered into by Yahweh and the kings than on the temple itself. The mutual fidelity of God and king will be more important in the history of the people than temple sacrifice. Later Christian tradition will recall this fact when the Church rejects the temple, because Christ has brought the relationship of love between the Messiah and his Father to unhoped-for perfection (cf. Is 66:1-2; Ac 7:48; Lk 23:44-45; Jn 2:19). Verse 11b is especially important as it leads to reflection on the importance of unity between God and his king for the existence and salvation of his people.

The first readings of this 4th Sunday of Advent recall the most important prophecies perhaps of the entire Old Testament. Nevertheless, not one of the three prophets in question was conscious of the sweep of his vision or the genius of his message. The first of their number is a simple court prophet who seeks to interpret these events in the manner most favorable to his master. The second seeks to attach the mad hopes of a miserable people to the person of a new-born king; the third cannot overcome his love for the land and the peasant mentality with which he was born.

In fact, each of them is limited by the necessity to read signs of God's presence into actual happenings. They simply lived the event with God and discerned his countenance there. For God is unique, unique in the history of salvation which he leads. The capacity to reveal the unique God in the meaningful happening is the key to the understanding of history. Faith universalizes the event, generalizes its essential traits and extends its meaning: it discerns the absolute in the relative, the divine in the human, the permanent in the ephemeral.

There must then be total involvement in the present in order to know the future, total immersion in the human in order to grasp the divine. The prophet is not by any means the dreaming mystic: he is very incarnate indeed.

III. Micah 5:2-5a   Micah is the spiritual heir of Isaiah and, as
  1st reading   did Isaiah before him announces a violent
  3rd cycle   judgment from which a select "remnant" will
                     emerge, in whom the promises will be fulfilled.

Micah depicts a messianic coming which is a study in contrasts. In 4:14, he covers Zion with ridicule as Assur lays siege to its fortress, contrasting it with the feeble Ephrathah, whence will come the Messiah. He compares the Judge of Israel, the king of the time, baffled by his enemies (4:14), with the future king, who has a glorious past (5:1), since his kingdom rests on the promises made to David (1 S 17:12-13; Mt 4:11-22), and whose future is no less glorious (5:3). He goes on to contrast Zion's grandiose fortifications (4:14) with the divine power which will raise up the future king and cover him with glory (5:3). Finally, he compares the people of his time which God will abandon, with the future Remnant (5:2).

Micah's messianic doctrine fits easily into the perspective of Isaiah, granted certain particular features. Micah is a peasant's son and does not therefore attribute the same importance to Zion as does the aristocratic Isaiah. The younger prophet does not consider Jerusalem's destruction a hindrance to God's plan. On the other hand, for him, as for Isaiah, the Messiah is a son of David (Mi 5, 2 alludes perhaps to Is 7:14); but he lays greater stress on the humble origins of the family of Jesse at Bethlehem than on the royal splendor of the palace in the nation's capital.

Finally, the scope of the restoration he envisages is more modest than that of Isaiah. It is sufficient that the remnant regain possession of the country and there is no idea of conquest in store for the weak Israel.

The prophecy of Is 7 was probably addressed to the mother of Hezekiah. Micah has now had the time to see that this king certainly did not possess a messianic character and so he refers messianic maternity to the eschatological future (5:2). His doctrine then shares the hopes of Israel in the davidic line but tempers them with the picture of the poor and humble David. It is the king-shepherd of Bethlehem (1 S 16) who will be the future guide of his people (5:3), not the glorious David of the royal city.

IV. Romans 1:1-7 Following contemporary conventions in letter
    2nd reading writing, Paul introduces himself before broach-
    1st cycle ing the real subject of his letter.

a) In his earlier letters, this introduction was rather short (see the salutations of 1 Th and 2 Th). But the doubts of the Galatians and Corinthians regarding his apostolic authority, at the time of his 3rd missionary journey (53-58), led him to speak of himself at greater length. In referring to himself as "servant," Paul is aware of taking over an honorific title reserved in the Old Testament for the great patriarchs (cf. Ex 24:31; Nb 12:7; Dt 34:5; Gn 26:24; 24:14; Jos 24:23). But he calls himself the "servant of Christ Jesus," which is not only a title but indicates a mission: the extension throughout the world of the "service" of Christ. Paul also takes pride in mentioning his second title "apostle," which Jewish Christians had refused him (1 Co 9; 2 Co 11:13, 23). He had already written many personal apologies explaining that this title "apostle" was not reserved to the Twelve, but rested on a personal call (Ga 1:1) and on a mission of "preaching the gospel" (1 Th 1:4; Ph 4:15; 2 Co 8:18). Here he goes on to say that the vocation depends on the Spirit and the resurrection of the "son of God," at a time when the apostles are still preoccupied with the "Son of David" and with "carnal" considerations.

b) The second part of the salutation describes the subject of this gospel: the Son of David, proclaimed Son of God. Paul characterizes it by the contrast "in the flesh . . . in the Spirit," one of the main themes of the letter to the Romans (Rm 8:1-13; cf. 4:23-29), which is not to be identified with the modern dualism: body-soul, or even with the opposition human-divine. For Paul flesh denoted the "world" before the resurrection of Christ, while "Spirit" is the "new world" strengthened by this resurrection. Here the contrast "flesh-Spirit" is applied to the terms: *Son of David and Son of God.*

The expression "proclaimed Son of God" is rather striking, if it refers to divine sonship, which Paul knows to be eternal (Rm 8:3, 29, 32; 5:10). In fact, he is probably not talking here so much of divine sonship itself as of the messianic title (Ps 2:7-8; cf. Ac 13:33; 4:25-28). Christ is son of David through his ancestors; but, being of the flesh, this title is empty unless God intervenes "in power" to make him Messiah (Son of God) and "give him all nations." To say that Christ is son of David is to assert that he belongs to Israel, and that Israel has a central place in the economy of redemption. To say that Christ is Son of God is to stress that the nations now have a "Lord."

Indeed Paul insists that his apostolic mission to the nations (v. 5) is the full realization of the universal messianism promised to the "Son of God" in Ps 2:7-8. And Paul is proud of bringing the good news of salvation to the citizens of the world capital.

The thought of Paul would therefore be distorted if we were to differentiate between son of David and Son of God just as we do between the humanity and divinity of Christ. Paul rather shows that the economy of redemption centered around the davidic dynasty for the sole benefit of Israel, is now displaced by a new order, which invites all nations to gather around the new Messiah.

The gospel of Paul thus presents Christ not only as God made man, but also as son of David and Son of God. Through the Incarnation, God not only espoused human nature, he also took upon himself the concrete human conditions, social and political, of Palestine at that time. The Messiah is thus a gift of God, but also the product of human history.

A belief in the son of David proclaimed Son of God nowadays amounts to a belief that civilization and history play a part in the building of the Church and of the Mystical Body. It also means a belief in the human aspect of Christ's mission, alongside its transcendence, and an understanding that the Eucharist must have definite human and cultural qualities in order to reveal its mystery more clearly.

V. Romans 16:25-27 *2nd reading 2nd cycle*   The relation of chapter 16 to the epistle to the Romans in general and the Pauline authenticity of this doxology (vv. 25-27) are still disputed matters, although the arguments in favor of Pauline authorship are gaining ground. At least it can be said that the Jewish and Pauline coloring of the doxology in an argument in favor.

Revelation of the *mystery* is the essential theme of the doxology. The mystery in question, as usual in Pauline literature, is that of the entry, at the beginning of the last times, of the

Gentiles to salvation (v. 26; cf. Ep 3:8-9; Rm 11:25; Col 1:25-27). The author of the mystery is the wisdom of God, who is the "sage *par excellence*" (v. 27). Throughout the vicissitudes of the ages, he can see the issue of history in the age that is to be (same sense in Dn 2:20, 28).

Prior to this the mystery was hidden in time (v. 25b; cf. 1 Co 2:6-8). Now it is made manifest, by Jesus Christ first of all and his death for all men (a central topic of the letter), then by Paul himself and the gospel he must proclaim to the world (theme of the beginning of the letter: Rm 1:5).

The mystery then is the secret of the world that is to be, the setting up of a humanity that will be reconciled with God and with itself. Through the wisdom of God it is realized in the cross of Christ, and the apostles are its witnesses and executants.

All that Paul has to say in this letter about the failure of Jewish and Gentile wisdom, about the absolutely gratuitous nature of the covenant and the faith, about the unity between men, Christian and non-Christian, which love has achieved, will only be clarified by the course of history, of which God alone possesses the secret. People may refuse to accept that this development depends upon a "mystery" reserved for the final times. But that would mean denying to God a part of his initiative, to the cross of Christ a part of its efficacy, to human love a part of its capacity to achieve unity on a scale altogether deeper than our world of disunity and pluralism.

VI. Hebrews
10:5-10
2nd reading
3rd cycle

In the preceding chapter (He 9:24-28) the author has analyzed the expiation ritual in order to show how it was fulfilled and surpassed in the sacrifice of Christ. Here we have an analysis of the whole sacrificial ritual of the temple as against the sacrifice of Christ.

a) This passage cannot be properly understood without consideration of the theology of the sacrifice of the poor, already developed in the Old Testament (cf. Dn 3:38-40). Trial and exile had put an end to the "quantitative" sacrifices of the old temple and substituted a sort of "poor" sacrifice. This was dictated by the poverty of the times, but the essential elements of thanksgiving, repentance and humility were present. The sacrifice consisted really of inner sentiment and commitment: God was no longer to be reached by means of bloody sacrifices but through obedience and love.

Among the many psalms which echo this doctrine one of the more important is Psalm 39/40. A person who has been at one time ill realizes that God does not expect sacrifices from him in thanksgiving for his cure, but an attitude of obedience and total fidelity to the law. From now on the whole center of cult, for him, will be his moral performance: worship and living have been fused together.

Because he puts this psalm in the mouth of Christ, the author indicates some definition of the sacrifice of the cross. The central thing is not the immolation of a victim, however select that victim is, but the communion with the Father which was evident in Jesus. From now on all that remains is a religion "in spirit and in truth" (cf. Ep 5:2).

b) We have still nevertheless to determine what was the *will of God* about Christ and what sort of obedience Jesus, on his part, showed. God could never have willed the death of his son. That would suggest a sanguinary God, appeasable only by the death of someone dear to him! What God wanted was acceptance in love by his Son of the human condition to the point where it could be transfigured. The human condition however includes death, and the Father did not exclude that, so that it might be shown that Jesus' fidelity to the human condition had the same dimensions as his love for the Father.

In order to describe the Father's will for his Son, the author uses a variant of the psalm (fashioned a body: v. 5) and he puts it in the mouth of Christ at the very moment of incarnation (v. 5: entering into the world). He is thus incorporating the sacrificial destiny of Christ in the Trinitarian godhead, anterior to incarnation. It is a detail which emphasizes the will of God and the infinite depth of the Son's obedience, and it leads us to the affirmation that the whole human life of Jesus was on continuous sacrifice of which Calvary was simply the culmination. For him worship and living were at all times fused, and at all times bore fruit.

VII. Matthew 1:18-24 *Gospel 1st cycle*   Interpretations given this passage have often misrepresented the religious character of Saint Joseph. It is therefore all the more important to grasp the essential points of Matthew's thought, giving special attention to the nuances qualifying the parallel text in Luke, and keeping in mind as well the particular literary genre. It is important to note that there exists within the bible a special literary form which deals with the announcement of birth. In each case, an angel appears on the scene and calls the person concerned by a name signifying his function (here: Joseph, *Son of David*, a title which will not be used again by the angel in other apparitions to Joseph). There is a certain difficulty to be overcome (generally, the mother's sterility; in this case, however, Joseph's reluctance to take Mary into his household); there is a sign given in pledge (in Lk 1:36, the pregnancy of Elizabeth, here the miraculous birth); finally, certain precisions are made concerning the name of the child (here: Jesus).

The literary form "announcement of birth" is evidently a manner of description only, while the event is real. Some details in the narrative ought to be noted.

When the angel appeared to the Virgin (Lk 1:26-38) he first informs Mary that her son would be the son of David (Lk 1:34-35). In the case of Joseph however, the angel proceeds differently: since Mary's pregnancy is a known fact, he simply affirms the davidic sonship of the baby (Mt 1:20-23).

Mary's immediate concern is naturally her virginal state; for Joseph, however, the problem is rather to discover what role he will play in regard to the child.

Mary was obviously the first to know that she would conceive her child while remaining a virgin. However the evangelists do not tell us whether or not she informed her fiance of this. Their silence cannot be interpreted as silence on God's part. It seems scarcely possible that Mary could have failed to inform Joseph of these conditions newly imposed which would affect their future life together. Joseph is in no way anxious concerning the virtue of his wife and it was not to assure him on this score that the angel appeared to him.

Joseph is a "man of honor" (Vulgate: a "just" man) (Mt 1:19) not in order to find in the law grounds for the repudiation of his wife. Nor was his an honor which would simply prevent him from injuring his fellow man. It was a fundamentally religious honor which would prevent him from attributing to himself a work of God. The angel intervened to signify to Joseph that God had need of him, that the child in Mary's womb was of the Holy Spirit, and that his role was to give that child a name and introduce him into the lineage of David.

Joseph is not, therefore, a man of honor because he is a model of resignation, or of obedience to legalistic requirements, but because he respected God in his works and was content to play the role God wished to give him.

Man's salvation is not exclusively dependent on the divine initiative in the sense that man becomes a completely passive instrument. God saves man only through the latter's cooperation and fidelity.

VIII. **Luke**   The particular form of this passage, a mid-
1:26-38   rash where each word and expression is
Gospel   charged with associations, calls for a verse
2nd cycle   by verse commentary so that the principal
themes can be analyzed.

a) *The setting and historical context* (vv. 26-27):

The appearance of the Archangel Gabriel places the event of
the Annunciation in a prophetic and eschatological context,
since tradition always associated him with the period of seventy
weeks which would usher in the final kingdom (cf. Dn 8:16;
9:21, 24-26). The angel appears first in the temple of Zechariah
(Lk 1:11), then to Mary, six months later (180 days) (Lk 1:26).
Nine months later (270 days) Christ is born, and forty days
afterwards he is presented in the temple. These sums add up to
a total of 490 days, or *seventy weeks*. Moreover, each stage is
opened by the expression: "When these days were accomplished . . ." (Lk 1:23; 2:6) which gives the events the significance of prophetic fulfillment.

Christ is truly the Messiah foreseen in Daniel 9, the human
Messiah but also the quasi-divine Son of man (Dn 7:13). The
events which herald his birth are simply the preparations for the
entrance of the glory of Yahweh, personified now in Jesus, into
the definitive temple.

b) *The titles of Mary* (vv. 27-28):

The simplicity of the annunciation in a small house in Galilee,
a region held in real contempt (Jn 1:46; 7:41) contrasts with
the ceremonial birth-announcement of the Baptist in the temple
(Lk 1:5-25), indicating straightaway the opposition between
Mary and Jerusalem, which is made clear in the angel's greeting.
He borrows his salutation in fact from Zp 3:16 and Zc 9:9 where
a messianic salutation to Jerusalem is formulated that proclaims
the approaching arrival of the Lord "in her womb" (the literal
sense of the formula of Zp 3:16). Thus, the angel transfers to
the virgin the privileges formerly attributed to *Jerusalem*. The

influence of Zephaniah extends throughout the narrative of the Annunciation (Lk 1:28 and Zp 3:15; Lk 1:30 and Zp 3:16; Lk 1:28 and Zp 3:14).

In the thought of St. Luke, the expression "full of grace" means simply that the virgin is "pleasing" as was Ruth to Boaz (Rt 2:2, 10, 13), Esther before Ahasuerus (Est 2:9, 15, 17; 5:2, 8; 7:3; 8:5) or woman in general in the eyes of her spouse (Pr 5:19; 7:5; 18:22, Sg 8:10). This matrimonial context has indeed profound meaning: God has long sought a *spouse* who would be faithful to him. He has repudiated Israel, his former spouse (Ho 1-3), but is well-disposed to "betrothal" once again. Addressed by means of an expression frequently used between spouses, Mary understands that God is about to realize in her the mystery of the promises of betrothal in the Old Testament, by bringing about the mysterious union of the two natures — divine and human — in the person of Jesus.

Today's gospel adds a phrase to the message of the angel which is peculiar to the Vulgate: "blessed are you." The phrase is actually attributed to Elizabeth at the time of the visitation, yet later Latin witnesses introduced it here, doubtless under the influence of such prayers as the *Ava Maria*. Such interpretations were important in the development of Mariology, introducing as they did the principal theme of the *woman victorious over evil*. They were initially inspired by the praise of Jael, the woman of Jg 5:24-27 who vanquished the enemy by crushing his head according to the promise made to the offspring of Eve (Gn 3:15). Influential as well was the hymn of praise offered Judith (Jdt 14:7).

c) *The titles of the Messiah* (vv. 31-33):

The first group of titles attributed to Jesus recalls the royal vocabulary of the messianic promises of Nathan (2 S 7:12-16). Jesus will be "great" (cf. 2 S 7:12), he will be the Son of the Most High, a title reserved for great personages (Pss 2:7; 28/29:1; 81/82:6; 88/89:7) and for the Messiah in 2 S 7:14. He shall sit upon the throne of David (2 S 7:16 and Is 9:6). Yet the angel transcends the limits of Nathan, for he predicts that Christ will extend his reign over the house of Jacob (the ten tribes of the North). He shall then achieve unity between Judah and Israel (Ez 37:15-28; Dn 7:14; Mi 5:4-7), as a preliminary to the unity he is destined to achieve between Jews and gentiles.

There is nothing extraordinary in the fact that the angel does not impose the name Immanuel on the son of Mary (Is 7:14). At least 10 names were foreseen for the Messiah, though no tradition had suggested "Jesus," which means "Yahweh or Savior." This name recalls two Old Testament figures who played important roles in the history of the people-elect: Joshua, the judge in the desert (Si 46:1-2) and Joshua, priest at the time of the return from the exile (Zc 3:1-10; Hg 2:1-9). In undergoing his passion and death, Jesus will in turn "merit" the name of mankind's "savior."

d) *The circumstances of the conception* (vv. 34-38):

The angel foretells the conception of the child in terms borrowed from Exodus 40:35, where God's presence is made manifest in the cloud. The child to be born will be the result of a special intervention by God: he belongs to the divine and celestial world generally symbolized by the cloud (v. 35).

However the divine intervention presupposes a free collaborator (v. 37). Apparently she proposed to remain a virgin. Young women could obtain this permission from their spouses, particularly in Essene circles. Mary's remark though about not knowing man (beyond her knowledge of Joseph) must be taken symbolically, like all of this midrash. Mary stands for Jerusalem, to which fruitfulness had been promised. For Jerusalem, not knowing man means the stagnation of rejection, abandonment, destitution (cf. Is 60:15; 62:1-4). What Mary is doing is taking upon herself the rejected city's desolation and asserting that there will be a new espousal, where God will take back, in her person, his spouse of former times. In the annunciation is accomplished the mysterious marriage between God and his people.

When Luke speaks of Mary and her virginity, he does so in

the very special context of espousal with God, and he is thinking particularly of the fruit of this espousal: the Messiah. When one believes in this virginity that characterizes the spiritual marriage with God, something is being affirmed about Jesus Christ. The point at issue is Christological.

The question remains whether Saint Luke, in using this particular literary genre, was alluding to the divinity of Jesus or only to the fulfillment of the scriptures.

Certain epithets such as "great" or "holy" (Lk 1:32, 35) are divine titles (Tb 13:4; Ps 47/48:2; 75/76:2; 85/86:10 etc.) especially when used in an absolute sense. However, they are also used relatively with reference to human persons (Lk 1:14, for example). On the other hand, the word "savior" apparent in the name of Jesus, and clearly indicated in Luke 2:11; 1:47, is a name almost exclusively reserved to God in the Old Testament. Thus we are oriented more directly toward the transcendent.

Finally, it would appear that it is verse 35, in spite of its ambiguous imagery, which really indicates the *divine personality* of the infant (cf. Lk 2:49 where the theme is again taken up). The evangelist discreetly evokes the divinity of Jesus, but clearly enough to enable believers to find there a solid basis for faith.

Saint Luke reveals as well the personality of Mary, whom he compares to the tent in the desert (v. 35). In her he sees the new Ark of the Covenant (vv. 39-46), the dwelling place of God in the last days. But, above all, she is compared, by reason of her maternity, to the new Jerusalem (v. 28), the city where God dwells.

Again, through the somewhat obscure imagery of Luke 1-2, the Christian is led to pose himself the question of Christ's personality, at once totally human and perfectly divine. The ambiguity of the themes employed by St. Luke compel us to keep these two aspects in focus. A Messiah who was not man could have no partnership with men in the work of salvation. A Messiah who was not the Son of God could not have directed us to the only possible means of salvation: filial attachment to the Father.

IX. Luke 1:39-45   The visitation narrative is presented by St.
   Gospel   Luke in a midrash style similar to the preced-
   3rd cycle   ing gospel (Lk 1:26-38).

a) The narrative is reminiscent of the *transfer of the Ark of the Covenant* to Jerusalem (2 S 6:2-11). Like the Ark, Mary undertakes the journey to Judah towards Jerusalem (v. 39; cf. 2 S 6:2). This takes place with similar manifestations of joy (vv. 42, 44, and 2 S 6:2), even the accompaniment of sacred "dances" (v. 44, where the infant "leaps" for joy in his mother's womb; cf. 2 S 6:12). She rests in the house of Zechariah as the Ark rested in the house of Obed-edom (2 S 6:10); Mary is a source of blessing, as had been the Ark previously (v. 41; cf. 2 S 6:11-12). The glad cry of Elizabeth as she greets Mary (v. 43) reproduces almost verbally that of David as he stands before the Ark (2 S 6:9). Finally, Mary, like the Ark, remains for three months in the home of her hosts (v. 56; cf. 2 S 6:11).

Beneath this somewhat belabored symbolism lies St. Luke's dominant theme: the events which surround the birth of Christ completely fulfill not only the prophecy of Malachi 3, but also that of the seventy weeks of Daniel. God has already sent his angel with the traits of Gabriel, into the temple (Ml 3:1 and Lk 1:5-25). Now it remains for God himself to appear in his temple (Ml 3:2). Mary's departure for the house of Elizabeth constitutes the first stage; the second will be the actual ascent to Jerusalem (Lk 2:22-38), consummated by the official presentation of the infant in the temple.

b) Though the chief symbol in the Ark of the Covenant is above all that of God's presence among his people, it was also the Ark that led the people into battle. Consequently the association brings us into the context of warfare which is emphasized by Mary's presentation as the *victorious woman*. In fact, then, verse 42, where Elizabeth blesses her cousin and the infant she carries, recalls the acclamation of Jael (Jg 5:2-31) after her victory over the enemy, and of Judith (Jdt 13:17-18; 15:9-10) after her defeat of Holofernes. Thus, Mary is seen here as the woman who assures her people of final victory over evil, and inaugurates the messianic era in which sin and unhappiness will be no more.

Mary is truly the dwelling place of God among men. Luke has shown her to be such by comparing her to the ark or to Zion itself. No more does God dwell in a temple of stone, but in living persons. After the example of Mary, every Christian is a sign of God's presence in the world: his attitudes and involvements build the divine dwelling-place on earth. However secular a Christian's life, it is now charged to an even greater degree with the divine presence than the consecrated temple or the Ark of the Covenant. In this sense, it becomes eucharistic.

B. DOCTRINE

1. The Theme of Messianism

The secular world has a messianism all its own. Modern man is the product of scientific and technological civilization, and more and more he becomes convinced that the achievement of salvation is the business of humanity itself. Not all however, it seems, play the same role in this historical evolution. To some — individuals, nations, social groups — history allots a decisive part in the future. Not all accept the idea of special functions, but for the people themselves it is a profound experience. The working classes for instance in our time believe that proper balance in the future requires great influence by themselves. We have instances of nations who are driven by inner compulsions that they have a duty to spread their way of life throughout the world, that the responsibility of shaping the human future belongs to them.

Earthly messianism like this, at first glance, seems totally in contrast with the Christian brand. There seems to be a direct conflict between two opposed principles: salvation coming from God, or from men. Must we then conclude that the conviction of modern man is something the Christian is bound to reject out of hand? Or ought we perhaps try to penetrate beyond this apparent conflict and ask ourselves whether Christian messianism does not imply something more than the descent of God among men?

In fact, when we consider the questionings of modern man, there is an urgent need for some rethinking of Christian messianism. The very essentials of our faith are concerned. Our concept of messianism, as we shall see, depends directly on our view of the mystery of Christ and the role of the Church in the future evolution of human history.

The messianic wait of the chosen people

Occasionally we have had biblical messianism interpreted

rather inadequately in terms exclusively of divine pedagogy. The history of Israel had to be punctuated by Yahweh with prophetic interventions which gave advance information about "Him who was to come," so that she would be prepared for the Messiah. And thus the study of biblical messianism becomes a matter of making inventories of prophetic utterances and demonstrating the verification of each in the Messiah who actually came.

But the real messianic wait of Israel, as lived, was quite otherwise. It is not wrong of course to speak of divine pedagogy, but this is by no means all. Messianic waiting pervades the whole Old Testament and clarifies the ultimate meaning of the religious search of Jewish man, because it is the focal point. Without it Israel's discovery of the God of Abraham, Isaac and Jacob would have altogether different implications.

As events, and history, shaped their faith, we understand how the Jewish people came to the conviction that their God was the Totally-Other, that an unbridgeable gap separated him from his creation. There was no question of reaching out and touching him; he saves his people altogether gratuitously, altogether freely, as he wishes, choosing the means himself. For Israel there could never be any doubt: man's salvation comes from God alone. Yet even in acknowledging that utter poverty was the only proper garb of the human being before Yahweh, that he must be completely at God's disposal, there was another insight: the realization that salvation must depend in a positive way on man, too, on his fidelity to the covenant. The whole tenor indeed of Jewish history gives the impression that seeing God as Totally-Other, seeing him too as Love, always meant an instinctive awareness that he was inviting man to be his partner in accomplishing the plan of salvation. Everything that happened indicates that Jewish man saw the risk of alienation implicit in the total otherness of God. One had to believe that only God saves, but it was equally true that in this process of salvation man was not obliterated. And so, in striking fashion, the evolution of faith brought two things into relief — the wholly gratuitous nature of salvation on the one hand, and on the other the necessary human contribution in the process.

Very early the history of Israel gives evidence of a passionate quest. A man was being sought who would make the proper response to the God of the covenant, who would be a savior just as Yahweh himself was intervening to save. Directed and furthered by the prophets, the quest permeates the history of the nation, and all the successive institutions where national self-consciousness was developed and deepened. The Messiah to be is a king's son, of the line of David, during the period of kings. His principal characteristic is that of a prophet during the exile, eventually a suffering prophet. It is a time when Israel loses all her institutions, and the security of her own territory. After the exile, because of the preponderant role played by the priests, the details of messianic expectation become more and more complex. Finally, in the second century B.C., comes the prophet Daniel with the figure of the Son of Man. So calamitous has the situation of Israel become, that it is only in someone unsullied by contact with the sinful earth people can see hope of salvation.

Jesus of Nazareth the messiah of Israel

Messianic expectation reached its culmination when the Messiah actually did come, when he identified himself with the Son of Man figure, and pointed out that he would assume the destiny of the suffering Servant. Yet in the high moment of culmination the decisive stumbling block had also to be encountered.

The facts were these. Jesus claimed to be Son of Man, but he was totally involved in the common human lot. He displayed messianic quality, but he made himself obedient, even unto death. And he demanded the same radical poverty from his disciples, the same total abandonment to the God who alone can save. Jewish man recoiled before a demand like this: he was subtly blinded by sin. If one accepted the demand it meant

that every human attempt to elicit salvation from human resources must be rejected as hopeless. It meant that sin must be
renounced, and that one must capitulate before the mystery of
Jesus. Although his lot is the human lot, although he becomes
obedient unto death, the death actually of the cross, he presents
himself as the expected Messiah. He is the one man among men
who is a savior, because the response he makes to the Father is
adequate. It is a filial response. For this the Messiah himself
had to be, by nature, the Son of God. Two things had to meet
and be perfectly blended, God's gratuitous initiative and man's
response. It was because of who he was that the response of
Jesus was a filial one.

But he was a stumbling block in the very act of fulfilling the
messianic hope of his people. He snatched from them the security
they most depended on, their privileges as a chosen people. The
Jewish messiah is actually the Savior of all humanity. The salvation he brings is the state of sonship, and here every man is
basically in the same position, that of sinner called to repentance.
To participate, for everyone, there is only one condition, to
follow Jesus by becoming obedient unto death. In concrete terms
this means putting into practice the new commandment of love
without limit. So that the task accomplished by Jesus of Nazareth,
when he intervened in history as the Messiah of Israel, is universal in the strictest sense.

The people of God as a messianic people

Every man and woman who agrees to follow Jesus Christ
and to be saved by his unique mediation becomes in turn a
savior. Set free from sin they obtain, in him, access to the Father:
he fulfills their aspirations. When they accept their creatural
condition, their "yes" acquires unsuspected depths; it is the
"yes" of the children of God. What Jesus accomplished once for
all is communicated to all those who believe in him.

When we remember this, we cannot overstress the importance
of the title which Vatican II gives the people of God: the

messianic people. Theirs is the mission of following out, in time and space, the messianic task undertaken by Jesus of Nazareth. In the success of this enterprise men and women of every race, of every spiritual and social condition, are called to play a decisive role.

When they describe themselves as messianic they are bringing a truth into sharp focus: that salvation is the result of two converging thrusts, God's initiative and man's cooperation. God only can give access to his own family the initiative is his, but men themselves, because they are sons by their living incorporation with the Risen Lord, should build salvation too. The people of God are responsible; their role is active, and most decisive, in the realization of the salvific plan. By baptism a man is charged with a mission for the benefit of all humanity. This is the first sign of his entry into the Church, and it is the justification for the legitimate pride a Christian feels.

Immediate stress however should be laid on one truth. If it is to be really recognized for what it is, the Church's messianic character, that of all Christians dispersed among other men, should reveal itself in the readiness to serve. That this does not happen automatically is very evident from Church history. Because of their seeming efficacy the instruments of power constitute a temptation for a Church which is aware of its responsibility. A ceaseless process of reform is needed so that the people of God can be faithful to the messianic vocation in the only way that is valid. The way of genuinely universal love that is; and this requires, from everyone, total self-renunciation. Such a love cannot but be vulnerable.

Messianic response to the expectation of peoples

By his intervention in history Jesus fulfilled the messianic hope of Israel. What he was for his own people the Church should be for all other peoples. When she evangelizes a people she makes her mark in their spiritual tradition, leading them into the mystery of Christ by the conversion that is necessary.

In our day, almost everywhere, the first phase of the Church's growth has been accomplished. There are nascent churches in Asia and Africa, on whom falls the responsibility of mission to our non-Catholic brethren. They are tender growths as yet, but only await increase. The evangelizing church in the world today transpires to be more and more a communion of particular churches, each one of which is an irreplaceable stone in the common edifice of the Kingdom.

There is a hierarchy of messianic responsibility for all such churches, and in the case of each of them details of basic importance should be kept in mind. A vivid awareness first of all of particular mission, of the duty to fulfill the spiritual destiny of whatever nation is in question. It is only in reference to the mystery of Christ, the pivot of creation, that such a demanding mission as this takes on meaning, and this is just as true of nascent churches as of the others. Everywhere the means of fulfilling the particular mission should be set in motion. Christians should come out from the ghetto where they have voluntarily enclosed themselves. They should deepen their lives of faith, hope and charity by sharing fully with their non-Christian brothers. In concrete terms, for each church, the opportunity for encounter with the living God of Jesus Christ is constituted by the spiritual destiny of the people where it finds itself. Religion is being put to the test everywhere in the world. Modern man will only become aware of what it means when he is confronted by genuine religious sentiment incarnate in human beings.

In this context, the need everywhere for communion is just as pressing. If the particular churches are to be faithful to their messianic task, there should be a constant interflow between them of life and energy. The people of God must bear witness in the world to the salvation acquired once for all in Jesus Christ. This will be impossible where the nonbelieving world is concerned, unless they have learned through their own diversities to experience these limitless fraternal ties that actually beget salvation. Charity is the material out of which the Church is built. It is hardly necessary to point out that exchange of life and energy in these terms will mean serious reconsideration of many roles and structures in our present ecclesiastical framework.

The fraternal meal of the messianic people

The progressive initiation of the people of God into the mystery of Christ is accomplished above all in the Eucharist. So too Christian awareness of crucial responsibility for the destiny of the whole human race ought to be renewed and deepened during those privileged moments.

Hence the importance of the liturgy of the Word. The fruits of the eucharistic celebration are not produced automatically. So many Christians attend only because they are searching for more security, or solutions for private religious needs. What the liturgy of the Word should really elicit, and always renew, is something deeper: a genuinely religious experience which embraces the world, and is knit into the texture of daily living. This will never be a bald commentary on scriptural texts. Scripture will be made the occasion for communicating the living Word, because it is this which sustains the people of God, the leaven amongst the whole.

Hence too the importance of the gathering itself; it is never an ordinary assembly. It is a gathering in which the Church tries to anticipate something. She would like to convey to her members a ritual experience of the universal fraternal love which characterizes the Kingdom. Moulded by this experience, Christians should return to their daily lives in a glow of real hope. Here too the ordinary ecclesial practice needs a measure of reform.

2. The Messianic Theme of Jesus, Son of David

Modern man is so insistent about happiness being the goal of history, and man himself the maker of history, that we could be misled. This is not totally new. As far back as we can go we see evidences of the human urge to participate somehow in the framing of human destiny. But of course, as the myth of Prometheus shows, all victories over nature were thought to involve anger on the part of the gods. Man doesn't have any such fears today: depending on divinity for salvation seems to him a useless, if not actually a harmful, procedure.

If the Christian is to have dialogue with modern man he must be able to show that his faith in the God of Jesus Christ does not set aside human responsibility in the search for salvation. On the contrary, authentic faith actually presumes such responsibility.

Jewish man in search of salvation

It is true that the Jewish concept of God as Totally-Other implied some danger of alienation for man. Did man have any function except passively to await the salvation that depended altogether on God's sovereign initiative? Her insight that without his own cooperation God would not save man is indeed a tribute to Israel's greatness.

All her investigation into the nature of the cooperation was made in the context of messianic hope, which literally pervades the Old Testament. It was only when he encountered from man the response of fidelity that Yahweh saved his people and saved humanity. Because fidelity always fell short of what it should be, the prophets would direct the gaze of Israel towards the future. Tomorrow would come the Messiah, the one capable of the proper human contribution in the task of divine salvation.

The "Son-of-David" aspect of the Messiah image is important. It is the richest aspect when we consider Jewish institutions; it is the most characteristically Israelite, the most human. The whole history of messianism is pervaded by it, so that other messianic figures are always influenced; but it illustrates too the formidable ambiguities that developed Jewish messianism.

Jesus of Nazareth, Son of David

It is worth noting how anxious the evangelists are to take account of Jesus' davidic ancestry. The death on the cross was already part of history when they wrote. Accordingly they were free to use a messianic title which Jesus himself preferred to avoid, lest he be misunderstood by audiences amongst whom nationalist interpretation of the phrase was very prevalent.

When Jesus is presented as Son of David, the point stressed is the profoundly human aspect of the Savior's intervention in history. It is not enough to say the Son of God became man. We must know in concrete terms who the man is. If we are too abstract in our concept of the hypostatic union, an essential dimension of the salvation acquired in Jesus Christ is liable to become obscured.

The precise moment in time and space when Jesus made his appearance was an exceptionally rich one in the human story. That particular environment in which he became incarnate molded him, provided the categories of thought and language which would enable him to declare what his mission was. In material terms, the emergence of Jesus just then among the Jewish population was an example of remarkable continuity. The radical discontinuity lay in the response he made to the hope of Israel. It meant a total and radical restructuring of the hope. It was unexpected, and it became a stumbling block because it deprived the chosen people of all their privileges. Yet in fact it had been deeply threaded into the texture of the history that began with Abraham.

We can look back even further. The religious experience of Israel is not isolated from that of the human race in general. There were many aeons of human history before it flowered. All this time had to pass before man achieved a minimal mastery over nature, developed viable forms of social organization, of moral and spiritual discipline, provided himself with speech and writing as means of communication. We should never forget that Christ's coming among us seemed to presuppose a relatively high degree of human culture, the use of writing for one thing. When he was born, Palestine was by no means the backward outpost we sometimes say it was.

The historical Church: people of God, body of Christ

Christ's body as well is made up of very tangible human beings. They show that the Church is something concrete and actual, in history, the people of God involved with human destiny. The members of his body are linked with Christ: they participate in his role as mediator and in his unique priesthood. The terms of participation, as they pursue their spiritual pilgrimage, are real and actual, even profane. The Church is more than the expression of the Father's gratuitous initiative. Ever and always it is the place of encounter between God who comes to man by his Spirit, and men who lift their lives to God through the Risen Lord. The Church wears the lineaments of her human members.

As Christ's body she continues to make salvation history, which had its true beginning with Jesus Christ, when he died and rose again for every man. Insofar as he engages his life, whatever its individual or collective dimensions, in the dynamics of Word and sacrament, each member is an irreplaceable stone in the edifice. Following Saint Paul, the Christian should invariably be able to say "For me to live is Christ;" because it is the expansion of this Christ-life in his members that day by day makes salvation history.

The development of secular history is not without its influence in this civilizing process. It does not make salvation history, but it is connected with it. Above all in these days the practical exercise of her catholicity by the Church is closely associated with modern man's great task, for which he is so much better equipped than his predecessors. The task, that is, of bringing into association with each other the different cultural blocs of humanity.

Because it is human the Church develops institutions. Initiating believers into salvation history means molding their whole lives, touching the very depths of their being. Ecclesial procedures are directed to this end, the Eucharist for instance, all that leads up to it and all that follows from it. The object always is to color the whole texture of living, but the method adopted is exclusively ritual. For the Church cannot aim by her practices at setting up another nation amongst the nations of the universe.

The human aspect of mission

Mission is the act of implanting, amongst all peoples, the mystery of Christ. It is to do again, for each people, what Christ did once for all for Israel. He, the Risen Lord, is the principal agent in every mission, but the task is accomplished by his body which is the Church.

The gospel is the key treasure of the Church which she must transmit to all peoples. Always it has two facets, the transcendental, and the relationship to a given culture at any time. It is the transcendental which makes possible the transplantation into new territory. In any given historical situation, where a people is not yet evangelized, it becomes the business of the Church to take on the particular spiritual ethos that is theirs. In the interior confrontation between Christ and this ethos the people is drawn to recognize the savior of humanity.

The foundation then on which missionaries build is never *tabula rasa*. The good news Paul announced to the Greeks was that Jesus had fulfilled in his resurrection the hope of his people Israel. And always, until the end of time, the good news we bring begins from this concrete work that has been done. We should be dubious about a mission which can be described as purely evangelical. Some missionaries think that because the gospel is universal, when we strip away the particular cultural growths with which centuries of Church history have loaded it, this is sufficient. This is incorrect. It tends to confuse evangelizations, which is the living tradition throughout all cultural changes of the mystery of Christ, with some sort of ideology about universal brotherhood.

The Eucharist in particular historical situations

The major act of the Christian community in assembly is the Eucharist. When we affirm its eschatological character, we are not denying the influence a particular culture must necessarily have on it. As in the case of the Church which celebrates it, here too the human lineaments will be visible. The formularies used, gestures and rites, liturgical style and structure: all these are stamped by particular history. The very scriptural texts which form the center of the rite are dated; the fact of Incarnation demands that it be so. This does not mean however that, where a church is engaged in evangelizing, she is free from the obligation of purifying celebrations from the cumbrous growths of history.

It should be added that the eucharistic assembly, like every Church practice, ought to have its own laws. The catholocity which is the strong note of the assembly suggests that it be a gathering easily open to all. Because if the Eucharist stands for the Kingdom of universal brotherhood on this earth, all those who participate in it must transcend in some way their own particular sociological framework.

LAST DAYS BEFORE CHRISTMAS

I. Genesis
49:2, 8-10
1st reading
December 17

This blessing of Judah is due to Elohist and Yahwist traditions. It comes from a poem attributed to the Patriarch Jacob, and cites the history of the Hebrew people and successive ascendancies of one or another tribe.

The blessing of Judah is all the more outstanding in that it follows the rebukes given to the three elder sons of Jacob. Judah appears as a lion satisfied after a particularly fruitful hunt. None dare approach him, his sovereignty is undisputed, and this sovereignty extends not only in space, overriding the other tribes, but also in time, right up to the messianic days. Verse 10 is indeed openly messianic: a descendant of Judah shall reign not only over the other tribes of the chosen people, but over the nations. It is generally accepted that this prophetic insight, so close to that of Isaiah or of Micah, was introduced into the poem just before, or at the time of, the exile.

II. Matthew
1:1-17
Gospel
December 17

While living among his people, Christ was rarely concerned with the matter of his davidic lineage. He is considered simply as the son of Joseph (Mt 13:55; Jn 6:42) or of Mary (Mk 6:3), origins which do not indicate a messianic genealogy (see Jn 7:40-42). In Luke's third chapter (which was for a time the first chapter), David is only mentioned incidentally, since it was not Luke's purpose to prove the davidic sonship of Jesus.

The fall of Jerusalem (70) seems to mark the time when Christian communities faced with Jewish criticism (as in Jerusalem: cf. Ac 2:25-36; Rome: see Rm 1:3-4; or Antioch: cf. Ac 13:22-24) busied themselves with establishing that Jesus belonged to the house of David. Matthew and Luke both added two new chapters at the beginning of their gospels to defend the davidic ancestry and the messianic mission of Jesus. Thus, at the very time when the Jewish hopes in the return of a davidic king were shattered, the Christian apologists assert that this son of David is none other than Christ, and liturgy inserts the title, "Son of David" in its revered formulas (Mt 9:27; 15:22; 20:30; 21:15).

a) In giving Jesus the title Christ (anointed; vv. 1 and 16), and David that of King (v. 6), Matthew's genealogy asserts that Christ belongs to the *royal line of David*. The four women who are mentioned for their important part in the Davidic hopes confirm the interpretation. It was through Bathsheba, Uriah's wife (v. 6), that Nathan's promise of an offspring to David was fulfilled (2 S 7:12-14). Tamar (v. 3) strove, even at the price of incest, to figure in the messianic line and to share in working out the royal dynasty. Ruth (v. 5) also prepared the way of David, through fidelity to her Jewish ancestry. We do not know, at present, why Matthew included Rahab (v. 5), but contemporary Jewish sources may one day reveal the messianic import.

The genealogy of Matthew is therefore an affirmation of the davidic origin of Christ. Approximations and considerable gaps noticeable throughout the list are unimportant (from Zerubbabel to Joseph, or a period of five hundred years, only eight generations are given). Matthew has arranged his list in order to prove that Jesus was the son of David, and to prepare his readers to understand the place of Joseph in this lineage (Mt 1:18-25).

b) The presence of the four women *sinners* in the genealogy has an added significance. Matthew recalls the incestuous Tamar, the prostitute Rahab, Ruth the foreigner, and Bathsheba the adulteress in order to emphasize that salvation is offered to all, even to sinners and foreigners. Coming from such a family, Christ cannot exclude from his kingdom, as intransigent Jews might have wished, sinners or women, the foreigner or the feeble. He is son of David, but also the son of sinners (cf. Mt 1:21).

From the evangelist's pains to insert Jesus into the lineage of David emerges an important doctrinal lesson. God could have sent a divine Messiah to reign secretly over hearts and establish a purely heavenly kingdom. By means of the Incarnation, he did establish a heavenly kingdom, but one deeply rooted in a human community of lowly origin and laborious growth, not uninvolved with sin.

That is why human ancestors, good and not so good, had to be provided for the Son of God. A geneology, even a continued one, was always, in Israel, a means of giving concrete expression to the idea of community of life and destiny.

III. Jeremiah   This oracle has been rather awkwardly in-
   23:5-8   serted in the violent diatribe delivered by
   1st reading   Jeremiah against the shepherds of the people,
   December 18 above all the kings of Judah.

The prophet's messianism is altogether theocratic: God himself will be the guide and director of his people. He was much too aware of the sad decadence evident in the davidic dynasty to give any credence to a role for it in the eschatological future.

Yet popular belief in a new *David* reacted against his overly theocratic view by inserting this oracle, which is obviously inspired by Isaiah 11:1-4. It is only by the mediation of a man that God will save his people. The theocratic ideal could indeed be wrongly emphasized, and it was important that popular feeling should react against the prophet's passivity. God who puts man in existence and makes him free by that very fact excludes all theocratic solutions to human problems. The solutions he approves are those of dialogue and collaboration, the solution, in a word, of incarnation.

IV. Matthew   The commentary for this gospel was given
    1:18-24   at the fourth Sunday of Advent, p. 140.
    Gospel
    December 18

V. Judges 13:2-7; The sage of Samson may have found its
    24-25a   origin in the story of a Palestinian country-
    1st reading   man renowned for extraordinary strength, a
    December 19   story that popular interest would embellish
    over and over. Behind the folklore there ap-
pears however a definitely religious purpose: whatever strength
man may have must come from God.

a) The principal interest of this *annunciation of the birth* of
Samson is the evidence that such annunciations were a very
distinct literary *genre*. We find it utilized for the annunciations
of Isaac (Gn 18:9-15), of John the Baptist and Jesus (Lk 1:5-25;
Mt. 1:18-25). In each case an angel appears to the father to tell
him the mission of the child to be. The father indicates an
obstacle that must be surmounted (old age and the barrenness of
his wife). Then the angel refers him to a sign that God will perform to show his part in the coming conception. Finally these
birth annunciations are frequently concluded by a commentary
on the child's name.

b) For the Hebrews, the classical way of stressing that a
man's strength is a gift of God is to say that it had been
promised before his birth under circumstances that actually
underline the weakness of man. Such is the case of Samson, of
John the Baptist, of Samuel, and of many others. In the case of
Samson, human weakness is seen in his mother's barrenness, his
father's old age, and his own refusal to use normal means of
sustenance (v. 7). His strength thus appears all the more a gift
of God, absolutely gratuitous, and therefore designed only to
carry out God's plan. Samson will indeed die on the very day he

uses this strength for his own profit, not as a gift of God, but for his personal glory.

The lesson could well be that God was not on the side of force. Weakness indeed might be the best indication he could give of himself. The whole life of Jesus on earth, lived in weakness, might not have been a mere interval in the eternal life of an all-powerful God, but a reflection of the greatest excellence in God, his love for men.

VI. Luke 1:5-25 It was long believed that the story of John
Gospel　　the Baptist's childhood in St. Luke reproduced
December 19 an original earlier than the evangelist, prob-
　　　　　　ably compiled among the Baptist's disciples.
This hypothesis is today abandoned. Luke actually composed the narrative himself, in a style intentionally biblical, full of reminiscences of the Septuagint. But he did so after the gospel was completed, at a time when he was contemplating the composition of the Acts. This explains the close literary and theological kinship between Lk 1-2 and Ac 1-12 and the presentation of the Baptist as forerunner of the aspostolic kerygma (Lk 1:76-80).

a) The first theme is the *heavenly announcement of the birth*. The advanced age of the couple and Elizabeth's barrenness (v. 7) have undoubtedly led Luke to see a parallel with Abraham and Sara (compare v. 7 and 18 with Gn 18:11; v. 13 with Gn 17:19; v. 18 with Gn 15:8). The parallel does not, however, go beyond the physical condition of the two couples. We cannot argue that Zechariah is a new Abraham or John the Baptist a new Isaac.

John is presented as a child of the priestly lineage of Abijah (v. 5). Now this family was despised at the time — to judge at least from disparaging remarks in the Talmud — a fact which could explain John's later break with the political and aristocratic priesthood of Jerusalem.

He is also introduced as a prophet. And he has all the characteristics of one: asceticism (v. 15; cf. Nb 6:1-8; Mt 11:18), vocation proclaimed at the moment of birth (v. 15b; cf. Jeremiah in Jr 1:5; The Servant in Is 49:1-5; Samuel in Is 1:11), and possession of the Spirit (Jl 3:1-3) which brings the Baptist astonishingly close to the apostles at Pentecost (Ac 4:8; 8:29; 6:3-5; 7:55). But it is to the figure of Samuel particularly that Luke turns to describe the gift of prophecy in the Baptist. Like Samuel (1 S 2:21), John is "great" in the sight of the Lord (v. 15). Like him, he is born of a barren womb (v. 15; cf. 1 S 1:11). Finally, John is priest and prophet, appointed to designate the Messiah, just as Samuel was priest and prophet appointed to designate the king (Lk 3:21-22; 1 S 16:12-13).

The Baptist then appears as converter (v. 16-17). St. Luke is here resuming the old prophetical theme of conversion, "return to the Lord" (2 Ch 15:4; 19:4; Ml 2:6; Os 3:5; 7:10 etc.), to which he will give basic emphasis in the piety of the primitive communities (Ac 4:4; 9:42; 17:12; 18:8).

Finally, John is a precursor (v. 17). Luke describes this function by quoting Ml 3:23-24 revised by Si 48:10-11.

b) The second theme of the narrative concerns the *mission of the angel messenger* (v. 19). Luke 1:39-47 has already revealed the messianic significance of the mission of Gabriel, the angel charged by Daniel with the interpretation and calculation of the seventy weeks (Dn 8:16; 9:21). Now he sees in John the Baptist this other angel heralded by Ml 3.

The messenger appears during a liturgy (v. 11), sacrifice being the ideal place of meeting between God and his people. Angels charged with communicating God's will to men normally appear in the smoke of sacrifice (Gn 22:11-15; Jg 6:20-22; 13:16-20; 1 Ch 21:18-30; Gn 28:12). There were indeed in Jewish Tradition marvelous tales of angelic apparitions during public worship, announcing the birth of high priests such as John Hyrcan or Ismael. They may have been the source of Luke's inspiration. But Luke sees in these apparitions (Lk 1-2, passim; Ac 1:10; 5:19;

8:26; 10:3) the sign of breach in the ancient barrier between heaven and earth, an epiphany of the celestial world irradiating men's abode.

Like that of Daniel, Zechariah's dumbness is caused by the overwhelming vision which he is granted. But the note of punishment added by Luke (v. 20) is new, and difficult to explain with certainty.

Thus the context of Luke's annunciation of the birth of John the Baptist is one of final preparation. The new Elias has come to herald the Messiah: the new Samuel is here to point out the future David. The precursor angel begins his ministry. Only seventy weeks remain until the inauguration of the final times.

VII. Isaiah
7:10-14
1st reading
Dec. 20

Commentary on this reading was given in that on the first reading of the first cycle of the fourth Sunday in Advent, p. 130.

VIII. Luke
1:26-38
Gospel
Dec. 20

Commentary on this reading was given in that on the gospel of the second cycle of the fourth Sunday in Advent, p. 142.

IX. Canticle
2:8-14
1st reading
December 21

Exegetes are not yet agreed about how the Canticle should be interpreted. Are the poems it contains a celebration of human love, of the encounter between man and woman, liberated now from the alienating magical practices with which ancient religions surrounded sexual love? Or are they just allegories which celebrate the love between God and his people?

The lovers have been separated by the rigors of winter; but now *spring* returns (v. 11). The suitor runs across the mountains of Judah (v. 1) and approaches the house of his beloved. She waits impatiently, watching behind the wall near the window, then at the door. Finally she hears his voice calling her to come to him (v. 10). The piece depicts the burning passion of the lovers who long to be reunited and wait with impatience. It is true that the final poems will propound a more adult view of love, which is marked by a fidelity stronger than death. But at no time is the freshness of young love disapproved. All the successive stages of human love are good in themselves. They can be used to deepen religious experience and become signs of God's love for his people.

The surprising prominence of the Canticle in scripture (something hardly acknowledged in the distribution of lessons in the new lectionary) serves as a reminder to man that his world is not exclusively one of technology and reason, science and politics. It is a world too of gratuitous giving, of love and sharing. We see that all the securities men seek, all men's categorizations of things and people, are shattered by the encounter of two hearts. The mutual giving of two persons.

God has not chosen clever, reasoning persons to communicate his message. He has selected those who were best capable of demonstrating encounter and relationship in their lives. The more numerous the relationships, so much the better, because encounter would be correspondingly enriched. The Kingdom of God is not the "one-dimensional" universe towards which our reasonable, shallow society tends. We find it whenever two human beings begin to understand one another, to respect and love one another.

X. Luke 1:39-45 This gospel has been commented on in that of
Gospel the 3rd cycle of the 4th Sunday in Advent,
December 21 p. 146.

XI. I Samuel   The greater part of chapters 1 to 3 of the 1st
1:24-28   Book of Samuel depends, it seems, on anti-
1st reading   royalist tradition. The notion of a child's
December 22   consecration to God was standard in those
days, but the ceremony is described mainly as
an introduction to the "canticle" of Hannah. Here we have a
psalm inspired from various sources: wisdom, pauperist, and
messianic. It celebrates the wisdom of God in the style of the
sages of Israel (v. 3), his great might in that of the poor of
Yahweh (v. 4-8) and the inauguration of the messianic kingdom
in that of the prophets (vv. 9-10).

A later editor doubtless put the psalm in the mouth of Hannah,
probably because the barren woman who bears child is mentioned.

XII. Luke 1:46-56   Literary analysis of the Magnificat reveals its
Gospel   different sources of inspiration. A first source
Dec. 22   appears in verses 46-47, 49b, and 50: they
reproduce formulas common in Jewish litur-
gical songs. Compare, for example, v. 49b with 1 S 2:2, Ps 98/99:
3, 5, 9; Ps 110/111:10, and v. 50 with the refrain of Ps 135/136
and Ps 99/100:5; 106/107:1; 117/118; 1-4; etc. The opening of
the canticle, too, is common in liturgical hymns (formulas in
"I"; Ps 102/103:1; 1 S 2:1; Ps 17/18:50; Hab 3:18).

In between such formulas, Mary's personal thanksgiving (v.
48-49a) is inspired by Israel's hymns of praise. Verse 48a recalls Dt 26:7, and v. 48b Ml 3:12. Verse 49 reproduces Dt 10:21.
Thus the Magnificat repeats the comparison between Israel and
Mary made by the evangelist throughout chapter 1 (cf. Lk
1:26-38; 39-47).

The Magnificat continues with acclamation borrowed from the
repertory of the poor (v. 51-53), particularly the canticle of
Hannah (1 S 2:4, 6-9 and Pss 146/147:3-9; 106/107:35-41; 112/
113:7-9; etc.). The poor made up the privileged section of the
messianic people (cf. relations between Ps 88/89 and verses

51-53 of Mary's canticle). Mary personifies them and becomes their mouthpiece.

The last part (v. 54-55) recalls the promise made to Abraham and draws its inspiration from second Isaiah (Is 41:8-9). Considered as the descendant of Abraham in whom the promises find their fulfillment, Mary is identified with the chosen people (compare Lk 1:38 with Gn 18:14; Lk 1:50 with Gn 18:3; 15:2; Lk 1:48 with Gn 12:3).

Thus the Magnificat attributes Israel's characteristics to Mary, the personification of the eschatological Israel of the poor, and of Abraham's race receiving the promises.

a) The comparison between the Virgin and Israel in St Luke invites us to see in Mary the image and mouthpiece of the Church. In fact, many an expression in the Magnificat is found in the vocabulary of the primitive community when it hymns its own mystery (cf. the word "exalt" in Lk 1:46, 48 and Ac 5:15; the word "Savior" in Lk 1:47, 69, 71, 77 and Ac 4:12; 5:31; 13:47; Ps 88/89 in Lk 1:51 and Ac 2:30; Lk 1:52 and Ac 2:22-38; 3:13). The eucharistic assembly, cell of eschatological Israel and object of the promises made to Abraham, is therefore entitled to repeat the Magnificat in its own right.

b) The Magnificat however belongs to a Christian society that is not yet sufficiently freed of the Jewish framework. The *reversal of situation* motif has no relevance now. True, we have poor who are oppressed by the rich and races oppressed by other races. It is also true that God's salvation means deliverance for the poor and the oppressed. But this deliverance should go *pari passu* with liberation for the rich and the oppressors as well. The alienation and slavery of the latter consists in their selfishness and their very need for power.

The Christian new order is not just one where the poor and the persecuted will be liberated. It is an order where everyone, rich and poor, oppressors and oppressed, will be delivered from

alienations of whatever kind. They will work together to build
new relationships, new encounters, new dialogue.

XIII. Malachi   Malachi (or someone concealed behind this
3:1-4; 4:5-6 name) writes his prophecies after the temple
1st reading has been rebuilt. But the priestly caste is far
Dec. 23   from being reformed, in spite of the legisla-
               tion in Leviticus (1st half of the 5th century).
The whole people, it is true, needs reform; but the prophet is
interested only in the temple and the cult. For the evil which
ravages the people reflects on the cult and, conversely, a de-
generate cult is the seed of decadence for the people. The in-
terdependence between cult and people is all the more pronounced in that Israel at the time had no leaders except religious
ones.

a) Malachi is resolutely in the tradition of *theocratic messianism*, which heralds the coming of Yahweh himself, not a
royal Messiah. It is true that at the time no person or function
seemed capable of arousing hope of a messianic character. Consequently Malachi prefers to depend altogether on Yahweh on
whom he confers the titles of "Lord" and "Angel of the Covenant."* However, Yahweh will be preceded by a forerunner —
his "messenger" (v. 1), a rather mysterious personage who
probaby fulfils the role determined by Isaiah 40:3; 57:14.

b) On the other hand, Malachi envisages a *theocracy of cult.*
The coming of Yahweh will be the occasion for a radical reform
of the priestly caste. The long anticipated "purification" (Is 1:25;
4:4-5; 48:10) will apply mainly to the levites (v. 3) who will
then return to the ideal of faithfulness their forefathers had
(v. 4), as recorded in Ex 32:26-29; Nb 25:7-13 or Dt 33:8-11.
Thus the messianic ideal of Malachi returns to that of Ezekiel

---

*On the relation between Yahweh and the angel, see, for example, Gn
16:7-11; Ex 3:2.

— a theocracy of cult with a strong bias toward perfection in rite and requiring as well moral purification by the exercise of more social justice (v. 5 inspired by Dt 14:29; 24:17).

However the reform of the priesthood which Malachi envisages is by no means ritualist and legalist. The priest, though he is a man of rite, can purify himself only by becoming a prophet, that is a man of the word (see the priestly ideal of Malachi 2:6-7).

c) This twofold role of the priest, at once man of rite (a rite made valid by moral attitude) and man of word (who incites to spiritual sacrifices) makes him, in Malachi's eyes, a *messenger of God* (Ml 2:7). The question arises whether the forerunner Yahweh sends (Ml 3:1) is not then a priest who perfectly fulfils the ideal of priest-prophet, a priest reformed who will prepare the tribe of Levi to play their part in the cult of the last days.

People wanted to know the identity of the messenger. Malachi, or one of his copyists, added two verses as appendix to the book (Ml 3:23-24), which specify that the personage will be a new Elijah. This prophet was believed to be bodily in heaven (2 K 2): accordingly, he would return to earth to spend the rest of his days. As easy step from this was the idea that he would prepare the reign of Yahweh. Furthermore, as Elijah had been engrossed in purifying the cult of his time (1 K 18:20-40), the idea that he should come back to purify the levitical priesthood and its sacrifices was pleasing to Malachi. He would thus "turn the hearts of children towards their fathers," that is, restore to the levites the ideal of the covenant of the desert, which Malachi highly prizes (Ml 2:4-5, 8, 10; 3:1).

The New Testament, under Christ's own inspiration, presents the messenger in the lineaments of John the Baptist (Mt 17:9-13; Lk 7:24-30). Now John was a member of the priestly family (Lk 1:5) and his conception had been announced in the temple (Lk 1:8-25). Even though he hardly ever exercised a strictly priestly function, still he was the priest-prophet foretold by Malachi.

The identification of Malachi's messenger with the Baptist is not absolute. Luke 1-2 sees in him the angel Gabriel himself Lk 1:5-25).

In resorting so eagerly to Ml 3, who presents a theocratic rather than a royal messianism, the New Testament invites its readers to see in Jesus not only the Son of David or the human Messiah, but the Lord himself, come to establish on earth a new and definitive priesthood and cult.

God has not come to overwhelm man by his power. On the contrary, he wants to make man an interlocutor, and for this reason he has decided that the theocratic reign should coincide with the messianic and human reign.

But the Man-God comes into the world to settle the conditions of the definitive cult, signified by the eucharistic assembly, source and summit of the spiritual sacrifice offered by the Christian. The messenger who purifies the cult continually and prevents it from lapsing into formalism and ritualism is present in the liturgy of the Word, the proclamation of the Kerygma, and the mission of the Church.

XIV. Luke
1:57-66
Gospel
Dec. 23

The announcement of John the Baptist's birth (v. 5-25) has put in relief the salient traits of his personality. The circumstances of his birth hardly add new elements. Neither the birth nor the circumcision are told for themselves. They serve only as a framework for the imposition of the name already proclaimed by the angel in verse 13.

Thanks to the unexpected agreement of Zechariah and Elizabeth, the name of John the Baptist appears to be willed by heaven. The healing of Zechariah's dumbness (cf. Is 32:3-4) too is sign of a heavenly manifestation.

Luke dwells on the astonishment and joy caused by the manifestation. These are characteristic symptoms of messianic times (for joy: Lk 1:14, 17, 57, 58; Zp 3:14-17; Jr 31:12-13; Is 51:3; for astonishment: Lk 1:21, 63; 2:18, 33; Ac 2:7; 3:12). The swiftness with which the news spreads, image of the swiftness of the spread of the gospel (Lk 1:65-66; 2:15, 17, 20), is also a sign of the presence of heaven among men.

At the very time these two first chapters of Luke were first put out, the contemporary world was singularly bereft of joy. The Jewish nation was crushed under the heel of an occupying power, while the Greek peoples were reduced by apathy to alienation.

Are things very different now, with uneasiness on every horizon, in a world where the majority of people are ignored and alienated? When people nowadays speak of joy, is it anything other than the escape of the music-hall, the thrill of sensual excitation, or the deliverance from depression offered by the psychotherapist?

Yet Luke's message remains valid. Joy resides in the assurance that one has communion with God, and that he is present even in human events.

It is not however an immediate consequence of belief in God's presence. The God of the Jansenists is not a joyful God, nor is the God of the pious. The God who gives joy is he who is present in the whole texture of a man's life, in secular activities, in the most private thoughts and the deepest encounters, in sufferings that surmount discouragement. The joy of messianic times is this joy.

XV. 2 Samuel 7:1-5, 8b-11, 16
1st reading
Dec. 24

We have already given an exegetical commentary on this reading in dealing with the first reading of the second cycle on the fourth Sunday of Advent, p. 131. Here we confine ourselves to a consideration of the place occupied by this prophecy in the general context of Jewish messianism.

The development of the theme of royal *messianism* is extremely revealing as an indication of how revelation progresses in the popular mind.

The primary text is the one we have in 2 Samuel 7, and the prophecy is designed to point out to David that there is a goal more important than the building of the temple: the establishment, that is, of the royal dynasty. Solomon is approved by Nathan as successor to David. There is nothing remote or ideal about the oracle. Solomon is the messiah envisaged (v. 12-14), an imperfect messiah (v. 14b) for whom prayers must be offered to God (v. 29), who receives no spiritual or universal mission.

In the parallel text however of 1 Chronicles 17, messianism has gone a step further. The idea of possible default is disregarded (v. 13): God's blessing on David's successor is not something to be prayed for, but an accomplished fact (v. 17): the promise is no longer confined to the "fruit of your entrails" but becomes precise — "one of your sons" (v. 11). And lastly the future king's stature is greater than that envisaged in 2 Samuel 7. He is the anointed of Yahweh (2 Ch 6:24), sits on the throne of Yahweh (2 Ch 9:8; 1 Ch 29:23) and appears side by side with the prophets (2 Ch 29:24-25).

Again, Psalm 131/132 gives another nuance to the basic text of 2 Samuel 7, by adding to the notion of a blessing by God that of an oath (v. 21), insisting on the part played by the merits of David in the appearance of the Messiah (vv. 10-13), and describing the messianic era as one of prosperity (crown, glory, horn, light: vv. 17-18).

A little later Psalm 88/89 will bring up once more the notion of God's oath (associated with mercy and with the covenant: vv. 3-4, 24, 29, 34-36). However, disillusioned no doubt with the Jerusalem dynasty, the author will base all hope on the quasi-immortal figure of David (vv. 5, 20-30, 37).

It remained for Jesus to give the final interpretation of 2 Samuel when, with the davidic theme, he associates that of the eschatological Son of man, or the suffering Servant.

XVI. Luke
1:67-79
Gospel
Dec. 24

The Benedictus predates Saint Luke perhaps. It has fewer characteristically Lucan phrases than the rest of the first chapter. Several words seem to be translated from a Hebrew original, and some others are a very Semitic type of Greek.

The most attractive theory sees in the Benedictus a Jewish messianic hymn which was modified somewhat and introduced into Christian liturgy in the Greek language. In fact one finds in it the vocabulary of the primitive community. The verb "raise up" (v. 69) means also "resuscitate" (Ac 3:15; 4:10). The title servant (pais) attributed to David is found too in the Christian liturgy of Jerusalem (Ac 4:25). The fulfillment of the scriptures (v. 70) is a constant theme in apostolic discourses (Ac 3:21).

To this christianized Jewish hymn, Luke has probably added the eulogy of the Baptist (vv. 76-77), referring to the message of the angel (Lk 1:15) and the prophecy of Malachi 3:1 (Lk 1:17). The manner in which he describes the ministry of John (knowledge of salvation and remission of sins) indicates personal composition (cf. parallels in Ac 4:10-12; 5:31-32; 13:26, 38). For him the apostles' mission is to "give the people knowledge of salvation, through the forgiveness of their sins." He attributes to John the same mission because he sees in him the precursor not only of Christ, but of the apostles and the Church. There is however a notable difference between the Baptist and the apostles. He gives knowledge of salvation; they provide salvation by knowledge.

Apart from the verses on the Baptist (76-77) there are three strophes in the canticle, each combining three ideas:
  a) *God is merciful* in his salvific acts: 1st strophe (v. 72), 3rd strophe (v. 78).
  b) *He fulfills the scriptures:* 1st strophe (vv. 69-70): the davidic promises; 2nd strophe (vv. 73-74): the covenant and the promise to Abraham; 3rd strophe (v. 79a): the

prophecy of Isaiah 9:1; 11:6; 42:7.

c) *He procures definitive salvation for men:* 1st strophe (v. 71): the deliverance from enemies won by David's warlike enterprise; 2nd strophe (v. 75): the service of God in holiness and justice; 3rd strophe (v. 79b): the progress of men in the way of peace.

The doxology then of ancient *Messianism*, this hymn celebrates the fulfillment of the prophecies and promises made to the patriarchs and David. The Messiah, designated by images: the "horn of salvation" (v. 69; cf. Ps 75:5): the "rising sun" (v. 78; Is 43:19; 45:8; 61:11; Nb 24:17) delivers from enemies (1st strophe), consecrates to the service of God (2nd strophe) and wins knowledge and peace for those who live in union with God (3rd strophe).

EVE AND FEAST OF CHRISTMAS

A. THE WORD

I. Isaiah 62:1-5   Cyrus has just issued an edict allowing the
1st reading   temple of Jerusalem to be rebuilt (538). A
Christmas Eve   first group of exiles has already left Babylon
on its way to Jerusalem, and a disciple of
Second-Isaiah sings of their hopes.

When they reached Jerusalem, the city was already restored
to a degree of its former activity, and had become a provincial
capital in the empire of Cyrus. But what could be the meaning
of a restoration intended for a population now indifferent to
Yahweh? The prophet revives the courage of the exiles by
directing their gaze towards the marvelous future of the city.

Zion will receive a new name (vv. 2 and 4) to denote a new
situation. No longer will she be called "forsaken," but *"spouse"*:
she will be like a young bride ready for her bridegroom (v. 5).

The source of happiness for this city lies in the presence of
Yahweh, whom the prophet sees sitting on Zion, with its ram-
parts around his forehead as a crown (v. 3).

The prophet inaugurates here a theme which will become
very important in scripture and in Christian symbol: the wedding
of Yahweh and Jerusalem. The love of God for his city is related
in terms of espousals because it is a form of love which expresses
mutual sharing and giving better than any other. The Incarnation, where Christ exchanges his divinity for our humanity, and
the Eucharist, where the exchange is carried on, are the brightest
moments of this sharing in love.

There is point in the comparison when the Bible, like so many
pagan myths, likens the city to a woman. Like the woman it is
drawn from man's own substance (or God's): it is a projection

of all those things which man has not yet come to be, of all that
moves him, spurs him to activity.

As it is by the instrumentality of woman that man discovers
himself, so is it with the city. As a woman teaches a man love,
sacrifice, how to transcend self, so is it with the city. In order to
act, to begin an enterprise, man (and God) needs something
living to love.

It is women who make the city. A military or a mining camp,
composed only of mercenaries and prostitutes, will never be a
city. The women give the city its tone and its tradition. As the
woman leads man into association and sympathy with other
living beings, so does the city.

II. Matthew   Commentary may be found in the analyses of
   1:1-25   the gospels of December 17 (p. 160) and the
   Gospel   fourth Sunday of Advent (p. 140).
   Christmas
   Eve

III. Isaiah 9:1-7   After the invasion of the eastern armies, the
   1st reading   Hebrews were being steadily deported to
   Midnight   Babylon (around 732). The darkness of cap-
                        tivity assailed them, sometimes quite literally,
for in those days the eyes of captives were often put out. The
captives indeed were like the dead reprieved, inhabiting already
a "land of shadow" (sheol).

Against this sombre background, Isaiah proclaims the light of
the Immanuel.

a) The theme of *light* indicates the approaching deliverance of
those provinces which have fallen into Assyrian hands, but it
makes that deliverance depend on the person of the future king.
Subsequent tradition was in fact quick to postpone to the
eschatological future this appearance of the light of salvation,

associated with the person of the Messiah (cf. Mt 4:12-17; Lk 1:76-79; Ep 5:8-14). Light thus becomes an essential property of happiness; it denotes liberation from evil and slavery, and participation in the glory of the Messiah.

b) This light is brought by a child (v. 5), who from the day of his birth receives the empire, an allusion of the oriental custom of counting a king's reign from the day of his birth. He receives a name, at once unique and composite. Like Solomon, he will be a "Wonder-Counselor" (v. 6), a "Prince-of-Peace"; like David a Mighty-God, an "Eternal-Father," as though he were coming to establish the dynasty without end (2 S 7:11-12) announced by Nathan.

Verse 6 specifies that the child is of the *lineage of David;* since he will sit on the throne of David and base his royal power on the justice and integrity, which constitute Isaiah's constant theme.

Who is this child? It must be a well known king, probably Hezekiah, whom Isaiah invests with superhuman power to bring salvation and light to a people in distress, a king who will assure his subjects peace and justice and lay the foundations of a dynasty dedicated to this ideal.

Disappointed by the later behavior of Hezekiah, Israel, and maybe Isaiah himself, transferred this portrait to the *Messiah.*

However close his ties with the house of David, Isaiah, like all the other prophets (Ho 3:4-5; Jr 21:22), was nevertheless aware that the dynasty faced imminent collapse, the kings being unable to live up to the standards expected from them. But loyalty to royal structure in the people helps him to envisage a messianic future true to the royalist ideal. As the exile and later disasters, particularly under the Asmonian dynasty, jeopardized such a future, the Jews referred this royalist ideal to the "last days," to be inaugurated by God's intervention. Apart from the Sadducees, compromised in Herodian politics, all Jewish sects, from the Pharisees to the Essenians, remained faithful to this messianic hope, never allowing themselves to be caught up in politics or present affairs. Unfortunately they were too involved in formalistic discussions, too given to materialism in their hope, to be able to see the Messiah in the child of Bethlehem, or the Lord in him who rose at Easter.

For Christians, the messianic character of Christ finds its fulfillment in the paschal Lordship. Bethlehem cannot be understood unless the unexpected fulfillment of Easter is taken into consideration.

IV. Isaiah   This passage is probably from the pen of
   62:11-12   Third-Isaiah, and celebrates the approaching
   1st reading restoration of Jerusalem.
   Dawn Mass

a) In the style of Isaiah 62:1-4, the author proclaims "good news" to Jerusalem. To emphasize the salvation that is destined for the city, he resorts to describing the thorough *reversal* of situation and the change of name (v. 12; cf. Is 62:4). From the very moment of his calling (Is 61:1-3) he had seen his future, and that of the people, as a reversal of situation. The poor will receive the good news, bruised hearts will be healed, captives set free, the afflicted consoled, the conquered avenged. Mourners will be restored to joy.

What he is proclaiming is the good news of the messianic era, which will be characterized by a reversal of situation, in favor of the poor particularly. Christ uses the same procedure in putting himself forward as the guarantee that the messianic era has come.

b) In the case of Jerusalem, a change of name goes with the reversal. For a Jew a name, in the case of persons or things, was more than a mere surface etiquette. It was deeply connected with the very essence of being. Changing a name was equivalent to becoming a new being. In a Jerusalem of changed name what we see is the advent, by God's will, of a totally new humanity.

The change of situation theme is an admirable illustration of how the poor and humble will be the prime beneficiaries of salvation. Christianity however has somewhat modified this idea of change. Though everything is indeed fundamentally changed in Jesus Christ, everything still remains to be done. A new situation or a new name is not the result of magic, but demands our free cooperation. Change is secured in Christ, but will only be accomplished after a slow growth. It is this thought that led the primitive community to introduce to the beatitudes of Christ important nuances, still noticeable in Matthew's version. We should not either give too literal an interpretation to texts such as today's reading, but rather look upon them as a call for our cooperation.

V. Isaiah 52:7-10 From the walls of Jerusalem the prophet
1st reading   watches the long train of Babylonian captives
Day   returning to Palestine. Under the eyes of the
                  watchmen, with whom the prophet is stand-
ing (v. 8), comes the vanguard with its good news (v. 7), proclaiming salvation. Then the watchmen shout for joy (v. 8),
and are joined by the whole city (v. 9).

This salvation is the victory of the Warrior-God, the same whose holy arm had vanquished the Egyptians (v. 10) and today subdues the nations. Messengers may herald peace indeed, but the peace has the bitter after-taste of crushing victories!

Another aspect of this return to Jerusalem is the solemn procession of *enthronement for Yahweh*. Previously, the prophet had described the long return as a sacred road, leading God back to his temple (Is 40:1-3), a notion of theocratic messianism. It is God himself who comes to rule and no longer just a son of David (v. 7). Second-Isaiah thus meets the theocratic visions of Malachi 3:1-5 (cf. 34:23-31).

In Jesus, God and Man, the twin aspects of the Messiah,

davidic and theocratic, will blend in an unexpected manner.

This passage, which is one of the earliest in the whole bible to mention "good news" or "gospel," suggests reflection in a particular way about the nature of the Word of God. We can distinguish in the passage a number of different kinds of word. We have the word of the *avant-garde* who proclaim the liberation while still involved in the happening, that of the watchmen who relay the news and make it official, lastly that of the city folk who comment on the event. There is even a further word, that of the prophet, who recounts the event and interprets it. Among all, where is the Word of God? It is not, as is too often believed in the inspired poem which is the prophet's commentary, nor yet in the "gospel" proclaimed by the *avant-garde* of the exiles. It is in the event itself; it consists in the fact that the exiled people, after many ups and downs, finds itself suddenly free and on the road home. In his word, God gives himself completely, not in piecemeal fashion. In this event, of which he is the author, in the "signs of the times," he manifests his plan. This is the primary word of God, the most fundamental, the only efficacious word in the full sense of the term.

All other words, those of the messengers, the watchmen, the crowd, even that of the prophet himself, are only words of God to the extent that they proclaim and interpret the event, refer us to the event.

It is through creation and history that God acts in order to accomplish his plan. And it is there we find his Word, his plan clarified. The primary thing is the event. Everything else, however essential, is no more than "service" and ministry (sometimes, no doubt, inspired) of this Word. If this realization were more widespread, the Church would avoid the dangers both of biblicism and intellectualism. She would realize that attention should be directed above all towards the event, towards the human beings who are God's handiwork. Everything else, her Word, and that of the prophets, is no more than the manifestation, in history, of God.

This is to say that the Christ-event, and the death-resurrection event, are more effectively the Word of God than the very gospels which proclaim and interpret them. These are only God's word to the extent that they share in the Word which is the resurrection.

It is to say also that grace is always anterior to intervention by the Church, to the ministry of the Word and catechesis. Altogether apart from the Church, Christ is active in the universe. True, the Church's mission is decisive in explaining the presence of Christ, but her word in evangelizing never takes precedence over the basic word of the Lord himself.

VI. **Titus 2:11-14** These two readings, taken from the letter to
and **and 3:4-7** Titus, are somewhat parallel. The first (Tt
VII. *2nd reading* 2:11-14) is the conclusion to an instruction
    Midnight on the duties of specific groups of Christians.
    and Dawn The second (Tt 3:3-7) follows an instruction
              of more general character. Both clearly demonstrate Paul's intention to base Christian witness in the world on strictly theological foundations.

a) Paul has enumerated the duties of older people, of women, of the young and slaves (Tt 2:1-10). This literary genre is borrowed from the *De Officiis* of contemporary Hellenism, and Paul thus writes the first Christian letter of guidance, rather commonplace, such as could have been directed to Stoics, there being nothing specifically Christian in these moral instructions. But is it possible for any list of virtues to be exclusively Christian? Since the birth of Christ, all human values have become Christian (cf 1 Co 3:22), if Christians bear witness in their moral life to the coming of salvation.

An interesting point here is that Paul is trying to express Christianity and its ethic, the product of Judaism with its "salvation" religion, in terms of stoic experience as a "courage-to-be" religion. We can see here an invitation to search for meaning for our life in existential thought, which is heir to stoicism, but all to often considered as marginal and incapable of manifesting the salvation of God.

In the eyes of the apostle, Christian morality finds its place between two divine "manifestations": goodness and glory (Tt 2:11 and 13; cf. 3:4). Christian life must be permeated by these, as it is itself a *manifestation of salvation to the world*. Whether or not the world will believe in salvation and hope for the final revelation of God will depend on the behavior of the Christian. His life will then reveal the victory of the blood of Christ over sin and his Lordship in the world (Tt 2:14).

b) Paul has recommended Christians to be kind and courteous to pagans (Tt 3:1-2), reminding them that they too were once like them (Tt 3:3). In the second text, he insists that God's kindness and love has shown itself to both Christians and pagans. Then how can a Christian be a sign of God's love for man and yet despise the unbeliever? This is all the more important since God's goodness is gratuitous and does not entitle the Christian to any glory (Tt 3:5).

c) God's goodness manifests itself most of all through *baptized Christians* (Tt 3:5) in whom the mystery of salvation, first seen in the birth of Christ (v. 4), is made actual. Baptism indeed offers men a rebirth (v. 5), making them sons of God and heirs of his life (v. 7). Baptism is not studied here in itself, but in its most important fruit: the interior regeneration which turns man into a new being, and the Christian into an "epiphany" of the salvation of God in the world.

Though not treating of the birth of Christ, these two extracts of the letter to Titus still see Christian life, both sacramental and moral, as a fruit of the manifestation of salvation in Christ Jesus. This revelation will be glorious only at the end of times; but even now it is at work in the sacraments that renew man, and in the moral conduct which makes him a witness to salvation in the world. Its origin lies in the appearance among us of God-made-man and in his saving sacrifice.

Thus this reading gives a complete synthesis of Christian life: the mystery of Christmas, the sacrifice of the cross, sacramental life, Christian witness, and hope in glory. This fully justifies our celebration of the Eucharist.

VIII. Hebrews
1:1-6
2nd reading
Day

The first verses of the letter to the Hebrews describe the enthronement of the Lord in heaven, in a vision that recalls the prologue of John's gospel.

The author's attention is centered on two consequences of this enthronement: Christ, become the Lord, is greater than the prophets (vv. 1-3) and rules over the angels (vv. 4-13).

One should remember that the letter to the Hebrews aimed at persuading Christians of Jewish background to give up some outdated notions, such as their hope for restoration of sacrifices in the temple, and return to the law of Moses. The law was good, but it was brought about through prophets and angels, who are now surpassed by Christ the Lord.

a) Centered on the *superiority of Christ over the prophets*, the opening verses give an outline of the history of redemption. God has never ceased to speak to man, until the day when his word was completely revealed in the person of his Son. Two steps mark this history ("the past — the last days"; "our ancestors — us"; "the prophets — the Son"; vv. 1-2). Today this history is fulfilled because Christ has appeared as beginning and end of all things (v. 2). The prophets may have helped in the evolution of history, but they are neither its source nor its end. As God-made-man, Christ has on the other hand become heir to all he had created as Word.

Moreover, from him radiates the light and glory of God (v. 3) prerogatives, it used to be thought, of the temple (Ex 40:34-35;

1 K 8:10-11). Finally, he has offered the decisive sacrifice, cleansing from sin (v. 3; cf. Heb 8-10) and enabling him to enter the Holy of Holies and sit at the right hand of the Father.

b) In the first century the angels were given an important place as intermediaries between God and man (cf. Ph 2:11; Rv 4:5). But the enthronement of the Son of God at the right hand of his Father assures him of *supremacy over the angels*, with a role far superior to that of any of those beings in the administration of the world. Christ indeed has received the name of "Son" (Ps 2:7; v. 5), which is a royal title denoting in the eyes of the author the Lordship attained by the resurrection (cf. Rm 1:4; Ac 13:33). But even this was only possible because Christ was the Word of God. This sonship, of nature and of Lordship, far exceeds the highest names ever given to angels, so that their power has become worthless by comparison.

Against a Jewish tradition which gave importance to the prophets and a considerable role in the evolution of the universe to the angels, Hebrews 1 proclaims the birth of a new world, resting on far more stable and universal foundations than the old, on the Lordship, that is, of God-made-man.

Today prophets and angels have probably lost the influence attributed to them in the past. Other mediators have now taken their place in the search for salvation: man, progress, modern technology.

Christ has obtained supremacy not only over the prophets and angels, but also over all other mediators. Although progress and human strivings for betterment may be necessary, man's salvation can be found only in deification through the Incarnation of God and filial attachment to God as Father.

The Eucharist gradually initiates man into divine life and human fulfillment; it enables him to accept his responsibility as creature and master of the universe in total union with the Father.

IX. Luke 2:1-14, The second chapter of the gospel of Saint
and and 15-20 Luke gives rise to several exegetical problems.
X. *Gospel* Since it was probably written after the year
Midnight 70, it cannot be based on the contemporary
and Dawn witnesses to whom Luke had recourse in the
rest of the gospel and in the Acts. The evan-
gelist is well aware of the fact: he will give definite historical
facts, but in the midrash form accepted by the Judeo-Christian
community, adding here and there his personal views of events.

We can therefore find three layers in this gospel: the historical facts, their midrash interpretation, and the original
thought of Luke.

a) Joseph and Mary's journey to Bethlehem, and the birth of
Jesus in utter poverty, are the two basic *historical facts.* Other
circumstances are presented in a more flexible way. Apparently
Luke combines several imperial edicts issued over a period
into just one, and he gives Quirinus a title which was to be his
only later. Historical accuracy was not so important in those
days. Luke's only aim is to describe the "man" whom authorities
will discover through taking a census of the world.

b) The *midrash* presents the marvelous aspects of these facts:
angels appearing, the divine glory announcing the last days, the
prophecies of Micah fulfilled.

The first of these prophecies (Mi 3:1-4) inspired verses
6, 8, 9, 14 where Christ is shown as the expected *davidic king.*
The second (Mi 4:7-10) influenced verses 4, 8, 11, where the
kingship is not only davidic, but God's own kingship, respond-
ing to the Jewish expectation of a davidic royalty, and yet
surpassing it. This same midrash may also have inspired the
contrast noted in the text between the poverty of Bethlehem
and the city of Jerusalem. Mary is seen as the new "daughter
of Zion" (Mi 4:10; 5:2) and the poor around her are enveloped
in the "glory" that had formerly been the privilege of the
temple (Ez 40:35).

c) Luke's *personal touch* appears chiefly in his choice of a *paschal* vocabulary (savior, first-born, Lord). The child is already Lord of all and his poverty that of the cross, "Mary pondered all these things in her heart" (cf. also Lk 2:51), because she saw in the birth of Bethlehem the prophetical sign of a deeper mystery that was to be revealed at Easter. The event has also the quality of foresight as in Gn 37:11, Dn 4:28; 7:28, Rev 22:7-10.

Other personal marks of Luke can be seen in the expression of wonder on the part of witnesses (cf. Lk 4:22; 8:25; 9:43; 11:14-16; 20:26), 41), and in the theme of praise of God (v. 20; cf. 1:64; 2:28, 38, etc.) which Luke also links with the manifestation of the Risen Christ (cf. Lk 23:47; 24:53; Ac 2:47).

The fact of the birth of Christ is more important than the circumstances. But, meditation on them by the midrash and Saint Luke helps us considerably in passing from fact to mystery, from history to the doctrine involved. Bearing at once on the human, Lordly, and divine character of the new-born child, such reflection urges us to beware of an inclination to see in Christ a mere human being, or in his gospel a simple humanistic system, or in the Church a human political and social institution. We must also avoid the other extreme which would see only the divine nature of Christ, disdaining creation, human nature, and even man's efforts.

It would be sad indeed if the feast of Christmas, which was instituted with the very purpose of fighting such heresies and deviations, should receive pastoral treatment that either turns exclusively towards human problems of peace and poverty, or is so preoccupied with the action of God that it forgets the human elements and delays.

A true estimate of Christ's personality will enable us to celebrate the Eucharist in a realization that it is not a magic rite, but an encounter with God, prepared and celebrated with the priest as intermediary.

XI. John 1:1-18   In a passage that is difficult and has under-
    Gospel   gone endless exegesis, Saint John praises the
    Day   Word, in a manner reminiscent of the O. T.
    treatment of Wisdom (Ws 9:9-12; Pr 8:22-32;
Si 24:5-11). Two themes give shape to the prologue: the Word of
God, and divine filiation. We shall here comment on the whole
prologue, although only part of it is read at Christmas.

a) Like Wisdom in the O.T., the Word seems to be both
transcendental and immanent: transcendental, because he was
before the world came into being (vv. 1-2; cf. Si 24:2-4; Pr 8:22-
33; Ws 9:10) and because he gives life to creation (vv. 1-2;
cf. Si 24:5-6; Pr 8:24-31; Ws 9:9); immanent, because he comes
to dwell among his people (vv. 9-11; cf. Si 24:8; Ws 9:10) and
brings his gifts (vv. 12-14; cf. Si 24:12-22; Pr 8:32-36; Ws
9:11-12).

Thus the Word is the *plan* of God, lives with God, is God (vv.
1-2), realizing itself gradually in all that comes to be (v. 3). It
could have been discerned in the world itself, but was not (v.
10; cf. Rm 1:18-32); it could have been discerned by God's own
people, the Jews who had the Law (v. 17) and the prophets, but
it was not (v. 11; cf. Rm 2:1-29). The Word was made flesh
in Jesus (v. 14) and those who receive him, whether Jews or
pagans, will become children of God (vv. 12-13).

The Word of God, in all its transcendence and glory revealed
itself in the creation and history of the world, and in the Law
and the prophets of Israel. The desire for immanence was realized
by becoming flesh in Jesus and by animating all who wish to
live as sons of God.

(b) Exegetes have long wondered whether the *Logos* mentioned in the prologue of Saint John is to be understood in a
Greek or in a biblical sense. In the former sense, it is principally
an intermediary between God and the world, making the world
intelligible and giving it recognizable laws. It is something

essentially objective to which man turns in an effort to comprehend it and pierce the mystery of the world. For the bible, on the other hand, the Logos denotes a word of challenge and command which confronts the free human being for his acceptance or rejection. It places man in an existential situation, forcing him to be creative and to give a concrete answer. The Logos in the Greek sense discovers itself to the philospher, while the biblical Logos is a matter of encounter between two freedoms. Pushing the contrast to its limit, the former can be described as purely objective, while the latter could dispense with objectivity, since it is not its contents that matters but rather the actual challenge given to man. If we follow the Greek notion, Christ would be the key to the intelligibility of things, the revelation of God's thought concerning them: in the biblical conception, Christ becomes the challenger of faith, more the living act of a saving God than a demonstration of truth.

Saint John apparently owes something to both cultures: he cannot speak and write in Greek without being saturated by its vocabulary. Then his biblical sources, the Wisdom literature and the Septuagint, are themselves largely dependent on certain Greek ideas. It does not therefore seem possible to say that the Word speaking to us in Jesus is a challenge in itself, independent of what he said and of his self-awareness, which is progressively identified with the Word. The Word is not given to us merely in connection with the coming of Jesus; it is substantially given in the person of God-made-man, of the Word-made-flesh. Jesus is not only bearer of the Word, he is also its content.

c) If we study the prologue in the light of semitic literary styles, a parabolic structure becomes evident, with its focus in verses 12-13.

a) The Word with God (1-2)   a') The Son with the Father (18)
b) His part in creation (3)   b') His part in the new creation (17)

c) His communication of life to man (4-5)

c') His communication of glory to man (16)

d) Witness: John the Baptist (6-8)

d') Witness: John the Baptist (15)

e) His coming in the World (9-11)

e') His coming in the flesh (14)

To make us children of God (12-13)

The verses on John the Baptist break the rhythm and the development of key words (*light:* vv. 5 and 9; *fullness:* vv. 14 and 16) and may have been added later by the evangelist. But the center on which rests the two parts of the prologue is in vv. 12 and 13: God's plan is to make us his *children* (cf. Ga 4:4-6). The coming of the Word into the world has no other meaning; the actual birth on earth of the Son of God prepares the mystery of our filiation.

d) The central theme of the second part of the prologue is the *Lord as man and God*. While verse 1 pointed to the Word in his eternity ("was"), in his divinity ("God"), and in his union with the Father ("with God"), verse 14 shows him in a state of becoming ("was made"), in touch with human weakness ("flesh"), and in communion with men ("among us").

Christ is indeed the only Son of the Father, enjoying the vision and glory of God (v. 14), but he is at the same time seen by men, and known by them (v. 18). As such he proves to be a *real mediator* capable of making God and man co-exist in a single life.

e) This notion of mediator introduces the figure of *Moses*, who was considered by the Jews as *the* mediator. But the final part of the prologue is a demonstration of the inferiority of Moses' mediation to that of Christ.

Moses brought the Law only; Christ brings grace, i.e. loving-kindness and fidelity (v. 17). Moses could not see the glory of God (Ex 33:18-23); in the case of Christ, that glory is his as the only Son (v. 14) and he shares it with us (v. 18). When contact with God made Moses radiate glory (Ex 34:28-35), he had to veil his face, but Christ allows the glory to be seen (v. 18: on the importance on this theme of vision, see Jn 1:43-51). Moses invoked Yahweh, asking for "kindness and faithfulness" (Ex 34:6-7), but Christ alone can guarantee it (v. 17). Finally, Moses had asked that Yahweh be present with his people (Ex 33:15-16), and God granted his wish by the construction of the ark and tabernacle, his dwelling place among men. But Christ comes to "live" (in Greek, to pitch his tent, v. 14) among men much more actually.

Like Matthew (Mt 2:13-20), John sees in Christ the Moses of a new covenant, bringing "grace in return for grace" (v. 16), i.e. a grace (or loving kindness) far superior to that of the old alliance. But his treatment of the point differs from Matthew's being above all doctrinal.

The gratuitous and unexpected appearance of the word of God in the flesh is the climax of other appearances in creation and history, in the Law and the prophets. Those who were unable to discover God's intervention there, who have not "known" or "received," will be unable too to see God in the flesh. Likewise those who believe in the Word made flesh are capable of discerning that Word in his work of creation, in his humanity, and in the writings he inspires.

St. John invites us to gather all creation round the Word of God. The best fulfillment of the prologue is the eucharist itself, which is creation in expectation, and reveals the sons of God (Rm 8:19).

B. DOCTRINE

1. The Theme of the New Adam

At Christmas we are commemorating the New Adam, the First Born of humanity in the true sense, willed by God from all eternity. However, the fulfillment he achieved in the flesh does not correspond to the kind of happiness that humanity on the natural level tends to seek. We need not consequently be surprised that celebration at Christmas is always liable to become pagan. What should be the Christmas of true peace, if we are not careful, can be a sort of escape into illusory happiness, unlasting, patterned upon the wisdom of the world.

In the fourth century there was a pagan festival of renewal at this time, which confronted the Church with a problem. She dealt with it by setting up the feast of the New Adam; but the problem has continued to be actual throughout the long history that has since elapsed. So, at Christmas, it is essential that we be able to see the true countenance of him who saved the world.

Man's actual state

Man according to God's design is Adam. He was created in God's image and likeness, so that his state is at once creatural and divine. Made for the God who loves him, his calling is to fulfill himself by relying on God's gratuitous initiative. This means acceptance of his creatural condition, and complete renunciation of his own powers as means to fulfillment. He is a "being-to-be-saved" and only divine intervention can bring him what he seeks. What man did in fact, instead of accepting his condition, was attempt his own salvation, thus involving himself in a basic contradiction.

The first chapters of Genesis are very much corroborated by what we know of human history from its earliest beginnings. To a greater or less degree human beings had always some inkling of the paradox implicit in their state. The deepest yearning was always for the absolute: the "sacral" held some fascination. Yet for the pursuit of his destiny the means at man's disposal are so frightfully limited: he is only a "profane" being and he knows it. He finds himself plunged into existence without any wish of his own: he is made for death. What happens when he confronts the paradox and attempts to resolve it without recourse to God's gratuitous intervention? The only way open apparently is to attempt to touch the "sacral." Thus, instead of accepting creature-hood, man makes absolute his profane existence. Most of all he gives absolute dimension to the secure or constant values that little by little he discovers in nature, in society, or in morals.

Jewish man's performance

With Abraham, with the chosen people who never ceased to intensify the initial experience of the Father of believers, comes something new, the way of Faith. The resolute choice of Israel was to await salvation from God alone. He is the Totally-Other, the universal Creator, the free Dispenser of every benefit. We cannot touch God; human salvation depends on this absolutely gratuitous initiative, which originates everything.

As a result of this choice Jewish man was led towards an ever deepened awareness of his creatural condition. He could appraise realistically all that is stable in that state, and all that is fragile. He knew that man by himself is profane, unable to reach the fulfillment towards which his whole being yearns.

Yet, though God saves man, he cannot do so apart from man himself. Man is not a "thing": in the process of salvation he should be the interlocutor that creation in the image and likeness of God makes him. That is why in Israel the discovery of the Totally-Other God led to a passionate quest: a scrutiny of events to uncover the nature of the human response required in God's plan. This developed into messianic hope, a state of waiting for the man who could bring salvation to men.

Nevertheless the essential question remained unanswered. How would the Messiah reconcile in his person the active cooperation that God's plan required, and the total self-despoliation demanded by faith?

The decisive achievement of the New Adam

When the man-God did intervene in history, the human yearning for divinization was realized beyond the wildest hopes. The paradox implicit in man's state was definitely resolved. Jesus of Nazareth, a creature, entered the Family of the Father freely, but by right. The reason was that he was God's son, and it was only for that reason. Simultaneously, by becoming obedient even to the death of the cross, he disclosed the true nature of the creatural condition.

In Jesus Christ man remains a creature, but becomes a child of God. His vocation is to enter into communion with God; but in the family of the Father his creatural task is the obedience of poverty. So the structure of salvation falls definitely into place. The Kingdom where human fulfillment is to be found is beyond every created power. But the "yes" of a man who accepts the creatural condition, becomes in Jesus Christ the filial "yes" of a child of God, the "yes" which builds the Kingdom. Once he *is* a child of God, man is equal to the creatural task, which prior to that threw him into confusion. That task does not bring about salvation; but it will always be the necessary basis for man's filial "yes" to God, and therein lies a worth that can never be denied.

Jesus showed us the destiny that awaits us in the Kingdom, and demands from us the total despoliation that ought to characterize the creature. In doing so he revealed to us the true meaning of man. He is the New Adam, the First Born of humanity according to God's will from all eternity. When we say Jesus is the New Adam we mean he is the true Adam: we do not mean that following man's sin God made a new plan. The newness comes from the fact that the way he followed ran counter to the procedures of sinful man.

This is the realization that begins to dawn on us when we see the Prologue of Saint John as a rewriting of the beginning of Genesis. It is in the mystery of the Incarnate Word that we find the real meaning of the creation of man.

The Church, spouse of the New Adam

The New Adam is the living center around which all men can come together. In Jesus Christ they are all called to enter the Family of the Father, and this Family is essentially one. But it is a unity that fully allows for human diversity, a unity of communion, the product of true catholicity.

Being as he is that center, the New Adam becomes the universal reconciliator, whose task is a task of Peace; and a feast centered on the New Adam becomes very naturally the feast par excellence of Peace. Peace in this real sense is simply the unity in diversity of the human family. It is at once a gift of God, and a work to accomplish, always in Jesus Christ.

Very naturally, too, the feast of the New Adam becomes the feast of the Church which is his spouse, she from whom he expects a contribution that is essential. He constitutes our Peace; but that peace is brought about by the efforts of all members of the new humanity. "Blessed are the peacemakers, for theirs is the Kingdom of God." When we say the Church is the spouse, we are insisting on the necessity of cooperation by Christians in building salvation history. When the Christian celebrates Christmas, he is perceiving clearly the exact contribution to peace demanded at this time; because working for peace is the primary task of a humanity redeemed in the New Adam.

Evangelization as a revelation of the true countenance of man

A Christian attitude frequently encountered suggests that there is serious misunderstanding where human values like peace, social and international justice or the like, are concerned. Just because these values are considered independently more and more, because they fall less and less under the direction of the

Church, the belief grows that the mystery of Christ is not concerned in this area. One hears from time to time the observation that a keener sense of human values, often a more realistic one, is found among contemporary pagans. There is the remarkable example of the working classes. Ecclesiastical influence is less evident here than anywhere. Yet, to an extent unknown in Christian circles, their lives show the influence of fundamental values like solidarity, and the efficacious desire for peace. What are we to say?

It is true that there is a rediscovery of human values in their own right, and that a decline of ecclesiastical influence has had to be accepted in recent centuries. But this does not by any means imply that our faith is unconnected with these values.

Consider the facts. Of all the children of men the New Adam is he who has shown us the true face of man. We see in him a harmonious blending of child of God with creature. So, by his link with the New Adam, the Christian man, at once creature and image of God, has the power to live the human vocation to the full. Above all he has the power to put into correct perspective his control over the future, or, if we wish, the power to promote human values with a proper understanding. The gospel, which is the book that demonstrates man's active acceptance of his creatural condition, provides the wisdom for such an understanding.

Evangelization means announcing the good news of the salvation acquired in the New Adam. If modern man, as he takes his destiny in hand, is again to have a sense of mission, Christians can give the first sign of true evangelization by demonstrating how they live their creatural responsibilities. It is their contribution to peace here below that brings news of the divine gift of peace.

The Eucharist of the new humanity

Essential moments of the never quite achieved initiation into the state that is at once creatural and filial are the hearing of the Word and the Breaking of the Bread. It is only by being linked with the New Adam that we can enter the ranks of the true humanity which God wills. Human achievement finds its source in the Eucharist; and the believer in following the New Adam's path of fulfillment must remain altogether under his tutelage.

When the Eucharist initiates the Christian into his state as "filial creature," it necessarily opens him too to the fraternal links which constitute the Kingdom. By assembling men into the familial unity of the Father it builds the new humanity, and in this sense it is directly doing the work of peace. Believers receive all men as brothers in the faith when they celebrate the Eucharist. Strong in the gift of grace, they exercise a mission as artisans of peace among men. For this purpose all they need do is act out their creatural responsibilities in truth and fidelity.

2. The Theme of Christian Liberty

Where modern man is concerned liberty and self-determination are almost obsessions. Such pursuits are all-absorbing both on the collective plane and on the individual: freedom of peoples, emancipation of women, of the working classes, and so on, all the causes that people nowadays regard as peculiarly their province. Slaveries of one kind or another continue to exist of course, but the idea is that all human resources should be mustered to deal with them.

Can we find any similarity between such notion of liberty and that which has been acquired once for all in Jesus Christ? Are they compatible, or mutually exclusive? If we are to engage unbelievers in frank dialogue about our faith it is essential that the point be clarified.

The slavery of sin and the victory of death

Man's sin is one of pride and jealousy. Though created in God's image and likeness, he seeks to divinize himself independently. He refuses to await from God the salvation that satisfies his yearning for the absolute. He wants to use some ritual means or other to put himself in touch with divine energies; in a word, he wants to depend on his own resources.

When he gives absolute value to things that are merely creatural and relative: to some sort of theory about cosmic cycles, to some determinist view of social or moral life, to individual or collective programs, he becomes a slave. He is binding himself to something that is not central to his true vocation.

The slavery becomes evident in the way that death constantly triumphs over sinful man; because earthly life is in fact deprived by death of meaning. Attempts at divinization by our own resources are attempts to curtain off death, to push it into the background. But it has its revenge. It causes all the seeming securities to collapse, sets up conflicts in man's psyche, in his relations with others. So is it the consequence of sin.

The slavery of the Law

When we enter the era of faith, Jewish man makes a decisive step forward towards true liberty. In a very real sense he begins to meet the challenge of death: for liberation he looks towards a God who is acknowledged as "Totally Other." Death will be vanquished on the "Day of Yahweh." The major events of Jewish history, the escape from Egypt, the return from exile, are really so many figures of the eschatological victory, of man's final delivery. Already indeed he would be free, were it not for Israel's infidelity by contrast with God's great acts of liberation.

Faith is shaped by fidelity, and the Law is designed to define the terms of fidelity. Later, Saint Paul will say that the Law would have given justification, if it could have communicated life. As it was, it remained exterior to man, and only emphasized his slavery by making him realize how deep were the roots of sin, from which his own resources offered no means of escape.

The Law meant slavery too because, in the case of man not yet justified by faith in Christ, it set up conflict. Law is made for observance, and the observance of a law however holy does not constitute fidelity to a saving God. It is only a stage. Israel's Law, because it insisted on the maintenance of Israel's privileges, did not open the way to the true realities of the Promise. Finally, because it became encumbered with so many merely human traditions, the Law was very far from being the codified expression of Yahweh's will for his people.

Jesus Christ, the free man *par excellence*

With Christ begins the era of true human liberty. His human nature was equipped for the proper sort of response to God. He was man created in the image and likeness of God, and his freedom as man was aligned to divine salvation precisely because he was the Son of God himself.

Because sin had no dominion over him his freedom was perfect. Neither death nor the Law could impose on him the yoke of slavery; the former was vanquished on his own domain, the latter henceforth was something subject to man's control. But obedience to the will of the Father, which was the constant expression of Jesus' liberty, has nothing to do with passivity or fatalism. It is discovery, spiritual adventure. It is something that takes place on the plane of love, a source of rejuvenation, of renewal.

Christ restored human liberty as a controlling factor over created things precisely because he laid open for it the path to the Family of the Father. It is a point on which modern man can be reassured. The liberty acquired once for all in Jesus Christ is not alone compatible with man's use of his own resources: it implies such a use. Man must not however have recourse to these resources in some sort of illusory attempt to divinize himself: he must do so in full acknowledgment of his creatural condition.

The Church and the task of human liberation

Membership in the Church extricates man from his involvement with sin, and introduces him as adoptive son to the Kingdom. As adoptive son the Christian is free. He has the power to achieve the destiny God has reserved for him, in Christ Jesus His own Son, from all eternity. He can address God and in very truth call him Father.

The adoptive son's liberty does not of course work automatically. We must actually behave as members of the Father's family; our freedom as sons is a freedom in principle, a source from which action springs. In the Church, where day by day we receive the sacraments and the Word, our action begins to flow from the proper source.

She reveals to her children the true meaning of liberty as sons of God. If we are free in Jesus Christ, it means that we have in him a true capacity of conversing with God as children. When we exercise our freedom we leave everything to God; we refuse to give absolute value to any created thing. Our freedom delivers us from sin; we are capable of using as we should a creatural power that is set in proper perspective. Experience adequately demonstrates this. What militates against liberty more than anything else is the disorder introduced by sin, the manner in which it confuses "sacred" with "profane."

The free man's imperatives are those of evangelic love. He is inspired by the obedience which overcomes death no matter where it manifests itself. There is an element of discovery in this obedience. It means a constant questioning of all established orders, because the tendency is to invest the established order with the aura of the sacral. The only service that avoids being alienating for free man is the service of God and man in obedience unto death.

Mission as a liberating enterprise

The spiritual energies of these cultures where the mystery of Christ has not yet been rooted are extraordinarily complex. It is the Church's business in her missionary endeavor to establish contact with such energies, to make it evident that Christ is the fulfillment of their deepest strivings. Her mission then is in itself liberating; because once the mystery of Christ is grafted into the spiritual tradition of a culture, it begins to exert a striking influence that is literally bond-breaking. The man who comes to faith in Jesus Christ, when summoned to adoptive sonship among all gathered in the Family of the Father, is unshackled from his sin. He escapes the natural tendency to confuse "sacred" and "profane." When he discovers what "filial" liberty means, gradually he comes to realize that the proper exercise of his creatural power demands poverty. This poverty surmounts the challenge of death by meeting it in obedience. And so a man comes to realize what it means, humanly speaking, to be truly free.

What is described, with understatement, as the "encounter of the cultures" is one of the most formidable tasks confronting man in modern times. It is an area virtually untouched, and it is here that the walls of separation raised between peoples are most impenetrable. If Christians approach the task as free men, armed, that is, with the power in Jesus Christ of surmounting the challenge, in whatever form, of death, they will be a sign to the modern world. They will demonstrate the nature of the "filial" liberty they have acquired in Jesus Christ.

The Eucharist an assembly of free men

The purpose of the eucharistic assembly is constantly to deepen the believer's awareness of his state as child of God. The Spirit animating the assembly makes him a free man. When the Word is proclaimed there, it reveals what that freedom is in very truth because there is always the risk for freedom, which does not conform to the wisdom of the world, of being degraded. Then, because he partakes of the Bread, the believer is gradually assimilated to Jesus Christ, the free man *par excellence*.

And because the assembly is essentially one of free men, freedom ought to characterize its celebration. The freedom of the believer must be demonstrated and witnessed. It is a point on which our conscience should regularly be examined.

SUNDAY WITHIN THE OCTAVE
OF CHRISTMAS
Feast of the Holy Family

I. Sirach 3:3-7,   Ben Sira lived in a prosperous Jerusalem
14-17a   family which did not lack adequate means
1st reading   for educating the children. As father of a
family, he takes his responsibilities seriously
and strives to mold his children according to his authority. At a
time when the pressure of Hellenist culture was beginning to be
felt, the family seemed the most effective bulwark against
paganism.

However, one should not make too much of Ben Sira's outlook.
As he sees it, the objective of the father of a family ought to be
the well being of his family, the assurance of a life of "long
days" (v. 6) and the boon of God's blessing (vv. 8-9). From all
this parents will glean honor and reputation (=glory: vv. 2-6),
if their children have been well educated.

Ben Sira's ideal for the family then is rather unambitious. It
is limited to the sort of happiness that can be obtained by
passive acceptance of the formation and education offered by
the previous generation. The child puts on the prefabricated
mold that calls itself wisdom or experience, and comfort of a
kind is held out to him as the ultimate reward.

That attitudes like this, fairly prevalent indeed in many contemporary families, are quite inadequate for the demands of the
time is amply demonstrated by the rebellion, practically everywhere, of young people.

But the culture of Ben Sira's epoch was a rural culture. Everything depended on the natural call of community. Family, clan
and village made one's whole social and cultural environment
stable. All duties were seen in this framework, conjugal relations,

relations between parents and children, attitudes and obligations towards one's neighbor. In our society horizons are considerably widened. Men are living less and less in natural communities, and are beginning to control the natural tendencies in grouping. Nowadays we have all sorts of artificial communities (based on city, profession, union membership), but men are far from being properly integrated in such groups.

The family still plays a very important role, but henceforth it must share importance with these new groups. It is precisely at this point that tension arises. Your middle class Christian family is scarcely as aware as it should be. The moral framework which it transmits, which is concerned with conjugal relationships, obedience of children, justice towards neighbors, family prosperity and comfort, is in fact of the rural, traditional mold. The children however are already involved in communities of far wider ambit, and have become involved with larger issues: world peace, assistance for under-developed countries, revolution, etc.

Because tendencies like this make the future precarious and challenging, some Christians are driven by fears into conservatism. Their chief concern is defense of natural groupings ("family and fatherland"); and this attitude proves distasteful to people who are already involved in artificial groupings, and concerned about the ethics of proper adjustment and integration.

II. Colossians 3:12-21 2nd reading Confronting the idols that hold men's attention stands the person of Christ. Through his victory over death, he is the one Lord capable of bringing man and the universe to perfection. This primacy of Christ, the main theme of the letter to the Colossians, has moral implications as well. The effort and self-denial demanded by the cult of idols or the search for material goods (Col 2:16-23) must now be totally supplanted by an asceticism based on acknowledgment of Christ's Lordship in the world (Col 3:1-4).

a) Christians must therefore lead a life that is a sign of Christ's Lordship. Saint Paul addresses them on this level by calling them saints and chosen ones (v. 12-15). But the notion of *holiness* also includes separation. In the Old Testament, God was the Holy One because he had nothing in common with man, and, in turn, the people of Israel were holy insofar as they were different and apart from other nations (Is 4:3; Dt 7:6). But in Jesus Christ the holiness of God has revealed itself as communication, his transcendence is shown through immanence. Therefore the holiness of Christians does not consist of superiority or disdain, it is rather communication and sharing. Saint Paul expresses this in terms which, in the Old Testament, were reserved to God's behavior towards man: "goodness" and "gentleness" proper to the Father (Pss 24/25:6-7; 39/40:11; 50/51:1; 68/69:17; 20/21:3; 30/31:20; 64/65:12; 118/119:65-68, etc.), "forgiveness" and "peace" proper to Christ (v. 13).

b) The Lordship of Christ must also be manifest in the *liturgical* celebration indicated in vv. 16-17. Here we find the basic form of these meetings: proclamation of, and commentary on, the Word of God, singing of psalms and hymns, and finally, thanksgiving (vv. 15b and 17). But liturgy cannot be an isolated act, and Paul is just as anxious to see the Word, songs and thanksgiving reecho in the heart and in daily life.

c) The Apostle then turns to various situations: conjugal and family relations, those between slaves and masters. Primitive catechesis often analyzed concrete situations in order to stress the requirements of common morality and the distinctiveness of Christian behavior (Ep 5:21-6:9; 1 P 3:1-7). Today's reading only deals with *conjugal and family relations* (vv. 18-21). The verses are rather disappointing at first encounter; Paul limits himself to the most commonplace moral requirements of the time: submission of women, loving authority of man, obedience of children, serenity of parents. Christian behavior does not seem different from that of others. Yet a short phrase: "in the Lord," adds a whole new dimension to Christian behavior. It is best understood when contrasted with another frequent phrase of Paul's: "in Adam" (1 Co 15:21-22; 2 Co 5:21; Rm 5:21). We are not confronted by two different humanities, one in Christ, the other in Adam, but by one common human race, motivated by the same desire for betterment and salvation. Some seek it "in Adam," that is by human means only, and that is sin. Others seek it "in Christ," that is by opening themselves up to God, which allows man to achieve his end by triumphing over sin and failure, and that is justice. Christian conjugal and family love need not be opposed to that of non-Christians, but Christians live "in Christ" in a new humanity where God's initiative meets human effort.

Living "in Christ" or "putting on Christ" does not demand isolation from other men. Christ really reveals man to himself, and asks for an openness to the initiative of God and the example of the Cross. Living in Christ means therefore living the human vocation at maximum intensity, taking on family and other personal relations, and using the means provided by Christ in order to attain this ideal.

The aim of the liturgical assembly is to imbue our hearts with this conviction and this faith, so that our acts may always be guided by the power of the "name of Jesus" (v. 17).

III. Matthew   We shall comment here on the entire passage
    2:13-14, 19-23   of Mt 2:13-23, which taken together is in effect
    Gospel   a kind of a midrash on the life of Moses. It pre-
    1st cycle   supposes knowledge of Jewish traditions concerning the main figure of the book of Exodus.

a) The theme of Christ the new Moses is highly significant. The circumstances under which the birth of Christ is announced to Herod, his magi and scribes, evokes those surrounding the announcement of Moses' birth to Pharaoh and his magi (Mt 2:4).

On hearing the news, Pharaoh had ordered all the first-born of the Hebrews to be killed (Ex 1:15, 22); Herod likewise has all the first-born in Bethlehem slain (v. 16). Moses escapes the massacre (Ex 2:1-10), and later flees abroad (Ex 2:11-15); Jesus also avoids the massacre of the innocents and flees into Egypt (vv. 13-15). When Joseph is recalled to Palestine with Mary and the Child (v. 20), the angel uses terms identical with those used to recall Moses to Egypt (Ex 4:19).

In the infancy gospel, Matthew probably did not intend to be strictly historical. He describes the event in a literary style which emphasizes certain characteristics of the Messiah, above all his function as legislator of the new alliance. The first gospel is indeed divided into five parts, obviously the counterpart of the Pentateuch of Moses, and Jesus represents more than anything else the fulfillment of the Law, to the point indeed of surpassing it (Mt 5-8).

b) The parallelism is not limited to Moses: Jesus is also compared to Jacob-Israel. The flight into Egypt recalls Genesis 46:2: "Do not be afraid of going down to Egypt, for I will make you a great nation there. . . . I will bring you back again." As Jacob went to Egypt, to return a sizable nation, so Jesus by way of Egypt becomes a large nation. The quotation of Hosea 11:1 in verse 15 confirms this view.

Jewish tradition (Gn 31) makes Jacob a fugitive from Laban to Egypt where, as a nation, he would await the star of deliverance; meanwhile Rachel, his wife, buried in Palestine (Gn 35: 19), would be weeping for her children until they return (v. 18; Jr 31:15).

The flight of Christ, the new Jacob, into Egypt, and his return to Palestine as a new and great people, introduces a paschal theme. Christ will one day go through death, but only to emerge as "Son of God" with the countless people of the redeemed ones. The mystery of Easter therefore animates these pages of Matthew.

The midrash is a literary genre which the modern mind scarcely comprehends. The early Christians made extensive use of it, because they found here a means of reinterpreting in a Christian sense the readings they went on hearing in the synagogue.

Modern mentality may be more critical, but it would be a great loss to reject those infancy narratives which point to the great missions of the Lord, legislative (new Moses), redemptive and paschal (new Jacob).

IV. Luke The reading combines two separate events: the
2:22, 39-40 first verse is related to the presentation of
Gospel Jesus in the temple, while the other two refer
2nd cycle to his hidden life at home. The purpose of
the liturgy in bringing these verses together can only be apologetic: family life is to be lived quite simply (vv. 39-40), but with an explicit reference to God (v. 22).

The lesson of these verses on the *hidden life* of Jesus is very important. Though he is God, he follows nature's law of growth, not only physically, but also in wisdom and knowledge. In childhood, puberty, and adolescence, he lives his mission in utter self-emptying. Though Son of God, he is content with a gradual understanding of his life's purpose, and with discovering the will of his Father through such relations and education as his particular family could provide in a small village from which "nothing good can come" (Jn 1:46). His appraisal of persons and things is normal for a developing intelligence; he does not want to know things that an average man could not know (Mt 24:36); his faithfulness to his Father is the result of his complete submission to his human condition, frail and limited. Throughout his life, from inarticulate infancy down to the horrible moment of his death, Jesus has splendidly inscribed on human life the Word of the Father. For the first time, an agreement as perfect as possible is established between the will of a man and the will of God.

V. Luke 2:41-52
Gospel
3rd cycle

This gospel, one of the hardest to interpret, is set between two verses (40 and 52), which relate the harmonious development and the wisdom of the Child Jesus. These verses may well be the key to proper understanding of the whole.

a) For a Jew, *wisdom* is above all a sharp mind, quick in repartee (Ac 6:10; Lk 12:12; 21:15). It often appears as a gift of God, and is connected with a mission: it helps people to understand the scriptures and to fulfill them (Pr 3:14-4:26).

The pilgrimage to Jerusalem revealed the precocity of Jesus (vv. 46-47), his emanicpation from family surroundings (v. 43) and his clear conscience of a special vocation (v. 49); but it also showed the anguish (v. 48) and lack of understanding (v. 50) of his parents.

b) These events must be read in the light of the *death and resurrection of the Lord*. The phrase "did not understand" occurs in Saint Luke whenever the disciples are unable to grasp the meaning of Jesus' statements that he is going up to Jerusalem (Lk 9:43-45; 18:34; 24:25-26) to undergo his passion and death.

On the other hand, the phrase "storing up things in one's heart" (v. 51) is generally used of people who feel intuitively the fulfillment of a prophetical pronouncement (Lk 1:66; 2:19, 51; Gn 37:11; Dn 4:28; 7:28 (LXX); Rv 22:7-10). And the words of Jesus to his parents: "Did you not know that I had to be . . ." (v. 49) lead us back to the scripture that he is to fulfill, more particularly to those passage dealing with his death and resurrection (Lk 9:22; 13:33; 17:25; 22:37; 24:7 and especially 24:27, 44). It is as if he were saying: "Haven't you read this in the scriptures, and how can the fulfillment of these prophecies be avoided?".

The first journey of Jesus to Jerusalem therefore foreshadows the last one. In both cases, he is sought (Lk 2:44 and Lk 24:3,

23-24) for three days (Lk 2:46, cf. Lk 24:7, 21, 46; Ac 10:40; Ho 6:2), the will of the Father determines his actions (Lk 2:49; cf. Lk 22:42), and the events take place during the paschal celebration (Lk 2:41; cf. Lk 22:1).

The wisdom of Christ then lay in understanding the plans of God and placing their fulfillment above all else. His parents, though lacking this wisdom, nevertheless respected in their child a vocation that was far beyond this.

c) The theme of the *search for God* also appears in the narrative, where "to look for" is used up to four times (vv. 45, 46, 48, 49). It is an important theme in the scriptures, because Yahweh, unlike the idols, is a God not easily found. The nomadic patriarchs began the quest, and they discovered the fulfillment of God's plan in history. Then the law pursued it in a more spiritual manner (*scrutare:* Ps 118/119). But it was still all too human in approach (Ho 5:6-7, 15), and it is not until the exile that the people find God in obedience to his will (Dt 4:29; Is 55:6; Jr 29:13-14; Ps 104/105:1-4 (observe in most of these texts the connection seek-find). This search for Yahweh was pursued especially in the temple, so that the expression actually denoted participation in its liturgy (Am 5:4-6; particularly Ps 26/27 with the phrase "seek his face").

With Christ, the search for God becomes a "search for the Lord", who will not easily be found on the human level of the family (Lk 2:44), but with the Father (v. 49). Because they are blinded by their legalism, the Jews will seek him without finding him (Jn 7:34; 8:21). Charity alone (Jn 13:33-34), prayer (Mt 7:7-8) and faith (Jn 20:11-15; Lk 24:5) will assure the searchers of finding him.

It is certain that Jesus' awareness about his approaching death became clear only at the beginning of his last year of public ministry. From his early years he had aligned himself "with his Father," and so entered upon his own search for God, but that did not entail a clear picture of where the road would lead. This is a fairly clear inference from his attitude towards the temple, and in the family.

In the temple, the place where Israel sought to discover the face of God, he reveals the nature of his own search. In him human will will be aligned absolutely with that of God. But, even for him, the will of God is the will of the Totally-Other, a will that baffles and disconcerts, that must be discovered day after day, until death.

En famille, Jesus "believes" in wisdom. He is destined one day to display the prophetic charism, and to reveal in an unprecedented way the presence of God in the decisive events of salvation, above all in his own mission. But, like every other man, the knowledge that he acquires about God and the universe is whatever can be naturally transmitted by his family background and culture. Because he was a perfect man people have argued that, in an infused way, he must have had full knowledge about God and the universe. This is tantamount to saying that he acquired by education what he already knew by grace. It is a mistaken view. Perfect knowledge for a human being does not consist in knowing everything, but in assimilating into oneself what one knows. A man who knows everything by means of a borrowed knowledge would not be a perfect man. Christ's perfection consisted precisely of this: that what human knowledge he had was acquired personally, and gradually, according to the development of his experience. In no other way is it possible to describe him as the brother of mankind.

In a word, when we say that Christ grew in age and wisdom, we are giving his knowledge a more human dimension. Humanly speaking, he inherits the Jewish religious tradition. His prophetic gift will enable him to transmute this knowledge in a totally unsuspected way. There is absolutely no necessity to insist that his knowledge about everything, including himself, was exhaustive.

This gradual ascent of Jesus towards the temple is really fulfilled in the Eucharist, because it celebrates the perfect adjustment of his will to that of the Father and associates with his perfect knowledge our feeble knowledge. If it could also be a celebration of the obedience of the members it assembles to the will of God, they too would find themselves possessed of a wisdom that would astonish the world, as his astonished the doctors of the temple.

B. DOCTRINE

1. The Theme of Family

When the liturgy of this day speaks of the "hidden life" of Jesus, it invites us to reflect in the light of faith on the true significance of those realities and structures which shape human existence. In particular we are to reflect about the family. We are sure of the fact that Jesus shared the common lot in every way, but his manner of doing so placed all the human situations he experienced in proper perspective. So we see him pass many years in the bosom of his family, and allow himself to be shaped there by the hope of Israel, but always the norm which determines his behavior is the will of the Father.

Today ideas about the family are undergoing a profound evolution. The whole process of secularization tends to deprive it of its sacral dimension. Whether we are pleased or disappointed about this, the trend is certainly irreversible, but it is not altogether deleterious. There are numerous dangers of dissolution confronting the family, but they are not insurmountable. Indeed it is possible that, restored to its true secular position, the family displays more than it did in the past its proper function in the building of the Kingdom.

The Family in Israel

In many ways the concept of the family in Israel is not different from the concept among neighboring peoples. It is the essential cell of clan, of tribe, of people. The cell answers a fundamental need of man to have a hearth, a line of descent for parents, of ascent for children. Deprived of family a man finds himself in the greatest insecurity and has no more stability in his life. The sacral character of human destiny is translated into the family. Many ritual ceremonies are developed, for marriage, for birth, for certain meals, for the building of the family home, for cult of ancestors and so on.

But in Israel a gradual transformation takes place. It begins with recognition of the "Totally-Other" God, because the believer now depends on Yahweh, not his ancestors, for security. The family turns to norms that are exterior to itself. Fecundity makes it responsible for the building of the chosen people. The education it provides has to inculcate in children an awareness of salvation history. For conjugal love and mutual fidelity the model, an unattainable ideal, is Yahweh's love for and fidelity to his people. In short there is a value higher than the family; and when necessary the family has to be sacrificed to it, as we learn from the martyrdom of the seven brothers and their mother during the persecution of Antiochus Epiphanes (2 M 7). Such is the obedience to his Law that the "Creator of the World" (2 M 7:23) has the right to demand.

The family of Jesus

For Jesus his own family was never an absolute. On every possible occasion he was careful to make it clear that the only absolute in his life was the business of his Father, and of the Kingdom he was to establish in his Father's name. "Whoever does the will of my Father who is in heaven, he is my brother, my sister and my mother" (Mt 12:50). It is not possible to be more precise.

The family of the Father was the only family commanding total allegiance. It was open to all men without distinction of race, sex or social condition. The earthly life of Jesus was lived under the aegis of a love that is universal, that goes the length of sacrificing life.

The Christian family

It is in the exercise of charity that we find the criterion *par excellence* of family life. This is the true source of family unity. By a recognition of the fundamental equality of all members we are capable of surmounting the challenges and enmities which tend to arise. In charity only can the other member become our neighbor, with recognition of his inalienable dignity.

Obviously, it is only when the true frontiers are those of the Kingdom of universal brotherhood, that family charity of this kind is possible. The prerequisite for genuine family life is openness. Christian households are challenged to constant effort by these demands. Otherwise, inevitably, there develops an inwardness, and the family takes on the sacral dimension again. Other responsibilities, just as essential, which we have undertaken towards all men in the charity of Christ, are sacrificed to it.

This concept of the family is not the one that emerges spontaneously. When Jesus said to his parents that he must be about his father's business, they did not understand (Lk 2:50). So all Christian meditation about family calls us to conversion. To begin with, we do not understand, because our natural tendency is not towards a fraternal charity that is universal.

The missionary meaning of family life

The family is a human institution, a work that will always be in progress. When Christians promote the values of the family, according to the patterns current in any age or any culture, they are inspired by the charity of Christ, and by the concept of human dignity which this implies. So the daily routine of the household, relationships both external and internal, can become a center of radiation. Witness is given there to the resurrection of Christ: the true nature of man and of the family are demonstrated.

Modern man too frequently tends to separate his professional responsibilities from his family life, the latter being, in his view, a completely private domain. It is a tendency which affects Christians as well. If the Christian yields to it he compromises seriously the mission with which he is charged, because it is from one and the same source, the charity of Christ, that he ought to draw inspiration for both social responsibilities and family life. The balance is difficult to achieve, but if we do not attempt it we are denying men the witness they have a right to expect from the Christian family.

The Eucharist as a means of communicating family values

The normal result of the eucharistic assembly is joint ascent in brotherhood towards the universal Kingdom. Participation means that we are established on the level of Christ's charity and that family life is restored to its rightful place. Precisely in proportion to the realization which the believer derives from the Eucharist of his pilgrim-state in the Kingdom here below, does the natural family tend to yield place to that genuine family so capital for the Christian, the Family of the Father, open to all. By dwelling on the hidden life of Jesus, the day's homily ought to emphasize these insights, and so the liturgy will inevitably lead the assembly to a true estimate of the charity of Christ. Proper direction of the celebration should produce a reaction, because the natural concept of the family that people have does not correspond to the Christian one.

When restored to its true state, family life will find the dynamism that is native to it. It will not be disturbed by the changes forced upon it by transformation in the world. On the contrary it will find there the source for new discovery and a new youth.

2. The Theme of Search for God

The search for God, to an intense degree, ought to be basic in the life of every believer. If the true horizons of our faith are not to fade from view, it is the lode-stone to which we must always return. However, from the conduct of numerous Christians, maybe the greater part, one does not glean the impression that the search for God is central in their lives. We Christians have the mission of bearing witness to God on this earth, but that God is not the law-giver, the ultimate guarantor of the established order.

Nor are we assured that the search will occupy its proper place in our lives if we say our prayers. Non-Christians for the most part are religious men and practice prayer. Of India, for instance, one has heard it said that it is the spiritual reservoir of humanity. The Christian's fundamental task is to search for the God of Jesus Christ. Thus it is important to examine the nature of the search, the conditions under which it can be properly conducted.

Israel in search of Yahweh

Though he does not himself belong to the sacral domain, man is fascinated by the sacral. The way towards it he most frequently chooses is the way of ritual; because by the liturgical act he is enabled to evade the hazards of daily life, and to insinuate himself as much as possible into the life of the gods. Pagan man can be successful in the search for God, and can reach the supreme being if he takes the means. Being is a sort of graded ascent where one can climb from the bottom to the top.

Approaching the age of faith we notice that Israel is ready to find the principal avenue of the search for God in the event, unforeseen and unpredictable. To Jewish man, before the meaninglessness of failure, suffering and death, his impotence was obvious. But Yahweh revealed himself as the Totally-Other, the absolute master of life, universal creator, unnameable because he is so transcendent, untouchable by any human hand. When man seeks to enclose him in categories he evades them. His will is unfathomable, unforeseeable. With absolute freedom he leads his people whithersoever he wishes.

Between him and man stretches a chasm which no one can bridge. We can know nothing of him except insofar as he takes the initiative in approach, in making himself known. As, one by one, the chosen people found their securities slip away (one thinks, for instance, of that memorable moment of the exile) the realization dawned that knowledge of God was possible under one condition only. The heart of man had to be transformed by God himself, and aligned to the impulses of his Spirit.

There were two main avenues in the Jewish search for God: the Jerusalem temple where Yahweh's cult was pursued and deepened, and secondly the observance of the Law, where his will was inscribed for the chosen people. But the fidelity required by the Covenant went further than ritual or legal observance. True knowledge of God would only become possible in the eschatological future.

Jesus of Nazareth and the will of the Father

From his very earliest years Jesus was wholly concerned with the business of his Father. To do the will of Him who sent him was his daily nourishment, and the constant motive of his action was the search for God.

He adored the Father in spirit and in truth, and so the two great Jewish avenues, the Temple and the Law, with him became precarious means. Everywhere and in everything the Father ought to be adored, which meant an alignment of our will to His in rendering thanks. Yet the search for God in spirit and in truth was fully realizable only in Jesus of Nazareth. Nowhere else could alignment of the human will to God's be invariably perfect. He was the man-God; his human action, because of the identity of person, was in fact the action of the Son of God.

We should, however, be under no misapprehension about the relation, in religious terms, between Jesus and the Father. His human will was always perfectly aligned with the divine will. Yet this did not happen automatically, not as if everything had been meticulously arranged beforehand. So far as his human awareness was concerned, as in the case of other men, God was the Totally-Other, whose will transcended the confines of human categories. Day after day, in the texture of events, Jesus discovered the precise will of God in his regard. He had his moment of recoil, when it became clear that this would entail his passion and death on the cross. Even for Jesus death meant a plunge into insecurity. "Father, let this chalice pass from me." But immediately he adds "Thy will be done."

The Church in search of the God of Jesus Christ

It is in the Church, the Body of Christ, that the believer can pursue his search for the true God in most authentic fashion, the God, that is, of Jesus Christ.

This is so in the first place because a constant Jewish principle, invariably observed, is continued in the Church. The insistence, that is, of the fundamental necessity of faith, if one is to encounter God in the event and in history. Men are withdrawn from the exclusive pursuit of security, and resolutely turned towards recognition of God as the Totally-Other. This sense of God acknowledges that he transcends all means of approach by human intellect, all moral or even mystical ascent. It implies that we see the direction of history as something which wholly defeats our comprehension, that God's designs are impenetrable, that it is only through the divine gift of faith that we are enabled to make contact with Him.

Secondly, we are brought to realize that it is through the mediation of Jesus Christ we must search for God and for his will in our regard. He alone can make us open unconditionally to the transforming action of the Spirit; because the God for whom the Christian searches is precisely his God. If we are to search in a genuine Christian way we must live the life of Christ, be modeled by his word day after day, be actually initiated into salvation history which had its true beginning with him. So for the authentic search for God church membership is of primary importance.

There are, in sum, two basic principles which must govern the Christian search for God, whether individual or collective. The first is what we call the "signs of the times", where the event communicates God's message to us and to the whole Christian community. The second is our actual relationship with the Church, the Body of Christ. Only in Christ and in the Church which is his Body are we enabled to read with accuracy the Word of God in the event.

Mission and the search for the God of Jesus Christ

As the human race continues its progress, the primary object of the Christian mission is to further, in genuine terms, the search for God. As the Good News is proclaimed to all peoples it entails essentially a summons to adoration of the Father in spirit and in truth. Nor does it imply any rejection of value in the search towards which racial or cultural tradition has already pointed. It is on the contrary a purifying of that search, a means of moving it forward, of turning it towards the God of Jesus Christ. All avenues of search have origin in the gift of the Spirit, who works in the heart of every man. The search is supported by the Church, the Body of Christ, which it is the purpose of mission to establish among all peoples and all cultures.

Indeed, the indications of multiple forms of the search for the God of Jesus Christ within the confines of the Church have great importance as evidence of her catholicity. The absolute originality of any people, its uniqueness, is demonstrated most effectively in the manner of God-seeking which characterizes its spiritual tradition. And when the different avenues intersect within the confines of the Church, when they are all directed towards the mystery of Jesus Christ as adorer of the Father, each is kept on proper lines and each is endlessly renewed.

The Eucharist in the search for God

It is in the eucharistic celebration that adoration of the Father in spirit and in truth finds its source and its greatest intensity. "Through him, with him and in him, in the unity of the Holy Spirit, all honor and glory to you, the Father Almighty forever and ever" (end of the eucharistic prayer).

The Liturgy of the Word, culminating in the celebrant's homily, gradually introduces the Christian to the will of the Father as revealed in the daily texture of living. The effect of the Word in the believer's life makes him more aware of God's "today".

Thanks to the sacrificial sharing of the bread, the Christian is associated with the only adoration which is agreeable to the Father, that of the one Mediator. The hearts of men are lead to the Holy Spirit, so that, being conformed to the image of the Son, they may also call God by his name and say: "Father, hallowed be thy name, thy Kingdom come, thy will be done on earth as it is in heaven."

OCTAVE OF CHRISTMAS

I. Acts 6:8-10 and 7:54-60
1st reading
December 26

We read today the opening and closing verses of the narrative of Saint Luke devoted to Stephen. It is generally accepted that Luke made use of an account Pauline in origin, centered on the conversion of the apostle, such as Ac 22:3-5 and 26:9-11. The witness of Stephen and his fortitude when faced with death must have impressed Paul, who considered it his first encounter with the Lord whom he was soon to proclaim.

On the other hand, Luke no doubt used a tradition echoing the controversy between Stephen and the Jews for the ideas found in the speech attributed to Stephen (Ac 7:1-53). The vocabulary however betrays his own hand.

a) Behind Stephen's speech and the account of his martyrdom, Luke sees the *development of Christ's trial and death*. False witnesses accuse Stephen of announcing the destruction of the temple (Ac 6:13) as others did at the trial of Jesus (Mk 14:56-61). In both cases the proceedings take place before the Sanhedrin (Ac 6:12; Mk 14:53), and the trials follow an identical pattern: evidence of false witnesses (Ac 6:13; Mk 14:56), interpellation of the accused by the president (Ac 7:1; Mk 14:60-61), the accused's reply alluding to the Son of Man superseding the temple (Ac 7:55-56; Mk 14:62), violent reaction of the audience (Ac 7:57; Mk 14:63-64), punishment "outside the city" (Ac 7:58; cf. Heb 13:12) and finally similar words uttered by Christ on the cross and by Stephen stoned to death (giving up the spirit: Ac 7:59; Jn 19:30; pardon of offences: Ac 7:60; Lk 23:34; a loud cry: Ac 7:60; Lk 23:46).

b) This way of relating martyrdom to Jesus is better understood in the light of the problems produced by persecution among early Christian communities. First, Christians saw the persecutions fomented by the Jews as a prolongation of those earlier inflicted on the messengers of the Lord (Mt 23:29-36; Ac 7:51-52). Later, persecution is situated in an eschatological context, and takes on a new dimension. It "finishes off the sins" of the Jews (1 Th 2:15-16) at the very time when the Son of man comes to judge and separate the good from the evil (cf. Mt 5:10-12). Persecution is then considered to be this judgment at work.

Still later, Christians are invited to suffer and die "on account of the Son of man" (Lk 6:22; cf. Mk 8:35; 13:8-13; Mt 10:39), or rather in imitation of his passion (cf. Mt 10:22-23; Mk 10:38). The account before us is clearly dependent on this concept: Stephen dies, not only for Christ, but like him, with him, and this sharing in the very mystery of the passion is the foundation of the martyr's faith: such a death places him in "the last days."

Martyrdom is thus seen not merely as a means of imitating Christ on the moral level, but as an essential element of eschatology centered around "the sign of the Son of man" (Mt 24:30), which is his death and resurrection.

c) Still another theme underlies the account of Stephen's death. The appearance of the Son of Man at God's right hand (v. 56) gives authenticity to Stephen's remarks against the temple and the holy places (Ac 6:14). So it is whenever in the New Testament Christ or the Christians attack the temple (cf. Mt 24:15 and 30; 26:61-64; 23:29). We can see in this the earliest instance of *substitution of the risen Lord for the Temple* in cultic functions and assemblies.

The early Christians of Jerusalem remained deeply attached indeed to the temple (Lk 24:53; Ac 3:1; 2:46; 21:26). They had not yet understood that henceforth the person of Christ was the place of cult "in spirit and in truth." The Hellenistic Christians, such as Stephen, were the first to part with the temple, thereby allowing the Christians of the Diaspora to build up a religion based on incorporation with and imitation of Christ, free from all traditional ties with the temple and its assemblies. On this ground the blood of Stephen was certainly not shed in vain.

II. Matthew
10:17-22
Gospel
December 26

The 10th chapter of Saint Matthew presents the instructions given to the Twelve by Christ when he sent them out as missionaries. But it is only in the first part (vv 6:16) that he seems to quote exactly the words of Christ, in a manner very similar to the other two synoptics. The second part (vv. 17-42) is mostly made up of additions by Matthew himself, which Mark reports in a different context, specifically in his eschatological discourse.

In any case, it seems that the very insertion of an eschatological discourse into the mission speech shows Matthew's intention of broadening the scope of the latter, making it a general treatise on missions.

a) Christ provides illustration from the animal world to make the Twelve understand that their mission will be surrounded by opposition and persecution. They had been sent to the sheep (v. 6), and now they themselves are sheep sent among wolves. The wolf theme often points to *false prophets* (Mt 7:15-16): doctors of the law who claim to consecrate their personal interpretations of the sacred text.

The disciples should not plunge headlong into the jaws of the wolf; in the face of danger they should, like the serpent, be suspicious and alert. Far, then, from seeking conflict, they should avoid it as much as possible by hiding themselves, or by fleeing! The disciple should indeed, be like a dove, taking off at the first alarm, though it is simple and blameless. The disciple too should have no desire to please the world; let him simply be dedicated to the gospel.

b) Pondering over this advice of Jesus, Matthew could hardly help thinking of the persecution already raging at the time he was writing. So he inserts here verses 17-22, taken from an eschatological discourse of Christ. Persecution is the normal lot of missionaries, since in announcing the coming of the kingdom of God they put an end to the religious claims of human empires, of synagogues, of governors and kings (vv. 17-18).

c) But the *Spirit* (v. 20) too is the normal portion of the missionaries. He will turn their preaching into witness (v. 18), because he has seen what they preach and bears witness to it through the person of the missionaries.

It is clear then that failure and hostility are not signs of bad faith in the missionary, or of his punishment. For those who want to be signs of the Word of God in the world, persecution is rather an opportunity for deeper union with the Lord, and especially with the Spirit. But the advice of Christ is not clear: who can judge that in one case the prudence of the serpent is to prevail, and in another the simplicity of the dove? Who can say when it is time to flee, and when it is time to resist?

The Spirit or the Word alone can teach the disciple to live in prudence and simplicity. Where the Spirit and the Word are present, there the missionary should be, thus finding the way of prudence and simplicity. Where they are not, the disciple shouldn't venture. But it is all a matter of purity of heart, of keen sight, and of openness to listen; in other words, of grace.

III. 1 John 1:1-4 The prologue of the first letter of John con-
     1st reading tains all the main themes of the letter, and
  December 27 reveals its argument.

a) To proclaim *union with God* is the aim and *raison d'etre* of John's apostolic ministry. The theme recurs in various forms throughout the letter: to be "begotten by God" (2:29; 4:7), to "live in God" (3: 5-6; 4:16), to "walk in the light" (which is God: 2:8-11), to "live in union with God" (1:5-7), to "know God" (4:7-8), all of which converge to the same argument. God manifests himself through certain qualities (justice, love, light), and the Christian who conforms his life to these qualities (who

is just, loves, walks in the light) enters into an existential relation
with God, which John calls union.

The letter will show elsewhere what this union actually consists in: a presence of God in man and of man in God through
a communication of life already fully realized in Christ but still
in a state of growth in the Christian (1 Jn 5:11-12; 2:5-6; 3:6,
24; 4:13-16; 5:19). This union is also an alliance, in which God
gives man a new heart that he may know him (Jr 31:31-34;
Ex 36:25-28; see 1 Jn 5:19; 2:27).

b) The second important theme is to *know God* (v. 1). It
almost coincides with that of union, but involves distinctive
aspects. For a Semite, knowledge is not intellectual: one knows
God by observing his marvels and interventions in the world;
but one cannot know him when he is silent, as during the exile.
And John boasts of just such an experimental knowledge: "he
has heard, he has seen, he has watched and touched" God in
the person of the Word, and he wants to share this knowledge
with his correspondents.

c) Within this context of union and knowledge, John places
the missionary proclamation, (v. 3) the role of an apostle. The
expressions describing this mission are to be noted; for: "testimony," "announcing," "joy" (vv. 2, 3, 5) place it on the existential
level. This mission is not teaching, but imparting an experience
and sharing in a life.

Such a program is a serious challenge to the witness of Christianity in the modern world. Man becomes atheistic because he
does not encounter God; he feels no need for him, either in-
tellectually, emotionally or morally. How then can Christians
who know God through a mere notional and intellectual teaching share with the atheist the experience of God, as proposed
by Saint John?

In fact, the Christian often talks of a union with God and of a
knowledge of God that cannot but offend modern man. He talks

of God sometimes because he cannot imagine a world without God; which is a vague notion, barely sufficient to back up sound morals or an explanation of events. It is not the God referred to in Saint John.

More often, the Christian talks of God in the Judeo-Christian manner, stressing the person to person encounter between God and man. Such a notion implies ideas like "plan of God," "Word of God," the ethical character of his Kingdom, alliance, prayer, etc., that is, most of the great themes of the Old Testament. Such a theism must be surpassed in order to bring a reply to the queries of modern man. It leads, indeed, to considering God as an "I" who comes into contact with a "Thou," as a cause distinct from its effect. God then becomes a being, he is no longer the being. He becomes a subject for man, who is in turn an object for God. But God as a subject makes me a mere object.

The God seen and heard by John (not with the eyes and ears of the flesh, but in faith) surpasses the God of theism and even the God of biblical "I-Thou" relationship. John has encountered the God of Jesus, to whom he could not say "Thou," since he was more self than himself, a self stronger than death, anguish and sin.

IV. John 20:2-8   This is a very late tradition, markedly distinct
    Gospel   from the synoptic witness. To begin with,
  December 27   Magdalen's motive for visiting the tomb is not
mentioned (v. 1). When she sees that the stone has been taken away she thinks it possible the corpse has been removed, doubtless by the officials (Jn 20:13). She hastens to tell the apostles, hoping they will be able to recover the body.

Since there is question of disappearance only, the apostles believe her and come themselves to verify the matter (vv. 2-5: differing from Lk 24:11 and Mk 16:11). The tomb is empty, but the cerements shrouding the body of Christ are on the ground (vv. 5-8). This precludes the hypothesis of removal.

So the apostles "begin to believe" (v. 8, a reading preferable to "he believed"). The body could not have been transported to another tomb. Could Jesus be arisen? The answer to this question was to be found in scripture (above all Ho 6:2; Ps 16/17:10); but at this moment the apostles did not have the key (v. 9).

What we are getting then in the account is the *progression* of the apostles towards faith in the resurrection. They first think of the possibility of removal. Then, realizing that this does not meet the case (the presence of the cerements) they "begin to believe." Nevertheless their pilgrimage will not be complete without the aid of the scriptures. In other words what is required from them is not mere verbal witness to something that happened, but the witness of faith, which must necessarily be based on the scriptures. The resurrection of Christ cannot be considered apart from the concrete, and totally unexpected, fashion in which it was an accomplishment of his messianic vocation. Indeed it is the fulfillment of the scriptures (v. 9) in Christ that constitutes the essential object of Christian faith. The apparitions of the Risen Lord must always be combined with reflection on the messianic hope that was realized in the earthly sojourn of Jesus.

It is for this reason the scriptural argument assumes such importance in the missionary discourses of the apostles. Their new insight in this domain made them realize that in Jesus Christ, always, mysteriously at work, each man is called to share the divine sonship and to cooperate in building up the messianic Kingdom.

V. 1 John 1:5-2:2 The first letter of John now becomes con-
1st reading   tinuous reading.
December 28

a) Two phrases summarize the whole passage. "To walk in darkness" is to live in sin; "to walk in the light" is to live in holiness. We can see here the usual Jewish phraseology of the "two ways," so frequently used in the bible (Ws 5:6-7; Pr 2:13; Ep 5:8-9; 1 Th 5:5; Rm 13:11-14). For the Jews the idea of light implies moral conduct, and the "way of light" is lit up by the lamp of the Law (Pr 6, 23; Ps 118/119: 104-105). But John introduces an original thought: our steps are not lit up by the Law but by God himself. Here John is still holding to a Jewish concept of light: it is equivalent to holiness; man practices virtue because he is in God's ambience: "Be holy, because I am holy," or "walk in the light, because I am light." As purifying ablutions restored the chosen people to holiness, so does the blood of Christ now purify Christians, bringing them back to the Way of light from which they had for a moment strayed (v. 7b).

b) There is however a new element. The light of God being shared by men leads them to *union with one another* (v. 7a): living in the light means living in charity (1 Jn 2:3-4, 8-11). Man cannot live in the light, and yet forget the fundamental precept of the new law of love.

c) By himself, man cannot remain in the light of God or be able to live in communion with him; "sin" is always impeding his progress and causing him to wander in the darkness. A holy realism should convince us of this. Christianity does not mix with spiritualistic sects which deny the sinful condition of man and to which John is probably referring (v. 8). The only real sin is the pride to want to be without sin, an attitude that cuts man off from the saving initiative of God in order to rely on himself. It separates him from all communion with God. The truth no longer lives "in him."

On the contrary, the confession of sins maintains him in the light and in communion with God since the same attitude with which he confesses his faults opens up the pardon of God (v. 9), offers him an advocate with the Father (v. 1), and causes him to make an act of confidence in the intercessory power of the death of Christ (v. 2).

To be in the light of God and live in communion with him is not something we acquire once and for all. It is rather a progression (walking in the light: v. 7) and a constant passage from darkness to light through conversion and the confession of sins. Sin is an occasion of communion with God by appealing to the pardon which he can give. Only the pretension of wanting to be without sin deprives us of this communion, since it withdraws from the saving intervention of God and makes of God a liar since he came to pardon us (v. 10)!

The kind of confession envisaged by John (1 Jn 1:9) is public. There is no question of secret avowal: the Greek word *exomologesis* actually supposes some public gesture. This may indicate the practice of a communal penitential liturgy at the end of the first century. It would be a confirmation of the Johannine doctrine that all communion with God means also communion with the brethren (1 Jn 1:7; 2:9-11).

John therefore establishes a close tie between his kerygma or "message" (v. 5: Jesus is the light of the world) and his parenetic catechesis ("walk therefore in the light"). In his gospel he proceeds from the kerygma to conclude with a moral exhortation. In his letter the procedure is often reversed: he begins with a moral message which he bases on the revelation of God in Jesus.

Hence the true light already shines in the world since the divine realities are revealed in the human. Chief among them is the union between the Father and the Son (1 Jn 1:3-4). Living in the light is living in union with it and with the brothers.

The Eucharist commemorates the manifestation of the light of the resurrection in the union between the Son and the Father, and invites participants to walk in this light of union, thus realizing both "message" and catechesis.

VI. Matthew The essential matter of this gospel has been
2:13-18 commented on on the Sunday after Christmas,
Gospel above, page 206.
December 28

VII. 1 John John has returned here to the central topic of
2:3-11 his letter, how to know God and enter in-
1st reading to communion with him. As he sees it all
December 29 knowledge has to do with observance of the
commandments.

a) The passage establishes a parallel between the phrases
"knowing God" and "living in him" (cf. 1 Jn 3:23; 4:13-16; Jn
6:56; 15:4-5).

The dwelling place of God — Ark, Temple or Tabernacle —
was already for the Jews a sign of divine presence, a source of
the action of Yahweh in favor of his people. The Christian sees
in it an active principle, allowing him to love, believe and avoid
sin (cf. 1 Jn 2:14; 3:5; 5:18).

To the notion of God's indwelling John links that of knowledge. In Ezekiel 36:25-27 and in Jeremiah 24:7 and 31:31-34, the
prophets already announced a new era, in which God would give
man "a heart to know him" (cf. 1 Jn 5:18). John borrows from
the prophets the verbs "keep" (Ez 36:26; cf. 1 Jn 2:4-5) and
"observe" or "live a kind of life" (Ez 36:27; cf. 1 Jn 2:6).

Thus we know God (as an experience which is the meaning
given in Jewish tradition) insofar as we are conscious of his
active living within us, of his presence urging us to keep his
word and radiate his love. Under the old alliance, as we have
seen, this active presence of God was extrinsic to man. Since
the incarnation of the Son of God man knows a God who works
within him and associates him in his own life. This is not at all
an intellectual knowledge: keeping the commandments is its
proof as well as its sign (v. 4).

b) But what *commandments*, one may ask, are we concerned with? John does not answer the question: we are only told that the commandment is one grasped by Christians "from the beginning," from the earliest stages that is of their initiation (v. 7). It is an ancient commandment because it belonged to the Jewish law (cf. Lv 19:18; Dt 6:4). It is new because, in Jesus, it has been fulfilled in a manner transcending expectation (in "him," v. 8), something possible now too for every Christian (in "you," v. 8).

The ancient commandment was of course one of love. But since the event of Christ the time that we live is the time of manifestation of the light, the retreat of sin (v. 8b), and the degree of accomplishment is so great that the commandment is "renewed." Christ transformed the Jewish law of love for the neighbor into love for all men, even enemies (Lk 10:25-37), and Christians now can love in these terms (Jn 15:12-13). And universal love of this kind has become the symbol and substance of God's love for us and ours for him (1 Jn 4:11-12).

This perfect fulfillment is described by the adjective "true" or "real" (v. 8) which John uses frequently in his gospel. We have the "true" vine (Jn 15:1), worship in "truth" (Jn 4:23), the "true" bread that comes down from heaven (Jn 6:32). In each instance there is question of a reality that has come into being in the last times, something that would be impossible were it not that God has made his dwelling in man.

People then can determine whether they are enjoying the privileges of these final times, or have relinquished them. It is impossible in other words to live in this "true" light that brings love to its culminating point, and still have hate (vv. 9-11) in one's soul. If a man hates his brother, he is walking in darkness, with a darkened conscience.

In Saint John the "commandment" has an even richer meaning than that disclosed by this single passage. To begin with he mentions the Father's commandment to the Son, the example of that which the Son gives to the disciples (Jn 10:17-18; 1 Jn 3:16). This commandment is inseparable from the communion in which Father and Son live, and is thus, inevitably, love. John goes on to say that, throughout salvation history, this commandment was being expressed before it was clearly manifested in Jesus and associated with the final times. This is the main idea behind our passage which makes the commandment a special characteristic of the final times where darkness disappears (v. 8). Finally, as John sees it, the commandment is not a regulation imposed from the outside. On the contrary it is a manifestation to the Christian in his inmost heart of what it means to be a new creature accepted by God.

The Eucharist commemorates the moment when the ancient commandment reached plenitude and newness in the Lord's Passion. It brings together all those who have decided to do their part in bringing the commandment to the most perfect stage of fulfillment.

**VIII. Luke
2:22-35
Gospel
Dec. 29**   On reading the first two chapters of Luke's gospel, one might be satisfied with exterior happenings: the Messiah is born of a poor woman, and submits to the Law that surrounds his birth. But the Old Testament texts that give texture to the narrative direct the mind towards the divinity of the Messiah, in midrash fashion. References are made to Malachi 3 (the coming of Yahweh to his temple), Daniel 9 (the prophecy of the seventy weeks before the appearance of God), and 2 Samuel 6 (the return of the ark to the temple of Jerusalem).

a) Mary went to the temple to be purified as laid down by the Law (Lv 12:2-8). She takes Jesus up with her to redeem him as first-born (Ex 13:11-13; 22:28-29; Lv 5:7). Now this presentation was to occur forty days after birth; and these forty days, together with the nine months of pregnancy and the six months that elapsed between the apparition of Gabriel in the temple and conception of Christ, amount to 70 weeks, or the period of time announced in Dn 9:21-26 as a prelude to the *coming of God* (cf. Lk 1:26-38).

Ml 3 also frequently enters this narrative (compare: Ml 3:1 and Lk 2:22; the "day" of Ml 3:2 and Lk 2:22; the "upright" of Ml 3:18-20 and Lk 2:25; the "light" of Ml 3:19 and Lk 2:32; the "offering" of Ml 3:3-4, 6-10 and Lk 2:22; the "nations" of Ml 3:12 and Lk 2:32). Thus Luke, who had seen in the appearance of the angel in the temple (Lk 1:11) the fulfillment of Ml 3:1a, now sees the coming of Jesus into the temple as the appearance of Yahweh foreseen in Ml 3:1b.

Finally the theme of the transfer of the ark is also brought in to show that God is really present in Jesus as he was formerly in the ark. In Lk 1:39-46, Mary bearing Jesus within her is compared with the ark. From the north, she proceeds to Judea, where she is greeted with rejoicings and dancing, stays for three months in a house before resuming her journey, and now accomplishes the last stage by going to Jerusalem. When the ark was transferred there it became the city of God.

As a final point, Luke inserts at the end of the account the canticle of Simeon, acclaiming Christ under the very term "glory" (v. 32; cf. Is 49:6; 60:1-3). In the Old Testament, that glory was God himself, a glory which brought death to those who looked upon it (Ex 19:21; 33:20; Gn 32:31; Dt 4:33; Ws 6:22-23). Now, in Jesus, God is among his people, and they can hear him and see him.

b) While stressing the divinity of Jesus, Luke also has in mind his redemptive and paschal role: though God, Jesus is *destined to humiliation and death.*

In his canticle Simeon sees at one glance both glory and death (vv. 26, 30, 32), as if he could only see the divine presence through the mystery of death, and the simple fact of seeing God drew man into the realm of the eschatological.

But it is mostly in the last verses of this prophecy (vv. 33-35) that the humiliation and suffering in store for Jesus are shown in close connection with his glory and his mission. Already in v. 32, Simeon, by using the phrase "light of the nations" was borrowing a theme proper to the theology of the suffering servant of Yahweh (Is 49:6), and Luke remains faithful to this theology when he ends his chapter with the description of the family life of Jesus (vv. 39-40).

The Messiah brings with him division and contradiction (v. 34; cf. Is 8:12-15). Because of him, a sword will pierce the soul of Mary (v. 35), in accordance with the prophecies of Ezekiel (Ez 5:1; 6:3; 21:1-22 and especially 14:17). The sword is a sign of the forthcoming punishment of Israel. Mary, the personification of Israel, is invited to take note of the fact that her personal suffering symbolizes that of the whole people.

So Christ will be a light for the nations, but also a cause of crisis among the people who will be torn by the kind of salvation proposed to them, and the kind of Messiah they will have to accept. This will rend the whole life of Mary right up to Calvary, not only because of the sorrow inflicted on her mother's heart at the death of her son, but because this is necessary for all progress in faith.

During the time which divides the actual writing of the gospel from his compilation of sources on the infancy of Jesus, Luke may well have become more fully aware, with the early community, of the divine fullness bodily present in the Lord, and also of the meaning of his emptying and death. By casting the light of the mysteries of the God-made-man and that of the Lordship of the servant on the most humble events of the life of Christ, Luke invites us to cast this same light on our lives as witnesses of Christ, and on the life of the whole Church. For through our eucharistic participation in the death and resurrection of the Lord, we are entitled to see in every event a step in the grand epic of salvation.

IX. 1 John   The first letter of John explains the means of
    2:12-17   union with God: to live with him in light, to
    1st reading   share his love by loving the brethren, in other
    December 30   words, to know him. But such a union neces-
    sarily follows a deliberate choice. For no one
can serve two masters: the Father and the world. Such is the
lesson of today's reading.

a) Every man, even a Christian, finds himself solicited by two
sources of life: *the Father and the world*. But whoever loves
the world cannot have the love of the Father in him (v. 15), and
whoever is led by the lures of the world (v. 16) cannot be following the will of the Father (v. 17).

Here, the world has for Saint John a pejorative meaning; it is
not the world for which Christ died (1 Jn 2:2; 4:14; Jn 3:17;
4:42; 12:47), which God has loved (Jn 3:16), but rather the
world which relies on itself for salvation, and refuses to admit
that its future depends on an encounter with God. It is the
world of which Satan is the prince (Jn 12:31).

The love of this world cannot be allied with the love of God;
how can any one even believe in the existence of the Father, if
he claims to rely on himself alone?

b) The love of the Father can be seen in the love for one's
brethren (1 Jn 2:8-11); being of the world means submitting to
desires (v. 16) which contradict the will of the Father.

The desires of the flesh (Rm 13:13-14) seem to denote sins of
sensuality and greediness, those of the eyes (Mt 5:28; 2 P 2:14)
the spectacles of the circus, those of life riches and possessions.
Without being exhaustive, this list indicates the behavior of a
man who looks upon himself as an absolute, and who turns
the object of his passions into an idol that turns him away from
God, as can hatred (1 Jn 2:11).

c) In opposition to the man who is slave to his passions, stands
the one who does the will of God and so enters into the *last
days* (v. 18). If a man refuses the attractions of the world in

order to choose the will of God, he has a share in promoting eschatology in the world. But if he considers himself as an absolute, and subordinates everything to his desire for power, riches, and pleasure, he belongs to the "passing world" and destroys himself.

The Christian does not flee the world; he knows that he is part and parcel of it, and that he can help to bring it to its eternal achievement through obedience to the will of God. But the world is sinful when it seeks to find in itself the means of its salvation.

Through the bread and wine, the Eucharist is also part of the world, as well as through the words there proclaimed, and the men who meet around it. But always the members of the assembly submit themselves to the initiative of God.

X. Luke 2:36-40   This reading combines two separate events:
Gospel   the first part completes the account of the
December 30   presentation of Christ in the Temple (vv.
            36-38), while the second describes his hidden
life at Nazareth (vv. 39-40).

a) The witness of Anna rightly confirms that of Simeon (Lk 2:25-35). Indeed the Law required that truth be established by two witnesses (Dt 17:6; 19:15; Nb 35:30), and the evangelists have taken great care to assure this dual evidence in the most important events of the life of Christ (Mt 18:16; 26:60; Jn 8:17).

But a witness must be reliable. And as a woman did not always have sufficient standing in Israel, Luke gives all the titles that will make Anna's evidence acceptable. An aged widow — Luke points out that she had remained a widow for many years, which was something quite respectable in those days — probably depending on the generosity of the community (Ex 22:21-23; Dt 24:17-21; 26:12-13; cf. Ac 6:1-6), she is one of the *poor of Yahweh* (Is 29:17-24; Lk 10:21-24). She then shares in messianic hope of the Remnant of Israel for the deliverance of Jerusalem (v. 38; cf. Is 52:9), and soon becomes a bearer of the good news of the coming of the Messiah (cf. Is 52:6-10; 40:9).

Perhaps it is only because of Is 52:6 and 40:9 that Anna is called a "prophetess" (v. 36); in which case the title would denote her constancy in hearing the Word of God, meditating over it and proclaiming it.

So in Anna, the poor of Yahweh see the fulfillment of their hopes in the person of Christ, and welcome him with joy and praise.

b) The other topic in this passage is that which is usually described as the *hidden life* of Jesus at Nazareth (vv. 39-40). The lesson of the verses is important. Jesus follows the natural course of human development, on the physical level, and also in acquiring knowledge. By undergoing childhood, puberty, adolescence in the usual way, he demonstrated in his mission an extraordinary *kenosis*. He accepted a condition of things wherein his knowledge of the Father's will would be progressive, in a family milieu from which "nothing good could come" (Jn 1:46), in the thousand and one ordinary events of living (Mt 26:42). What he would know of men and things would be the ordinary knowledge that comes with human development; he had renounced any knowledge over and above this (Mt 24:36). The fidelity to the Father which he displayed consisted of absolute fidelity to the human condition, however limited that was, and however frail.

These two separate events find a deep unity in the theme of poverty. But there is quite a difference between the spiritual and moral poverty of Anna, the old prophetess, and the ontological poverty of Christ. Anna's poverty is an attitude of man faithful to God, with his will open to the saving initiative of God. But in his poverty, the God-made-man is ready to rediscover his exclusive relation to the Father in the limited, inarticulate awareness of a child, or in the frightened awareness of a dying man!

Today other poor have inherited Anna's function. All the members of the eucharistic assembly who live as children of God and learn in association with other men to appreciate it as a gift of God, despite the frailties of daily life.

When poverty puts us completely at God's disposal, it becomes practically identical with love. This is why after all, the two readings of the day bring us a common message.

XI. 1 John 2:18-21 Here John puts his correspondents on guard
1st reading   against false doctors (vv. 18-29). This topic
December 31 is extremely important for John, and he devotes his letter to the knowledge of God.

a) John's notion of history and of the Latter Days (v. 18) leads him to compare the *false doctors* to those antichrists which the Judeo-Christian eschatology expected before the Coming of the Lord (cf. 2 Th 2:1-12). But John gives a personal touch, since his insistence on "several antichrists" shows in itself that one should be on guard not so much against a concrete individual, but against a doctrine, a cast of mind. In the book of Revelation, he will discern the antichrist in the political powers of the day. Jesus, too, mentioned false prophets and false messiahs before the decisive moment (Mt 24:23-24). The Old Testament had rather confused ideas on the subject (cf. Ez 38-39; Zc 14). This will show that here we can only surmise; we cannot erect opinion into doctrine. Yet it remains true that a doctrine that appears erroneous on a merely human level, such as false spiritualism or false humanism, will delineate more sharply the Kingdom, and the fullness of response it brings to men who seek it. Viewed in this light, error may be considered a negative sign of the reality of the Kingdom.

b) The false doctors did not stay with the community (v. 19); so they are easily recognizable. Though they were baptized and anointed like those who stay in the Church, they are distinct from them. They were baptized, but did not "know"; while the

faithful were baptized and "received all knowledge" (v. 20).
John approaches here the problem of *faith and sacrament*. The
sacrament alone can become otiose or waste away.

The incidents mentioned by John, which culminated in the
departure of the heretics and a conscious separation between
the faithful who "know" and the unfaithful who are "liars" should
never lead us to divide the world of today into two groups: the
knowers and the unknowing, into truth and error.

One should always remember the basic truth that God wills
(and his will is efficacious) that all men be saved (1 Tm 2:4).
No man, whether pagan or Christian, whether agnostic or religious, escapes this will. Without any infringement of human
liberty, God constantly summons every member of the human
race in a thousand and one ways. Each one responds in a
different way, anonymous or pseudonymous, conscious or un-
conscious, with or without a personal relationship to God.

But there is one special way in which God has chosen to manifest his will to be known to the whole world: Jesus Christ himself (Hb 1:1-2). Those who adhere to the Son of God are not
just people in touch with a truth out of reach for others; they
rather constitute a meaningful community, bearing the Word
destined for all men, through which God reveals himself to men
within their particular environment.

The fact that the Christian, by conscious membership in the
Church, is a meaningful member bearing the Word of God, does
not imply that those not so favored are necessarily in the darkness, and are liars. The Christian is a missionary of the Word.
He has knowledge of the Word, yes; but how can he be a missionary if he is not solidly with all human effort, rejecting
absolutely all idea of separation?

XII. John 1:1-18   Commentary on this gospel will be found
    Gospel   above, p. 189, gospel for Christmas Day.
    December 31

JANUARY 1 – COMMEMORATION
OF THE HOLY VIRGIN

A. THE WORD

I. Numbers
6:22-27
1st reading

This brief formula reproduces the blessing that the priests of Israel gave the people at the end of liturgical ceremonies (cf. Pss 127/128; 121/122) and especially at the New Year (Feast of Tabernacles), the most important feast in the Jewish calendar.

In the bible, man becomes aware of the fact that he is not master of the happiness toward which he feels drawn. The *blessing* is a way for man to recognize that this thirst cannot be fulfilled without admitting the divine origin of all good and accepting a life in communion with God (as expressed in such phrases as: the face of God, the name of God, etc., in vv. 25-27).

The gifts brought by this blessing are often material: peace, for instance (v. 26), denotes an assured welfare. Yet slowly, man realizes that true happiness will be the very presence of God in his life, whatever its circumstances (Pss 23/24:4-5; 127/128; 131/132:13-15).

Christ is the true blessing, not only because through him man can attain the divine blessings (Ep 1:3; Ac 3:26), but most of all because he has given mankind the Spirit of God, which is the source of true communion with God, and crowns the search undertaken by man for happiness.

II. Galatians
4:4-7
2nd reading

In the 3rd chapter, Paul had discovered the role of the Law in the salvation of mankind: in the plan of God, it has never been a decisive instrument of justification, since the

241

Spirit alone can bring about salvation (Ga 3:2-5; 3:14).

The first verses of chapter 4 describe the turn of events "when the appointed time came" (v. 4). A child or slave formerly under the Law (vv. 1-3), man comes of age with Jesus Christ, obtaining the state of sonship described in today's reading.

a) Verse 4 is based on a double antithesis: God sends his *Son* to be *subject to the Law* so that those subject to the Law may be adopted as sons. In stressing the fact that Christ is "born of a woman," Paul recalls that the Son had submitted himself to the servitudes of nature — not only of the Law — in order to free man from the "elemental principles of this world" (v. 3) and to grant him divine sonship.

Now, this sonship is acquired by the mission both of the Son, born of a woman and subject to the Law, and of the Spirit, who came into our hearts (v. 6). Once again the argument of Jn 1:1-14 applies: the ultimate reason for the incarnation is the gift of divine sonship to all men. The Father initiates the gift, but realizes it in two successive missions. He sends his Son to be a slave, that slaves may become sons, and he sends the Spirit to fulfill this sonship deep in our hearts (cf. Rm 8:14-15).

b) The context of the letter to the Galatians adds to the idea of sonship that of *liberation* (v. 7).

Man is first subject to the "elemental principles of the world" (v. 3): servant to nature and slave to the powers believed to govern the world (cf. Ga 3:19; Col 2:15-18). God frees Israel from this fate through gratuitous interventions such as the Promise and the Law (cf. Ga 2:16-17; 19-21). But the Law again turns the Jew into a slave (Ga 2:4; 3:23; 4:21-31; 5:1), confirming him in sin without any possibility of being freed. Besides, it was given by angels, mysterious beings somewhat similar to the "principles of the world," holding man under their control.

Then Christ comes, liberating man from all the negative exigencies of the Law. Whoever joins with him in the bond of the Spirit becomes an adopted son, and therefore heir to a new world where all is gift and freedom (v. 7; cf. Rm 8:14-17; Ep 1:1-5).*

c) These themes of liberation and sonship are for Paul characteristic of the fullness of time (v. 4). How should we understand this fullness, when nothing is changed in the course of times and seasons, wars and famines, births and deaths? It is because a man, born of a woman, hence subject to nature and its events, subject also to laws (vv. 4-5) has lived every moment of his life with a dimension of eternity, discovering in it the divine presence that makes it decisive and accepting it in all freedom. This divine presence is called Wisdom in the first reading; here it is called the Spirit poured into our hearts (v. 6), a Spirit that gives an eternal value to the most ordinary events of life, a Spirit that all men possess within themselves, but which is perceived only by those who led by Jesus have sufficient insight, and with Jesus live in the present time of decision.

Modern man believes in freedom, and wants to liberate his brethren. But Christ will always remain the first man to be truly free. Free where nature and law are concerned, because he has made use of both in his loving plan. Free of death and sin, which have no hold on him. Free too in his obedience to his Father; for this is not passive and resigned, but so filled that it develops in the structure of discovery and spiritual adventure.

Every Christian must reveal this filial freedom to the world showing by his behavior how unexpectedly it fulfills the deepest wishes of all freedom movements of the day. The Eucharist should thus be an assembly of free men, brought together not by a political Messiah who could not have given them such freedom, but by the Spirit of God itself, who alone knows the secret of freedom, because he also knows the secret of sonship.

The Christian is in fact free, but not yet sufficiently mature to devote his freedom properly to the service of love. That is why

* See the doctrinal theme: *the liberty of the Christian*, p. 198.

he must depend on the charity of the community (which is the Body of Christ), and more especially on the Eucharist, if he is to realize how love permits him to express better his freedom. The ecclesial community should never be the sort that excludes expression of freedom, and, consequently, of love. Recent events, reactions for instance to *Humanae Vitae*, overly authoritarian measures taken by certain bishops, the fact that we have in many countries an underground Church, are sufficient evidence that our structures nowadays fall short of the ideal.

Reform in this domain must take account of numerous rights to freedom that the Christian has. These are defined not only in the basic charter of human rights, but in ecclesial documents such as *Pacem in Terris* or *Gaudium et Spes*, or the decrees of Vatican II. To be specific, we might mention the freedom to seek the truth among the various ideologies which purport to explain a developing universe; freedom to express a private opinion, above all in an area where one has competence, even if some noninfallible teaching is thereby jeopardized; freedom to give expression to one's own personality even in areas that are strictly ecclesial; freedom on the part of non-Western cultures, or for that matter of subgroups in the Western framework, to define their faith in terms of the problems and values they actually experience.

Freedoms of this kind are not of course absolute. They derive meaning from the service they render to love, and the witness they give to sonship. But today, if ecclesial communities are to become vital centers of freedom and love, they are very necessary indeed.

III. **Luke 2:16-21** This gospel is that of the Dawn Mass for
    Gospel   Christmas. Today's liturgy adds to it verse 21,
                relating two facts: the circumcision of Jesus
and the imposition of his name. Our commentary here will be limited to these two points.

a) The Hebrews practiced circumcision to show that they were engaged in an alliance with God for the fulfillment of the promises (Gn 17:2-27); they also hoped that this rite might help them share in the renewal of all things. But the prophets and the law had always insisted on the "circumcision of heart" as a condition for participation in the renewed world (Dt 10:16; 30:6; Jr 4:4; 6:10; 9:24-25).

A sign of membership in the chosen people, circumcision engaged all Hebrews to the same destiny and the same manner of life. For Jesus, it can only signify his belonging to the Jewish race. His true circumcision, that of the heart, will consist in loving acceptance of his passion (Col 2:11-15). On that day he will truly have made vain the ritual circumcision.

Jewish traditions saw in the blood shed a blood that renewed the alliance. The blood of Christ, shed in the circumcision of the heart, will be the blood of the new alliance capable of leading all men towards the promised gifts.

b) Circumcision placed the individual in a special relationship with God and the Jewish community. The rite usually ended with the imposition of a name which signified this. Abraham, John and Jesus all received their names at the time of their circumcision (Gn 17:2-11; Lk 1:59; 2:21).

Christ's relationship to God in the alliance contracted with him is indicated by his name. Jesus, a name ratified by the will of God (Lk 1:31; Mt 1:21), means "God saves." It had been the name of Joshua (written like Jesus) through whose ministry the people left the desert (Nb 13:8, 16; Jos 1:1-5) and by another Joshua who played an important part in the restoration of Israel after the exile (Zc 3:1-10; Hg 2:1-9). It was also borne by Jesse, the ancestor of Jesus (Is 11:1).

By immersing us in the mystery of the death of Christ, baptism renders unnecessary the circumcision of the flesh, which was accomplished once for all on the cross (Col 2:11-15), but not the circumcision of the heart, which is the renewal in faith of our whole being.

It does not obliterate either the significance of circumcision. If we no longer carry in our flesh the concrete evidence of Church membership, this does not mean that we can rest content with a purely mystical membership. Christians are not divided from other human beings, because the Church is not a secular kingdom. And indeed they should avoid any understanding of ecclesial membership in institutional or secular terms. Nevertheless their initiation into the mystery of Christ must be visibly demonstrated by participation in the Eucharist, which commemorates the blood poured out in the new covenant.

B. DOCTRINE

The Theme of Membership in the Church

There is nothing sociological about membership in the Church. We are not Catholics because of our nationality, or our place in life, not even because we are Western. Nevertheless through reaction against such sociological ideas, some lean towards denial of the historical character of the Church. Accordingly it is important that we ask ourselves what Church membership really means in the Christian life.

Circumcision, the sign of the covenant

Circumcision was by no means an exclusively Jewish practice; among many other contemporary peoples it was the concrete sign of membership in the community. It proved that the community was no mere fortuitous juxtaposition of individuals, but a physical and spiritual unit. Membership in this sense meant that you shared the community's destiny, its history, its hope, its difficulties, its rites, its manner of life. Unconsciously, prior to any choice of your own, you were drawn into fruitful association. You belonged, just as a limb belongs to the physical body: you were bound by functional, organic and stable ties. The notion people had of membership went deeper than the juridical, the mystical or the ideological. Circumcision was a permanent fleshly sign of the vital link binding an individual to the group.

For a man in search of his sacred destiny membership in this sense was the chief source of security. Always the group would be seen by its members as related in a special fashion to their god, as the agency which determined an alliance of some sort. The rite of circumcision which proved group membership was then a particularly apt indication that individuals were embraced in the alliance between the group and its god.

Among the Jews however the concept of alliance took on, more and more, a particular significance. Israel's God was not like other gods: he was acknowledged as the Totally-Other. Where other divinities were simply idols fashioned by the hand of man, he was absolute master of destiny for everyone. Similarly, the alliance between Yahweh and Israel tended more and more towards interiority. Because he required from his people a moral fidelity transcending all particular situations, mere membership was no longer of itself sufficient security. Thus we see the prophets appealing for a circumcision of the heart as distinct from that of the flesh. The latter had no validity in the eyes of Yahweh unless it led to the former. The Covenant is not something merely material; what Yahweh demands from the faithful is total personal engagement.

Jesus of Nazareth, first born of the spiritual Israel

On the eighth day after his birth Jesus was circumcised. The fleshly sign demonstrated his membership of the Jewish people, and indicated his sharing in their destiny, their history, their cult, their hope. The prophetic summons to circumcision of the heart was basic so far as he was concerned: he perceived more clearly than anyone that without it circumcision of the flesh had no meaning. By total obedience to the will of the Father in this regard he practiced circumcision of the heart, and demonstrated how deficient was the fleshly brand where salvation was concerned. When, in Jesus, the privileges of the chosen people disappeared, their physical rite of membership was shorn of its salvific value.

The spiritual Israel, the Kingdom inaugurated by Jesus in his person, is universal. It does not depend any longer on membership of a people. He saves Israel, not because he belongs to the chosen people, but because his humanity as a Jew is the humanity of the Son of God. Salvation through him is a right available to all men and to all peoples. The important thing for each person is his vital link with Jesus Christ, the First Born of true humanity. The source from which man elicits an authentic response to the plan of God's love, circumcision of the heart, is a gift of the Spirit. By right it belongs only to the man-God. By sharing in the life which the First Born offers them, all other men can make it theirs.

Membership in the Church, the People of God

The people of the New Covenant, of the Church, are not just another people among peoples of the earth. Always, however, they do constitute a historical group, fully involved in the human adventure. The Church summons all men to salvation, and always she will inevitably display the human lineaments of those who answer the summons. It was in the framework of actual membership of the Jewish people that Christ demonstrated the universality of the Kingdom. So must the Church in her own framework, with the members she actually has. The people of the New Covenant are not transcendent because they are "superimposed" on the peoples of the earth. Their transcendence springs from human diversity, from the various peoples among whom the Church has taken root.

So it is that membership in the Church is not just some sort of "mystical" association. That would indeed be the case if the Church were of exclusively spiritual character, if the sociological forms it assumed were divorced from its essential reality, in a word accidental, and irrelevant even, where some people are concerned.

Nor can this membership be described as something purely ideological. True we find Christians very frequently nowadays, extremely altruistic people indeed, who seek only one thing in the Church, the gospel. That means for them a certain vision of the universe, a particularly noble ideal of human existence; and the Christian's obligation is to bear testimony by his life to that vision and that ideal.

It would also be wrong to confuse Church membership with membership in any terrestrial group or secular community. The concepts cannot be identified: they are of different orders, but never mutually exclusive. Indeed, membership in the Church actually presupposes that participation in secular groups will be undertaken for its own sake according to the customary norms. Phrases like "Christian people" or above all "Christian community" are suitable enough in ordinary parlance, but can be misleading if one is not careful. The group which forms a church is never to be identified with the secular community in which it is developed; it should never be the occasion for setting up an artificial association of human beings.

How then can we determine what Church membership really is? The Christian is a pilgrim of the Kingdom here below. The Family of the Father, and the universal brotherhood which constitutes it, is the only absolute that absorbs his energies. Because he can perceive, at this high level, the decisive element in his life, every other association that he has is undertaken as something real, though secular, something which, as such, contributes nothing to his pursuit of eternal destiny.

The sign of Church membership

If the Christian lives up to the demands of his Church membership, and can give a good account of himself on that score, he bears witness to the Risen Christ. In the ordinary texture of living it is the dynamism of Christ's charity which will demonstrate his membership. Every action that he does, in fulfillment of individual or social responsibilities, is motivated by a spirit of universal brotherhood; and because this has its source in another by whom he lives, Jesus Christ that is, it can confront the numerous challenges presented by death.

It is not possible to fulfill the demands of Church membership properly without full and adequate participation in secular groupings. The Christian must be a man who takes his secular obligations very seriously indeed, cooperates to the full in the task of human advancement, and in associations demanded by this. When engaged in such pursuits he has a clear perception of their secular character, and is indeed better equipped than others in the field. He is less likely to sacralize, to drain such pursuits of the dynamism that ought to characterize them.

Christians will demonstrate their witness more adequately in ordinary life if they avoid expressing the brotherhood that unites them in institutional ties. This sort of thing is often an obstacle to evangelization. Always they must exclude from their pattern of living the inwardness that is exclusive.

The development of membership in the Eucharist

Once we understand all this there is a point that ought to be made, very emphatically. As we live out our lives, it is only by constant expression in rite that Church membership can be adequately lived and witnessed. Through constantly renewed initiation into the mystery of Christ by means of Church ceremonies, the life of the Christian is gradually permeated by awareness of his inclusion in the Kingdom. This does not happen automatically. It is only in relation to life that Christian cult can have its specific effect. The conclusion is that ritual, particularly eucharistic ritual, is the constructive element in deepening our participation in the Church.

Wherever celebrated the Eucharist is a mysterious summons, in universal terms, to the Kingdom. Whatever their sociological circumstances it brings men together just as they are, and provides entry into the universal brotherhood that is already established in Jesus Christ, the first born of humanity in the truest sense. By means of it each Christian assumes his status as pilgrim here below of the Kingdom. It restores him to life, and in the framework of ordinary human relations he will demonstrate the transcendence of the people of the New Covenant where he is a member. From now on he acts from a living principle, the circumcision of the heart, of which the Spirit of the Risen Christ is the source.

SECOND SUNDAY AFTER CHRISTMAS
FEAST OF THE EPIPHANY*

A. THE WORD

I. Isaiah 60:1-6   Meditation of a prophet on the plight of
1st reading   Jerusalem. Perhaps he is watching a sunrise
over the city, a spectacle still available for
visitors today. While the valleys all around are as yet en-
shrouded in darkness, the city walls, already reflecting the glare
of the rising sun, appear all bright with light. Transposing this
spectacle to the eschatological plane — a process common among
prophets of Zion (Ez 40-68; Ps 86/87) — Isaiah imagines Jerusalem as the light of the world; her radiance no longer comes from
the sun, but from Yahweh himself.

The characteristics of this new Jerusalem are above all liturgical: the "glory" is the manifestation of God's "presence" in his
temples (Ez 1:4-28; 43:1-5; Pss 25/26:8; 62/63:3), which is
proper to the religion of Zion (Dt 12:5). The Law demands
that all tribes be assembled together (2 K 23; Dt 4:9-13; Ps
121/122:4) for the principle feasts of the Jewish calendar and
all nations bring to Jerusalem the spices required for the sacrifices of incense, for which Yahweh has made known his prefer-
ence (Ml 1:11). But these characteristics take on a new dimension: if the elements of the cult are reestablished at Jerusalem,
around the glory of Yahweh returned to Zion, the gathering (v. 4)
is no longer made up of the tribes only, but of the nations as
well (v. 3). The new liturgy concerns the whole world. However, the nations' participation in this "assembly" (Za 14:15-20)
is still understood as subordinated to the Jewish tribes, and the
role of the nations consists mainly in bringing back the sons of

---

*When the Epiphany is celebrated on January 6, the readings are inter-
changed. The commentary will be found on pages 278-281.

Jerusalem into the walls of the city. This nevertheless is the first step along the road of Christian universalism.

The grandiose vision of the prophet as he describes the nations' upward climb towards Jerusalem does not entirely conceal the particularism which still inspires this text. As Ps 71/72 promises a king to whom all other kings of the earth will pay tribute, so the prophet, under the influence of a process familiar in Oriental literature, sees in Zion the city to which the whole universe gathers to bestow its riches and offer its sacrifices. But this universalism is too centripetal; it is still around Zion that it takes shapè. (Dt 7:1-16; 23:4-9; Ne 10; Si 36:1-17). For a while the first Christians believed that Jerusalem would be the center of religious unity. Paul himself seemed to hold the same view. When he took up collections for Jerusalem he obviously was thinking of the prophecy which we are considering: all riches will flow toward Zion (Rm 15:26-28; 1 Co 16:4). But soon Christians had to give up this narrow idea of centralization and recognize in each local church, as a eucharistic assembly, an efficacious sign of the universal gathering. The central bodies are nothing but a service at the disposal of the local assemblies and the source of their unity.

II. Ephesians   This passage begins the conclusion to the doc-
  3:2-3a, 5-6   trinal portion of the letter, and indicates the
  2nd reading   prayer which is to follow (Ep 3:14-20). Once
                  more Paul is concerned with the "mystery"
(v. 3) of the inclusion of Gentiles in the Church, and of the apostolic ministry (v. 7), that has fallen to his lot, in order that God's will may be fulfilled (cf. Ep 1:3-14; Ep 1:18-23; 2:1-2, 14-22).

As God sees it, the *mystery* of the Church consists in its relationship with the world. The central function of the Church is the reception of men into the Kingdom of God. Apostolic ministry is a service whereby men are constantly reminded of the dialogue with the world that must go on, of how all human mentalities, all cultures, must be welcomed.

Paul calls this mission a "mystery" because God's purpose in setting up such a Church is not immediately evident. The choice of Israel seemed to indicate that God's will was directed towards a particular people. The universalist prophets, with whom the Old Testament culminated, could not effect any considerable change, because their listeners were inured to particularism.

Throughout all Israel's history God's will remained hidden; but in the person of Jesus it was finally made manifest. Throughout his life he had shown concern even for the Gentiles; and after the resurrection there were no longer limitations to his body. He would encounter all men and attach them to himself in love.

III. Matthew 2:1-12 Gospel   In Matthew 1:18 to Matthew 2:23 the evangelist assembles five episodes of the childhood of Christ, juxtaposing them with five texts of the Old Testament (preceded by the midrash). His purpose is to discover in the childhood of Jesus the signs and presentiments of a vocation which fulfills all past vocations. *Christ is a new Moses,* like him escaping massacre; like him, called from Egypt and miraculously illumined at the moment of his birth (if we accept one Jewish tradition: Sota 12); a *new David* who fulfills the prophecy of the Immanuel (Mt 1:20-24), and on whom will shine the messianic star of Numbers 24:17; a *new Solomon* whose wisdom draws the wise men of the East as the wisdom of the king draws the Queen of Sheba (1 K 10:1-13); a *new Elijah,* practicing the prophetic asceticism (Mt 2:23).

a) But the narrative of the adoration of the Magi serves another purpose. Matthew writes for the Christians of Palestine.

Jews passing to belief in Christ, they need to support their new faith with the conviction that they remain loyal to ancient prophecies. The evangelist wants to prove to them that the birth of Christ is surrounded with the glitter of the *royal dynasty*. By combining 2 Samuel 5:2 and Micah 5:1 (v. 6), Matthew shows that Christ belongs to the davidic dynasty, and solves the painful question of the unity of the people, which was divided between Judah and Israel. Hence Jesus fulfills simultaneously a prophecy on the restoration of Judah (Mi 5) and a tradition among the northern tribes (Israel), which summoned David to rule over them (2 Samuel). The Jews' trust in the prophecies leads them to recognize Jesus as the Messiah they have been awaiting.

b) How, then, explain the fact that the Jews do not become Christians? In answer, Matthew tells the story of the visit of the Magi, in which the pagans are the first to be concerned about the birth of the Messiah, and go 'in search" of him (important theme of the approach to faith; cf. Lk 2:41-51). On the other hand, the scribes and priests, whose knowledge enables them to determine the very spot where the Messiah is to be born, have a faith so weak that they do not take the trouble to go and see the child. As for Herod, he is quite eager to go to Bethlehem, but with a criminal intent.

The essential point of the narrative hinges therefore on the opposition between the *refusal of the Jews and the faith of the pagans*. The sight of pagans adoring Jesus recalls to Matthew's mind Isaiah's prophecy (60:6, the gifts) and he points out its fulfillment. So the converted pagans have another motive to strengthen their faith. The actual Jewish prophecies by announcing their conversion, justify the action. As a matter of fact the whole gospel of Matthew is characterized by anxiety to justify the refusal of the Jews and the approach of pagans to the Christian faith. After the resurrection Matthew reintroduces the unbelieving priests (Mt 28:11-15) opposing to them the mission of the apostles to the nations (Mt 28:16-20).

The lesson of this gospel seems clear, even though it conceals an older midrash: the Jews know the prophecies but do not recognize the Messiah. This lack of faith dispossesses them of their rights. On the contrary, the nations who do not know the prophets, enter immediately into faith. Is it not sometimes the unbeliever who reveals to Christians the true countenance of Christ?

c) In this episode of the Magi, Matthew's purpose was to give a commentary on the *Balaam* episode. In both instances the Magi were summoned by a foreign king (Nb 22:2-4) to pronounce a malediction on the people (or their king). In both instances they take an opposite viewpoint and bless the one they have been charged to condemn. In both instances they mention a luminous star (Nb 24:17; cf. Mt 2:2). In both instances they return undisturbed to whence they came (Nb 24:25; cf. Mt 2:12).

By this sort of midrash on the Balaam story Matthew makes his intention very clear. He wants to associate the Gentiles with the universal kingdom of Jesus from its very beginnings.

Popular midrash, the narrative of Matthew 2:1-12 stresses the universalism of the new reign. Whether or not all its elements be historical, the purpose remains unchallenged. Science may some day show that the Magi never came to Bethlehem and the star never appeared. But we know that the literary sense of the midrash allows the use of legends to advance a good cause. Let us keep to the essential: the child worshiped by the Magi inaugurates a universal kingdom.

B. DOCTRINE

1. The Theme of Catholicity

Is it true that the Church has failed in her mission of universalism? Her purpose is to make all peoples feel at home within her confines. Yet, after twenty centuries of history, what we actually find is almost exclusive association with white-man cultures. Looked at from the viewpoint of Asian and African peoples, Christianity seems a European religion, and that of the European extension in America. The Asian and African minorities we do have seem to manifest their faith in categories and institutions that are Western in character.

When, because of this, people challenge the universalist pretensions of the Church, the Christian should be ready with some adequate response, some explanation why the catholicity so essential to the Church has been apparently without fruit.

We must consider the matter from two angles. In the first place we must be perfectly clear about the principle that universalism is an absolutely essential characteristic of Christianity. To the Kingdom inaugurated in Jesus Christ, entry is offered to all peoples. The Church's missionary obligation is absolutely primal. In our treatment of the Epiphany this will be the first topic of study. It will also be necessary to demonstrate that faith in Jesus Christ implies universalism by its own internal logic. Seen from this angle, the Church's catholicity appears a historical task of quite extraordinary duration and dimension. The second portion of our study will be devoted to it. Having investigated both avenues, we shall understand more clearly the urgency on the one hand, and the slow progress on the other, of missionary endeavor.

Israel and the nations

Was there, from the Jewish viewpoint, any place for other peoples in Yahweh's salvific plan? Before attempting an answer, we should make the point that Israel was never in fact an isolated people. She had very many contacts with other nations, interior and exterior associations, not alone with local and neighboring tribes, but with the great international groupings of the time, Egypt, Assyria, Babylon and the like. When Samaria and Jerusalem were captured, an Israel of the Diaspora comes into being. Rather generally throughout Eastern Asia and the Mediterranean Jewish communities were established.

Like all small peoples, to safeguard her political and religious identity, Israel had to defend herself. At times the threat of political absorption was serious. But even during periods of political peace, particularly indeed at such times, there was the danger of religious lapse. There was always the temptation to revert to paganism, and among the chosen people themselves there were elements who favored this.

However, Israel did not develop a theology of universalism because of actual contacts with other peoples. The operative factor was the deepened dimension of faith which these contacts brought about, chiefly during the exile. Acknowledgment of Yahweh as the Totally-Other, the absolute master of human destiny, meant seeing him as the universal creator. It meant that all nations as well as Israel were subject to him. He had his plans for all peoples: in the salvation to come they would have their place, as well as in the judgment. With a keener appreciation of the implications of universal creation came a better realization of the universal dimension of God's plan. But all the time the idea was that in the Kingdom to be Israel had a special place.

While waiting for the day of Yahweh the role of other peoples in salvation history was a sporadic one only. Yahweh's use of them, in the final analysis, was to help the chosen people, or chastize them for their faults. Israel was the people of witness, the unique race chosen from among others as the avenue towards faith in Yahweh.

After the exile Palestinian Israel became recessionist: it

severed its contacts with the pagan world as far as possible. Israel of the Diaspora on the contrary did not hesitate to seek integration in its surrounding environment, to make a strenuous effort of assimilation with other cultures. With full awareness it began to open the doors to pagans of goodwill. Nevertheless its mission, we should note, was not one of proselytism: the overall purpose was to increase the numbers of the chosen people.

Christ, the light of the nations

It was in universalist terms, a Kingdom open to all, that Jesus actually did inaugurate the expected Kingdom. Cultic exclusiveness is abolished. The blind, the lame, the leprous are invited to the banquet. He associates with publicans and sinners, it is for their sake he has come. Even the Gentiles receive the summons. He did concentrate his ministry on the chosen people themselves; he wanted to make them the missionary instrument in the Kingdom. But while they constantly tended to regard God's gratuitous choice as a privilege, Jesus tried to make them understand that choice by God meant responsibility more than anything else.

One fact was soon to become evident, the refusal by the chosen people to follow God's design, and it is this which brings the universalism of Jesus' teaching into sharper focus. The Kingdom, which was designed for the heirs, will be taken from them and given to the Gentiles. When gospel episodes tell of Jesus' contacts with pagans, there is emphasis on the manner in which he is struck by their faith, their unreserved acceptance of the good news.

As the universalist angle becomes prominent, the true nature of the Kingdom becomes evident. It is open to all: it is not of this world: it has appeared among men, but is totally beyond their control. Access to the Family of the Father is a completely gratuitous gift from God, and the consequence is that all privileges are abolished.

The pivotal point of the Kingdom is Jesus himself. In his

person it is established in its true character, at once transcendent and immanent. He is rejected by his own people; but he
gives up his life for the benefit of all. The paschal mystery
means that there is an end once for all to Jewish particularism.

The universal Church

Little by little the first generation of Christians came to realize
what is entailed in the abolition of Jewish privileges. Time had
to elapse before the terrestrial Jerusalem actually ceded to the
celestial, before Christians born in paganism obtained full rights
of citizenship in the pentecostal Church. The consequences of
Christian universalism were gradually realized, and it was
essential that the realization should come. Saint Paul helped a
great deal. He really saw the cross of Christ as the definitive
razing of barriers between Jew and Gentile.

In the domain of doctrine there was a corresponding development. In the case of Saint Paul it was not until the letters of the
captivity that the Church was disentangled from those overly
terrestrial links to the mother church of Jerusalem, and could be
seen in terms of ascent with Christ to the Father.

Universalism then in the Church has a double dimension. She
cannot be reckoned in the ordinary roster of terrestrial groupings; individuals, peoples, cultures are summoned to take their
place in her fold. She is none the less a historical reality. Constantly, to achieve her mission, she draws upon the riches of
the nations. She assumes the lineaments of the national group
where she finds herself established. What Jesus did for Israel she
does for various cultural groups. She becomes rooted in their
spiritual tradition, but her manner of doing so demonstrates her
essential transcendence. The universal Church may be rooted in
a local environment, but her business is to demonstrate in this
environment that she is open to all.

Let us not deceive ourselves. Wherever she is established the
possibility of regression will beset the Church. We Christians
always run the risk of confusing the universal Church with the

actual visage she presents in our particular environment. Genuine universalism will be jeopardized in all these cases. The spiritual extension of the Church, on the other hand, the assimilation within her confines of people of very great diversity, is the guarantee of genuine universalism. And it is towards this end that ecumenical activity is directed.

The universal call to salvation

Missionary activity is the inevitable outcome of universalism in the Church. At the very origins, realization of the urgency of such activity grew in direct proportion to awareness of the implications of genuine universalism. The "going out" from Jerusalem was dictated at the beginning by the turn of events. But when the Antioch church was established, the community in full assembly dispatched its chiefs, Barnabas and Paul, as missioners, and from then on it was clear that missionary enterprise was essential to the whole idea.

It remains essential because the non-Christian world is essentially related to the Church. She is obliged to establish herself wherever the divine summons to salvation in Jesus Christ brings men together, irrespective of their religious or sociological circumstances. So she must always be taking on new aspects, always adapting herself to new cultures. The treasure of living tradition she possesses strengthens her for this task, and also the readiness to recognize the grace at work in the non-Christian world, which can bear fruit within her fold.

Everyone ought to be concerned with missionary endeavor, but not every member has the same role to fulfill. A missionary function in the strictest sense will be the province of some. Wherever they find themselves, wherever they are sent, in their persons genuine Church membership will have to be combined with membership of the non-Christian world. The means of transmitting the mystery of Christ to the people being evangelized will depend on their fulfillment of this delicate double role. And if all cannot be missionaries in the strict sense, nevertheless the regulative principle of their daily lives must be the overall missionary endeavor. This is not just one obligation among many others laid on the Church; it is the keystone of the whole structure.

We have clear evidence from Church history that whenever the Christian world extended its spatial frontiers, or whenever a new order took the place of an old one, people were inspired to undertake the missionary charge imposed. Each time, however, success in the enterprise depended upon whether the general body of Christians followed in the missionaries' footsteps.

Every Christian generation faces a new missionary task. The one confronting our generation is difficult. For the first time in history the cultural groups are unavoidably involved with one another. In this context, our task is to point out that Jesus Christ by his cross (which is also that of the Church) has razed all barriers of separation between men. In view of all this the missioners of tomorrow, it could well be, will be agents of intercommunion above all, carrying out a universal mission that is unique.

The Eucharist, the mystery of catholicity

Each celebration of the Eucharist has a thrust towards universalism, because the most continuous tradition unites the Eucharist and the Church. There is a sense in which celebration of the Eucharist is a bringing to birth of the Church, a propagation of the mystery of universal summons to salvation in Jesus Christ. Whatever be the diversity between them, the barriers of separation, those hearing the summons are invited to the Feast. In other words, what is actualized in the celebration is catholicity itself.

In the mode of celebration, and indeed, on a broader scale, in the whole tenor of ecclesial practices, it is vitally important that the element of catholicity be evident. Too often eucharistic celebrations carry the sociological stamp, too exclusively, of the participants. In principle, they are open to all, but in fact they are not. The regular congregation feels at home; others feel like strangers. We know from history why such celebrations were frequently indifferent expressions of catholicity. In our day the success of missionary endeavor will depend on the extent to which the Eucharist becomes the distinctive sign of catholicity, the witness *par excellence*. If Christians assemble to partake of the Word and the Bread, they should realize that the whole of humanity is included in the communion offered.

2. The Theme of Universalism of Faith

Here the purpose is to show that universalism is of the very essence of faith in Jesus Christ. We shall see how it is displayed in missionary endeavor among all humanity, and thus we can hope to understand why the missionary task is one of such extraordinary depth and duration.

Ideologies of universal thrust are by no means infrequent in human history. Christians indeed, with some idea of rapprochement with such ideologies, show a tendency to modify the universalism of their faith, thinking in terms of some kind of universal brotherhood. That the gospel *can* be manipulated in this way is fully demonstrated by the life of someone like Gandhi, say. Yet that sort of understanding will not penetrate its secret, the mystery of the man-God, Jesus Christ. Nor will it lead to the efficacious living of the gospel, man's participation in the divine life.

The particularism of faith in Israel

The spiritual pilgrimage of Israel led to acknowledgement of God as the Totally-Other, the universal Creator, the absolute Master of destiny in the case of all peoples. The plan of Yahweh included, of necessity, all nations; there was no escape from his all-powerful intervention. This was not their original theology, but onwards from the Babylonian exile we can say that it became the accepted view. If one considered God's approach to men, universalism was evidently of the essence of faith.

But what about man's approach to God? Recognition of a saving God required fidelity on the part of Israel. According to the terms of the Covenant the response to the divine gift on the part of man was not made adequate by mere membership of the chosen people. But what *did* constitute the required fidelity? This was the very question which brought about, under the guidance of the prophets, a period of intense interiorization, so that gradually the moral requirements of the Covenant became clear. Few enough met the requirements, and so developed the idea of the small Remnant. These were the Poor of Yahweh, who would reap the fruit of the promises, because they placed everything in God's hands and observed the Law with love. True, God's plan is universal, but only the remnant will be saved. Others will incur the judgment.

An obvious consequence of this was that practice of Israelite faith did not inculcate any sense of mission. Nowhere indeed was particularism more in evidence. It is true that after the exile Jewish communities of the Diaspora made a considerable effort to be open to their environment, and to become assimilated. They looked for followers. But the motive was not conversion. They wanted to swell the ranks of the chosen people, not to direct Gentiles towards the living God by paths other than membership in this group.

Christ and the universalism of faith

With the intervention of Christ the essentially universalist character of faith became clear. Here the response of faith to God's loving initiative emanated from a person whose condition was a 'filial' one, by virtue of the hypostatic union. The response derived its value from the fact that he was the only Son, not from any creatural power. It was not based in other words on any moral quality, however sublime, but on his quality as Son. His achievement in the moral order was of course attuned to this perfect "yes"; but it was not its source.

So it was that in the salvation brought by Jesus Christ no cognizance was taken of privilege arising from race, intelligence or virtue. Whatever their condition, or their situation, all men, by virtue of their adoptive sonship, are called to answer the filial "yes" to God in Jesus Christ. No one is excluded from the invitation — it is the expression of the greatest love possible.

There is abundant evidence of this universalism in the life of Jesus. He takes his place in the ranks of the poor of Yahweh, but he does not hesitate to break through all forms of particularism. He keeps company with publicans and sinners, rejecting the prohibitions which set people into special social categories. The pagans he encounters, who live by faith, he is always ready to praise.

The universal Church of believers

When we reflect on the universalism of faith we are inevitably led towards a deeper understanding of the catholicity of the Church in all its mystery. The mere affirmation that the Church is open to all peoples, adaptable to all cultures because it is bound to none, is of itself by no means sufficient. The sense in which all men have the right to feel at home in the Church must be clarified, and the manner in which she honors the claim she makes.

We have already seen that recognition of the Savior of the world does not imply any cultural uprooting. The only thing required is conversion, renouncement that is of any form of particularism in one's native religious tradition. When the mystery of Christ takes root among a people, the effect is constructive, not destructive. The human beings that are called are called in all their diversity. Any avenue of search for God, once the necessary purification has taken place, can be successfully pursued within the confines of the Church.

The accommodation of such avenues of religious search, in all their diversity, which lead to the discovery of God in Jesus Christ, depends on the degree of realization among the people of God of the universalist dimension of faith. If we live our faith in this sense, we shall be demonstrating as perfectly as possible our fidelity to the commandment of unlimited brotherly love. This is more than merely accepting others as different to ourselves. It means the desire to promote otherness, renouncement of any attempt to annex. Only on the basis of such true love can we adequately honor the claims of universalism. It is the deep level at which catholicity is manifested as a requirement of communion. As they grow in numbers what we must find among the people of God is exchange of life and energy. So will the multiplicity of avenues of religious seeking, all leading to the unique mystery of Jesus Christ, become a reality in the Church.

Universalism of faith and missionary obligation

We have much rich teaching on this matter in the history of the primitive community. From the moment when events compelled the infant church to shed all vestiges of Jewish particularism, mission was perceived to be a requirement of the faith. The decisive change of front on this issue took place in fact at Antioch. Prior to that the majority of Christians were convert Jews; there was little understanding of the fact that pagans who wished to be disciples of the Risen Lord would not wish to accept the obligations of Mosaic Law. Antioch was the third city of the Empire, and convert pagans were sufficiently numerous to confront the local community with the real problems posed by entry into the Church. It was due to them that Christianity made contact with a world other than the Jewish one; the environment led them to see the genuine universalism implied by faith in Jesus Christ. Barnabas and Paul proclaimed that one did not need to become a Jew before becoming Christian, and they saw to it that this was ratified by the apostolic Church of Jerusalem. Soon afterwards there was an event of quite incalculable importance, the dispatch of its leaders by the community as missionaries. A faith shorn of all particularism, if genuinely practiced, was seen to lead naturally to missionary endeavor. In fact, the only way to live up to such a faith is to attempt to spread it among others, to apply the new commandment of unlimited love.

The situation in the Church today is not unlike that we have just described. Everywhere we encounter men and women, whose cultural environment is not that of the Church. Some of them actually constitute the young churches of Asia and Africa. Under the influence of science and technology the whole complex of cultures is undergoing a profound transformation. A new world is coming to birth, and the fact that more and more Christians show the influence of this change gives the Church itself a new look. In such circumstances we ought to shed any vestiges, as the Church did in Antioch, of particularism, and display in full clarity the universalism of our faith. The task is a difficult one, because the strong Graeco-Roman heritage has become as it were a second nature.

We know that Vatican II has initiated a profound renewal in this domain. At the Council the idea of large diversity among the people of God was accepted quite deliberately. If, however, the different members are to coexist in a single Church, if each is to constitute an irreplaceable stone in the common edifice, there must be constant interchange. When the Council speaks of dialogue this is what it means, displaying a charity, the quality of which appears in the developments it inspires. The dialogue should take place in the texture of daily living, with all the human confrontations that it implies. It is not a domestic ecclesiastical affair; it is the mind of the Church that this should serve the cause of peace among all men. So, unity in diversity can become the great ecclesial sign, convincing the world that walls of separation between peoples have been effectively razed by Jesus Christ. When missionary endeavor is understood in such terms, manifestly it is an outgrowth of universalism in our faith. The dialogue, of which the charity of Christ is the living source and inspiration, must necessarily ensue among all human beings. When we see the missionary enterprise measured against the long vicissitudes of human history, we comprehend why it is a task always urgent, but yet of extraordinary duration.

The Eucharist as source of universalism in the faith

The believer enters into living contact, of the most intimate kind, with the mystery of Christ in the eucharistic celebration. At this hallowed moment the baptized Christian finds himself capable of realizing fully what universalism means, what it demands. It is only the adoptive son who can follow the First Born into this realization.

It would be wrong however to believe that all this will happen automatically. The actual mode of celebration, and of participation, are very important. The lesson that should be inculcated is that the Kingdom into which the believer is initiated is the gift of universal brotherhood acquired once for all in Jesus Christ. When we receive that gift it means that we discover for ourselves the great gap that divides what is already accomplished from what, in terms of human history, remains to be done.

As the celebration concludes, everyone should be clearly conscious of the universal brotherhood in Jesus Christ, and of what they still have to do. If universal brotherhood is to be a reality in the lives of men, their awareness should be clear and without compromise. So can the members of the Church hope to be bearers of the Good News of salvation as they live their daily lives.

FIRST DAYS OF THE YEAR

I. 1 John 2:22-28
1st reading
January 2
With this passage John concludes his diatribe against false doctors who deny that Jesus is the Christ (v. 22). He is not thinking of the Jews who denied that Jesus was the Messiah, but of Cerinthus who like the Docetists and Gnostics denied the divinity of Christ. He considered him a demiurge, an instrument in the hands of God, but not in himself God.

a) John's main contention is that whoever denies the divinity of the *Son* cuts himself off from the Father (v. 23) and therefore also from eternal life (v. 25). To "acknowledge" the Son (v. 23) is indeed more than a speculative admission of his divinity, it means adherence to his commandment of love. It therefore involves clinging to his innermost life and to the Father who unceasingly gives it to him. The theology here is typically Johannine: no one can go to the Father except through the Son (Jn 14:6); the Son alone can reveal the Father (Jn 1:8; 14:7); to know the Son is to know the Father (Jn 8:19).

b) The conclusion of the passage read today is of sacramental character; it is through instruction as catechumens (v. 24) and through the baptismal anointing (v. 27) that the knowledge of Christ is acquired, a knowledge that develops into communion with him (such is the theme of "dwelling") and therefore into communion with the Father. Though he repeat the words of this catechesis, the heretic can know no union either with Christ or with the Father. Adherence to Christ, on the other hand, leads one into the movement of the Spirit (represented here by the anointing), who constantly instructs the faithful from within (v. 27), thus also constantly increasing the instruction received originally.

II. John 1:19-28
Gospel
January 2
The commentary on this gospel was made at the third Sunday of Advent, gospel of the second cycle.

III. 1 John   These verses begin the second part of John's
2:29-3:6   first letter. So far he has mainly treated of
1st reading   union with God and knowledge of Him. He
January 3   now deals more fully with the same ideas,
                  but from the angle of filiation.

a) The preceding verse (1 Jn 2:29) talks of our being be-gotten by God, a strong expression of God's gift of life (cf. 1 Jn 3:9; 4:7; 5:1, 4, 18). Already in his gospel John had stressed the necessity of rebirth in baptism (Jn 3:3-8).

Because of this, Christians have a right to be called God's children (v. 1). But because this expression might seem am-biguous since Jewish liturgy (Dt 14:1) and mystagogic religions also gave this title to their initiates, John insists on the fact that the Christian is truly a child of God, because he actually shares in the divine life ("that is what we are," v. 1).

Our sonship is a reality, though it is still in a state of growth. That is why the world which refuses to know God cannot per-ceive it either.

b) A growing reality, the divine sonship of the Christian is also an *eschatological reality* (v. 2). Unknown to the world, it sometimes goes unnoticed even by the Christian himself whose life is often commonplace and superficial. He should know that his sonship, now only perceived in a confused manner, will reach its fullness in the world to come. Unlike human religions and techniques of divinization which purport to confer upon man an equality with God through processes full of pride, John teaches his correspondents that the way to deification (cf. Gn 5:5) requires purification (v. 3): for only the pure of heart shall see God (Mt 5:8; Heb 12:14).

c) This notion of *purification as condition for the vision of God* and hence for our filiation probably originates in some ritual. The High Priest of the Jews went through numerous ablutions and purifications before entering into the Holy of Holies to "see the face of the Lord" (Pss 10/11:7; 16/17:15; 41/42: 1-5). But the priest of the new alliance, purified by his filial obedience (Heb 9:11-14; 10:11-18), also purifies those in union with him, insofar as they share with him in a priesthood of love and filial obedience.

The Eucharist works this purification in us, making us worthy of being God's children, because it recalls to the assembly how the son lived his sonship in death and rejection of sin.

IV. John 1:29-34
Gospel
January 3

John the Baptist diverts attention from his own person to that of Christ, who is now present among men, but not "known" (Jn 1:26).

Originally the text of the passage probably ran thus:
(31) And I too did not know him; but it is in order that he be manifested to Israel that I have come to baptize (33b, c, d) and he who sent me to baptize said to me "He on whom you shall see the Spirit descending and remaining it is he. . ." (34) Yes, I have seen and bear witness that it is the Chosen One (the Son) of God. (29 and 35) The following day John was still there with two of his disciples; seeing Jesus coming to him he said "Behold the lamb of God who takes away the sin of the world"

To this primitive account certain items from the synoptic tradition were added, like the allusion to baptism of water and the contrast between this and baptism of the Spirit (vv. 31-33). The link with the context was assured by another hand which dates the episode ("the following day", vv. 29 and 35) with a view to grouping the events in one week, and recalls at verse 30 a prophecy already cited at verse 27.

Thus the primitive account is centered on the *knowledge of the human-divine personality* of Christ. He is in the world, but no one has the means of knowing him (Jn 1:26), not even John (Jn 1:31, 33) who is on this account the least in the Kingdom (Mt 11:8-10; Lk 7:28 and Jn 5:33-36).

But an insight makes him realize that Christ is "Son of God" in the royal sense of the phrase (v. 34), and while baptizing Jesus he actually comes to understand the texts of Isaiah, 11:2; 42:1-7 and 61:1. He discerns that the baptism had the character of a messianic investiture. In the Baptist's declaration the "descent of the Spirit" had a messianic significance, but for the evangelist the Spirit is really a divine person, a divinizing force (Jn 15:26) who invests the risen one with his lordly powers.

The Baptist concludes his testimony by saying that he has actually discovered the "Chosen One of God" or the "Servant" of God of Isaiah 42:1-2 (v. 34). What the evangelist does is take advantage of ambiguity in the Aramaic word, penetrate beyond the Baptist's meaning, and attribute to him the affirmation "I have seen the *Son* of God." In verses 29 and 35 the Baptist uses the Aramaic word *talia* to designate Christ. Doubtless he had in mind the Servant of Isaiah 42:1-2, and meant by this that Christ is actually the Servant who will inaugurate messianic times, disseminate a Spirit who will help men toward sinlessness and thus really "take away" sin from the world (v. 29). *Talia* however could also mean *lamb*, and the designation of the Messiah as lamb had a special relevance. It suggested at once the suffering servant and the paschal mystery, both fulfilled in the person of him who takes away the sin of the world.

The Christian should make the evangelist's view his own. Man cannot be saved by man, even though he be Messiah, or by anyone except God. He must become the interlocutor of God, and the dialogue must be that which informs from all eternity the relation between the Son and the Father. The Messiah is Savior because he is man and Son of God, holding eternal colloquy with his Father.

V. 1 John 3:7-10
1st reading
January 4

Having dealt with the likeness to God which is the privilege of his children, John goes on to contrast these with the children of sin, whose life shows a likeness to the devil.

a) He first implores Christians not to be led astray by false doctors; pointing out the test by which they can be recognized: their manner of living. The believer is characterized by justice (observation of the law and particularly of love; vv. 7 and 10); while the unbeliever leads a sinful life and does not observe the law (v. 8).

John here adopts a semitic approach: he contrasts the *mystical union* of the sinner with the devil with the mystical union of the believer with God. Obviously, these unions are not of the same order; the latter belongs to God through a real regeneration, the former belongs to the devil because he shares the evil that has prevailed among men since the beginning (cf. Jn 8:44). If belonging to the devil keeps man a sinner, belonging to God puts him outside sin (v. 9), not that the Christian will not sin (cf. 1 Jn 2:1; 5:16), but his basic condition is no longer evil.

b) The expression *child of God* (v. 10), contrasted with the child of the devil, is a Hebraism which in translation ("child of" is a rendering of the Hebrew "Ben") is liable to be misleading. The Hebrew phrase is in fact somewhat vague, and the idea could be just as well covered by terms like "dependent on," or "in communion with." To be a child of God then is to accept his life and his word, to decide to live one's life in communion with his word and in his Spirit.

VI. John 1:35-42
Gospel
January 4

The first events of Jesus' public life are fitted by Saint John somewhat artificially into a single week (cf.: "the next day," "the following day" in vv. 29, 35, 43; "three days later" in Jn 2:1). Thus the events read today cover two days, and in some cases even the exact time of day is known (v. 39b: the tenth hour; v. 41: early next morning, though the text is here not certain). Such remarkable chronological precisions, as well as the use of words with a double meaning (as "to live" in v. 38), leads us to assume that John intends a deeper and more mysterious message than the mere events.

a) The obvious message of the narrative is quite simple. A couple of friends, Andrew and probably Philip (whom we always find together in the gospel: Jn 2:40-45; 6:5-9; 12:20-21; Ac 1:13), both of them disciples of the Baptist (v. 35) discover the Messiah and follow him. Such is the origin of their *apostolic vocation*. In passing on the information to their brothers and acquaintances (vv. 41 and 45), they bring about the call of Peter and Nathanael.

Underlying the narrative is a whole theology of vocation. Human relations can foster the birth of a vocation: friendship, common neighborhood, sharing of a similar ideal as disciples of the Baptist, and family ties are all circumstances which lead to the vocation of the four disciples.

Yet vocation remains a call of God and of Christ. The authority of Jesus when he changes Simon's name (v. 42b), his hard look at him (v. 42a), his mysterious knowledge of Nathanael (v. 48) and particularly his magnetism in drawing the two disciples of John to himself (v. 38) all show very clearly that, though it may have deep human roots, vocation is an initiative of God. As a call of God and a human attitude, it communicates the mystery of the God-made-Man to the life of all who are called.

b) John then proceeds to important doctrinal developments, valid for all disciples of Christ. To define the basic attitude of a disciple, he uses two key words: *follow* and *search* (vv. 37 and 38); he also uses three other key words to express their reward: *find, see* and *remain* (vv. 39 and 41).

For John the phrase "to follow Christ" has deeper implications than for the other evangelists: it implies taking all necessary steps to arrive one day where Christ "remains" (Jn 12:26; 10:9-

10). As Christ lives in a glory obtained through the cross, it seems normal that the disciple should also carry his own cross in order to follow him (Mt 16:24; Jn 12:26).

The theme of "remaining" is also close to that of glory (Jn 14:1-3; 14:10), and Andrew and Philip's stay with Christ at the end of their search (vv. 35-39) calls to mind the house of the Father where all disciples of Christ will one day join in his glory.

The "search-find" theme is just as meaningful (cf. Lk 2:41-51). Here we find an allusion to the discovery of Wisdom, found by those who seek it (Ws 6:12), as Christ was found by Andrew and his friend (v. 37), "early" (Ws 6:14), at the same time that Christ was found by Peter (v. 41). Wisdom also goes forward to meet those searching for it (Ws 6:16), as Christ meets Philip and Nathanael on the road (v. 43, 47). In this way, the theme takes on a sapiential character, not excluded either in Lk 2:41-51, where the narrative occurs in the context of praises for the wisdom of Jesus (Lk 2:40, 52).

Whether in the case of an apostle or a Christian, vocation follows an identical road and demands the same dispositions of the soul and the same attitude of God. He it is who invites us to share in his life and glory. But the road leading man to this glory has to be the way of the cross, where all egoism dies.

VII. 1 John   John has stressed that the condition of child
3:11-21   of God involves separation from a world that
1st reading   refuses to acknowledge the initiative of God.
January 5   Mankind is thus divided into the children of
   God and the children of the devil or of sin
(v. 9-10). But this distinction often turns into opposition, as those of John's audience who undergo persecution well know.

a) Mutual love is characteristic of Christians; it is the commandment they have known since the time of their conversion (v. 11). The opposite is true of hatred (v. 15). Both hatred and love have marked mankind ever since its origin: Abel was just and Cain impious; and the latter hated the former (v. 12). Christ too was hated by the world which put him to death. And Christians are likewise exposed to the hatred of the world because they are witnesses of love (v. 13).

Hatred can lead the Christian to death (v. 15), but it cannot hurt those who, having passed out of death into life (v. 14), prove this by the love that shines in their lives.

In his gospel John had already noted that whoever listens to the Word of Jesus has passed from death into life (Jn 5:24). Here he makes it clear that this Word of Christ is the commandment of love (v. 11). Whoever has love also has life; even if he is deprived of the life of the body, nothing can wrest eternal life from him.

b) John has seen *love exemplified in Jesus Christ* (v. 16a), who gave up his life for men. Love is therefore not a theory, but an example to be imitated (v. 16b). Here again we find the dimension of experience which John always gives to knowledge.

He also goes on to an immediate application: if we are to imitate the love of Christ by giving our lives for others, should we not all the more imitate him in sharing our goods with the poor (v. 17)?

Then he concludes: there can be no abstract knowledge of Christ, as there can be no love in mere words (v. 18).

The victory of love over hatred is shared by Christians in the Bread and Word of the Eucharist. But any witness of universal love will encounter opposition, and the Christian is aware that hatred — both in himself and in others — hinders this love.

Every eucharistic assembly helps him to emerge victorious, not only because of the strength and patience he draws from it but mostly because of the bonds of brotherly love forged in it.

VIII. John
1:43-51
Gospel
January 5

The narrative of the vocation of the first disciples is carried on today in the call of Philip and Nathanael (not necessarily to be identified with Bartholomew). This passage goes beyond the theme of vocation in its mysterious allusion to a new ladder of Jacob (v. 51). We need not return to the theme of vocation (commented on in the reading of Jn 1:35-42).

a) Nathanael was probably known as a doctor of the law. This would explain why Philip invites him to meet "the one Moses wrote about in the Law" (v. 45). He was also sitting under a fig tree in the manner of the teachers of the day (v. 48-49), and shared their disdain for anything coming from Nazareth (v. 46; cf. Jn 7:52; 7:41-42).

Philip is offering him a conversion: "Come and *see*." (v. 46; cf. Jn 1:39). For John, seeing implies more than a physical look at the human nature of Christ; it means contemplation of his glory and divinity. This is how John the Baptist "saw" the Spirit coming down on Christ (Jn 1:32; cf. Jn 14:19; 1 Jn 3:2; etc.).

b) What Christ asks of Nathanael is precisely this change of outlook; he wants him to pass beyond his humanity to the contemplation of his glory. By calling him a "true Israelite" (v. 47), Christ shows him that he will be able to realize fully what the patriarch Israel (Jacob) could only glimpse. This is the usual meaning of "true" in Saint John. As Jacob saw Yahweh at Bethel (Gn 28:10-17), so will Nathanael see God in the person of Christ (v. 51). But the change will be gradual; he has seen Jesus, the son of Joseph (v. 45), he will soon see the Messiah (v. 49), and eventually he will discover both the divinity (heaven laid open, angels, etc.) and the humiliation of Christ (Son of Man: v. 51; cf. Jn 3:14; 8:28; 12:22-34; 13:31).

In analyzing the progress of Nathanael's conversion, John is somehow sketching an outline for catechesis: from the humanity of Christ to his Messiahship, and from this Messiahship to the Paschal mystery of humiliation and exaltation.

A mere look can show the humanity of Christ, but this may often lead to disdain and lack of understanding. A further step must be taken to see Christ in the signs he has given us as the Messiah (v. 48; cf. Jn 2:11, 23; 4:54). But only true faith can decipher the greatest of all signs: the humiliation and glorification of the Son of Man in the Paschal mystery (Jn 2:18-21; 8:28; 3:12-15).

Angels are ascending and descending above the Son of Man (v. 51) to show the dual movement of the Paschal mystery. Who can go up to heaven but the one who came down from there (Jn 3:13)?

All of this urges the Christian to check the degree of his faith. Is he still considering Christ as man? Is he moved by the poverty and weakness of the child of Bethlehem? His religion may be mere sentimentality. Does he now understand the "signs" and miracles of Christ, and see in him the One sent by God? He may then run the risk of getting lost in apologetics. May he rather simply "see," in the Johannine meaning of the word, the complex humiliation and glorification of Christ in his Pasch, and agree in all simplicity to follow him and find out where he lives.

IX. Sirach   This praise of wisdom is inspired by that of
24:1-4, 12-16   Proverbs 8. The same themes appear in both
1st reading   instances, but in a much sharper light here
January 6   in the words of Ben Sira.

a) The main idea is that transcendence and immanence come together in Wisdom, whether in the assembly of the Most High (v. 12) or in the midst of the people (v. 1). It stands outside all time (v. 9: the phrase does not imply divinity) and yet it enters into the time of men (v. 8). It dwells in God's holy tabernacle (v. 10), and yet pitches its tent among men (v. 8).

b) It is difficult to be both transcendent and immanent; such an achievement indicates divinity. But it is still harder for man to understand this alliance of life and death, of the absolute and of limitation. So we see how Israel, the first to profit from divine immanence, found in this a pretext for hoisting itself to some kind of transcendence above other peoples. Verses 10-12 indeed wrongly render the mystery of incarnate transcendence as a privilege and monopoly for the people of Israel.

It may sometimes happen that the Church fails to understand properly the definitive association of transcendence and immanence in Christ Jesus. If she judges the world (which is her right), but isolates herself from it, refusing to judge herself as she judges the world; if she loses sight of those ties that set her in the world though not of it, she is failing in her essential mission. She preserves transcendence at the price of immanence; she adopts a monophysite attitude that is longer a witness to God-made-man.

X. Ephesians
1:36; 15-18
2nd reading
January 6

There are extracts from the blessing with which Paul begins his letter to the Ephesians. They correspond exactly with the classical form of Jewish thanksgiving: first, an introduction (v. 3), then a stanza ending with a blessing of God (vv. 4-6), a further stanza which also ends with a glorification of God (vv. 7-12), (not in today's reading), and finally an epiclesis imploring God to grant his faithful knowledge of his plan (vv. 13-18). This thanksgiving is probably inspired by a prayer from the daily Jewish ritual, deriving from it themes like the Fatherhood of God (v. 3), and the choice of God (v. 4). These are even phrases taken word for word, as praise (v. 6), love or grace (v. 6), etc. There is still however an important difference while the Jewish ritual thanked God for giving the Law, Paul gives thanks for the gift of his Son.

a) The introduction concentrates straight away not only on

prayer, but on the main themes underlying the whole letter. It is a veritable thanksgiving for salvation (presented here as a blessing), willed by the Father, merited by Christ, and realized by the Spirit.

The saving *blessings* for which God is praised are the death (v. 7) and glorification of Christ (v. 10), and the birth of divine life in man, through faith and baptism (v. 13), and in the world, because Christ is made Lord of all (v. 10). The phrase "of heaven" denotes everything other than the "human enemies" (Ep 6:12) or the "heavenly powers" superseded by Christ (Ep 4:7-16; 5:23). The phrase "in Christ," on the other hand, refers to the mediation by which the Father's blessings are realized, since Christ has supplanted the "flesh" and the "spirits" in the order of salvation.

b) The first stanza (vv. 4-6) shows how God's blessing benefits men who are called by Christ to holiness. It means choosing the Father's love, and it leads men to be sons of God. Here the stress is on the initiative of God in the work of salvation and consequently on the certainty of salvation. The object of this choice is holiness, i.e. sharing the life of God (Lv 19:2). The sharing is brought about by love, a love that goes the length of adopting man as son.

c) The *wisdom* Paul asks from God for his faithful (v. 17) is the supernatural gift already known to the sages of the Old Testament (cf. Pr 3:13-18) but considerably amplified in its Christian meaning. It is now the knowledge of the Father given in Christ Jesus (v. 17); it is knowledge of eschatology (v. 18), of the glory to be inherited, (cf. Ep 1:14) which (cf. Rom 9:23) contrasts so strongly with the misery of human existence (cf. Rm 8:20). Finally, it is the discovery of the power of God, shown first in the Resurrection of Christ (v. 20), but still at work in our own transformation.

d) Paul lingers a moment to contemplate this *divine power*, which he describes in synonymous terms: power, strength (v. 19).

This is not only the power displayed by God in creating the

world and imposing his will on it (Jb 38). It will even reverse these laws; since it can change a crucified into a risen Lord (v. 20), can place a man above all angels (v. 21b), and establish here and now the laws of the world to come (v. 21b).

e) But the power of God will display itself not only in the future. Here and now, everything is accomplished by it; it has made Christ the head of all things in the very mystery of the Church, the fullness of Christ (v. 22-23). Paul begs for his correspondents the gift of wisdom, because they must understand before all else that the Church is the sign of this power of God, displayed in Christ Jesus. It is indeed the unprecedented privilege of the Church to have as head the Lord of the universe, and to be his Body. The Church is not only subject to the Lord, as is the universe; she is indissolubly united to him, as a body is to its head. She is the fullness of Christ, in that she is the vessel holding his graces and his gifts. The phrase "all in all" suggests that this vessel is without limits. Such graces are conferred upon the Church with a view to her growth (Ep 4:11-13), so that she may reach one day the state of "perfect Man," which is the condition of humanity united in Christ, and enjoying the fullness of divine life.

XI. John 1:1-18
Gospel
January 6

Commentary to be found at the gospel for Christmas day, p. 189.

XII. 1 John 3:22-4, 6
1st reading
January 7

If true communion with God is reserved for eternity (1 Jn 3:2), how can we know whether it is with us already in this world? What assurance can we obtain from God if we do not even feel his presence? This passage provides an answer to such questions.

We can know that God dwells in us (v. 24) by the way we observe his commandments. If we observe them our heart will not accuse us (v. 21), we will be in security before God (ibid.), and we will pray to him with the conviction of being heard (v. 21; same teaching in Jn 15:15-17).

The commandment which gives assurance before God and guarantees his dwelling among us is twofold: believe in the name of Jesus Christ and love one another (v. 23). John presents these two precepts in such manner that they seem to form only one. The apostle's view in effect is that they do not make up two distinct virtues — faith on the one hand, and charity on the other. They are the vertical and horizontal dimensions of the same attitude (cf. Jn 13:34-36; 15:12-17): by our faith we are children of God, and from this filiation stems our brotherly love (1 Jn 2:3-11).

It is not easy to hold on to both the horizontal and vertical dimensions of God's commandment. Today more than ever, the Christian is prone to seek a brotherly love more authentic and more universal, but without necessary reference to God, thus forgetting that love is rooted deep in the life of God Himself.

To believe in Jesus Christ as St. John demands is to believe that the Father loves all men through his own Son; it is willing participation in this mediation of love, recognizing that Jesus has responded to the Father's love in an unprecedented manner, and being ready to follow his renunciation and his filial obedience.

Each Eucharist puts Christians in simultaneous relation with God and all men. It does not gather them in order that they may first give thanks to God and then turn their attention to others: the simultaneousness of the two attitudes makes up its essence.

XIII. Matthew 4:12-17, 23-25
Gospel
January 7

This passage inaugurates the first ministry of Christ in Galilee. The message and ministry of John the Baptist have been an occasion for Jesus to discover the will of his Father. Christ let himself be baptized (Mt 3:13-17) because he felt that the Father wanted him to be a disciple of the Baptist. He will be a roving rabbi, thus taking over the torch abandoned by John (v. 12; cf. Mk 1:14); but he will leave Judea and the valley of the Jordan, so dear to John, to go after the lost sheep of the North and of Galilee.

Thus awakened to his role, Christ becomes a preaching rabbi, loyal to the Baptist's message of conversion (cf. v. 17, compared with Mt. 3:2) but spreading it, if not among the pagans proper, at least among those Jews who are no longer Jews except in name, so deeply immersed are they in the darkness of paganism.

Particularly sensitive though he is to this universalist intention, Matthew nevertheless feels the need to justify it; for his contemporaries believed that the Kingdom was to be made known only to the Jews, who would remain true and unsullied. He introduces therefore verses 13-16 and the quotation from Isaiah 8:23-9:1 (which he modifies by adding the word "sit" in the darkness; v. 16), to strengthen further the impression that the Syro-Palestinian regions are really embedded in paganism.

Christ's faithfulness to the Baptist's message is thus coupled with a great independence with regard to his Essenian master. He does not want to gather round him only the "pure" ones, nor submissive disciples: his message must reach everyone. That is why he does not hesitate to break with John, not on the substance of the message, but on the way of preaching it. He leaves Judea, does not impose the baptismal rite, and becomes itinerant to be sure of meeting men in all walks of life.

Christ therefore takes a stand in favor of God's universalist plan, and to this end breaks away from the communities of "pure" and "practicing" Jews in Judea. Should not our parishes and eucharistic assemblies strip themselves a little more, and open up more widely to people who are not too interested in the Christian message?

XIV. 1 John   After a parenthesis, in which he warns his
4:7-10   readers against error (1 Jn 4:1-6), John re-
1st reading   turns to the subject of his letter: God, source
January 8   and model of brotherly love.

We already know that John gives the terms "to beget" and "to know" (v. 7) the meaning of communion with God (cf. 1 Jn 1:1-4). Now the sign of this communion is love, since in the eyes of John love finds *its source in God* (vv. 7-8). Our sonship and our knowledge (faith) are therefore the principles of our charity.

But how can we be sure that God is love? For John the most luminous proof is the Incarnation of the Son (v. 9) most beloved (one of the meanings of the Johannine expression "only Son"; cf. Jn 1:14-18), whose mission it is to make us live the very life of God (v. 9; cf. Col 3:4; Ph 1:21) and to be a propitiation for our sins (v. 10: cf. Ep 2:4-5). John is not speculating on the nature of God; he is thinking about the diverse manifestations of his love in Jesus Christ.

But what is there specifically divine in this love? Verse 10 answers the question: true love is the one that takes the initiative. God alone can do it. Our human love is nothing but a response to this love which existed before us (Jn 15:16).

Experience of sin is one of the ways that lead to the discovery of the love of God, because the sinner who returns to God feels that he has been awaited from the first. Furthermore, he feels that it is the love of God that has urged him to return.

Even though this love be divine it can be lived by man (v. 7) insofar as he is ready to take the initiative, and that will sometimes entail forgiveness and forgetting faults.

XV. Mark 6:34-44   This passage begins a new section in the
Gospel   gospel of Mark. We are no longer concerned
January 8   with the first apostolic gestures of the rabbi
Jesus, with his triumphs over disease and de-

mons. This is a particular section, the over-all unity of which depends on the theme of bread. We have two multiplications of bread (Mk 6:30-44; 8:1-10), discussions about the meaning of ablutions before eating bread, and about false leaven (Mk 7:1-23; 8:11-20), a discussion with a Gentile about the crumbs of bread she requests (Mk 7:24-30), and so on. For this reason the section is sometimes called the "section of bread." What we are dealing with is more probably a collection of narratives that were already for the most part put together before the composition of the gospels. The purpose of the collection was initiation into the mystery of Christ in its original dimensions.

The beginning of the passage (vv. 30-34) is introductory, and indicates the importance of the apostolic group in Jesus' system of catechesis. Verse 34, which is proper to Mark, is highly significant. The image of sheep without a shepherd is borrowed from Numbers 27:17 where it reflects the anxiety of Moses to find a successor lest the people be without leadership (cf. Ez 34:5). Christ thus is presenting himself as *Moses successor*. He can take control of the flock, nourish the sheep and lead them to safe pasturage. The whole "section of bread" seems to be designed to show Christ as the new Moses who offers true manna (vv. 35-44; Mk 8:1-10), triumphs like Moses over the waters of the sea (Mk 6:45-52), frees the people from the legalism to which the Pharisees had reduced the law of Moses (Mk 7:1-13), and opens the way to the Promised Land even for the Gentiles (Mk 7:24-37).

b) Jesus performs the miracle of the multiplication of loaves in favor of a multitude whom he pities. But he has in mind also the *formation of his apostles,* whose services he uses in the preparatory stages (vv. 35-39, 41b), and whom he induces afterwards to reflect on the meaning of the miracle (Mk 8:14-21). This educative aspect of a miracle is, in Saint Mark, a new departure. No longer does Christ work wonders merely to satisfy people's material needs: he does so to reveal his mission among men, and to prepare his disciples for an understanding of the Eucharist.

c) In fact it is Mark above all who gives a eucharistic emphasis to the whole happening. The three synoptics take liberties, relatively speaking, with their versions of the general narrative (only 20% of the words are common); but in describing Christ's gestures (v. 41) their language is 80% identical. Here, without doubt, we have evidence of the veneration attached already to this central detail, where Christ's gestures are the very ones he used at the Supper.

The other synoptic accounts mention at the beginning loaves and fishes; but, as they proceed, they gradually concentrate on the bread only (Mt 14:17; Lk 9:13; Jn 6:9; Mt 15:34), thus indicating their eucharistic bias. Mark, who to the end keeps mentioning the fish (vv. 41b and 43b; cf. too Mk 8:7, a strictly Marcan text), is an exception to the rule. But the mentions of fish are clearly later additions, awkwardly inserted in the text. For the thanksgiving Mark 8:7 uses *eulogein*, a phrase of Greek origin, where in Matthew 8:6 we have *eucharistein*, a Palestinian phrase. There is every reason to believe that the additions were made by someone more concerned about historical accuracy than eucharistic symbolism. If they were made by Mark himself, this would indicate that the source he was using had already a eucharistic bias. So we have evidence that the eucharistic interpretation of the multiplication miracle goes back to oral tradition. Even before the composition of the gospels the primitive community was eucharistic in worship. This deals effectively with the suggestions sometimes made that the Eucharist is a later invention by the Church.

d) It might be urged that in the multiplication miracle there is no formula of benediction for wine, and consequently a eucharistic interpretation for it becomes problematic. The fact is however that one of the principal notes in the chalice-blessing, that of *multitude* (Mk 14:24) is found here in the multiplication, expressly in verse 44, and elsewhere (v. 43) symbolically, to indicate that the nourishment offered by Jesus is destined for many other banqueters, who have not partaken of this repast. There are precisely twelve baskets of fragments (v. 43); because the twelve apostles who have ministered to the assembly, are destined to become missionaries to other guests not now present. So that the missionary aspect of the Eucharist is indicated: it only brings together those "already assembled" in order that they will go to gather the others.

It is clear then that the primitive catechetical tradition interpreted the multiplication narrative as symbolic of the Eucharist from the very beginning. The Supper repast was not seen as a farewell banquet for the few disciples and friends who were present. On the contrary, it was a meal for the host of believers that was destined to grow continuously as the Christian mission spread. Whatever length of time in years it took for this concept to take full shape in primitive Christian circles, we can regard it as fully developed in the source that Mark used. That would date it just twenty or thirty years after the crucifixion.

XVI. 1 John   After showing how God is the source of love
    4:11-18   (1 Jn 4:7-10), John defines the signs of com-
   1st reading   munion with God: charity (v. 12) and con-
   January 9   fession of faith (v. 15).

a) The knowledge we have of God's saving love for us (faith) induces us to love too (morals). Thus *dogma creates ethics.* True, faith and love here below are in a frail condition: faith rests on nothing but testimony (v. 14); for no one has ever seen God, nor can anyone see him before eternity (v. 12). As for love, it is our adventure, since one cannot feel God's love.

Nevertheless faith and love are the criteria of our communion with God (theme of indwelling: vv. 12, 15). For John, in the person of the Christian, these two virtues become fused. A de-

cision of faith implies love because it implies the sort of conversion that is impossible without giving oneself. The Christian
life is at once vertical and horizontal. Vertical, because we are
made aware that God is love (v. 16), that he has loved us to
the point of sending his Son (v. 14), that he wants to dwell in
us (vv. 15-16). Horizontal, because we are induced to love our
brothers as God loves us (v. 12).

b) Even though the passage contemplates fear (v. 18), or its
alternative, *confidence*, at the final judgment, the assertion is
made that love in its plentitude is offered the Christian in this
life. This is possible because the Christian can live in full communion with the Father and the Son, is without the fear of
punishment, and can approach God confidently, without fear.
This sort of assurance is not based on Christian sinlessness,
which would be illusory (1 Jn 1:8), but on God himself, the
all-knowing God who is aware of our weakness.

Love then drives out fear, not only where the perfect are
concerned, and the saints. The same sort of love can become the
possession of the weak because its power to annihilate fear is
based on God, not on relative clarity of conscience.

The most fundamental psychological states, love and fear, are
contemplated here. Man is basically a fearful being: he lacks
assurance in a hostile world. The pagan will try to liberate himself by concocting security rites. The atheist uses his own techniques: his self and his skills are divinized. The Jew exorcises
fear by finding the love and mercy of Yahweh in all events,
good or bad. For the Jew fear of the sacral ceases to be blind:
it becomes a desire to know God, to respond to his love.

With Jesus Christ man finds himself an active partner with
God in bringing about salvation. Consequently the Christian can
share atheist attitudes, where hunger is concerned, war, social
and international injustice. He bears witness to the transcendence of God, which is verified in the incarnation of Jesus Christ.

XVII. Mark
6:45-52
Gospel
January 9

Mark's account of the walking on the waters is to be distinguished from Matthew 14:22-33 because of the details he recounts and the commentary he gives (vv. 51-52). The narrative is awkward in its context. Verse 45 is contradicted by Mark 6:32 and 6:53. This seems to indicate that the walking on the waters did not follow the multiplication of loaves, and that the evangelist's attempt to connect the two incidents (v. 52) so that Jesus might be presented as provider of manna and conquerer of the waters, a new Moses, is contrived.

a) God's *victory over the waters* is an extremely important theme in Jewish cosmogony. Following ancient semitic traditions, the bible describes the creation of the world as a victory by God over the sea and the evil monsters it shelters (Pss 103/104:5-9; 105/106:9; 73/74:13-14; 88/89:9-11; Ha 3:8-15; Is 51:9-10). Then the victory over the Red Sea (Ps 105/106:9) and the eschatological victory over the Lake (Rv 20, 9-15) were taken as decisive stages in salvation history.

Consequently the first Christians interpreted the stilling of the tempest (Mk 4:35-41) and the walking on the waters as manifestations of him who was bringing the work of creation to fulfillment, and as signs of the advent of the Day of Yahweh (Ha 3:8-15; Is 51:9-10). Walking on water is an epiphany as it were of the divine power that dwells in Christ. By placing the episode though in this particular context Mark is stressing the fact that this power is the power of the new Moses.

b) The apostles however did not understand this epiphany: fear blinded their spirit. By Mark, Jesus is presented as the victim of absolute *incomprehension* (cf. again Mk 8:20-21). He had separated his apostles from the crowd, withdrawn them in order to give them a special training (v. 45), but now he realizes that, if they are to be gradually made aware of the mystery of his mission and his person, he must begin again at the beginning.

A proper understanding of the walking on the waters, an

affirmation that Christ has overcome the power of evil, means a realization of the cosmic dimensions of his achievement. Prior to him all creation was imprisoned in the solidarity of sin: he burst the bonds.

The Christian's victory is more than a victory over himself: it has cosmic reverberations. He really does overcome the world, the forces of which he can control. His mission is to roll back the onset of evil in those areas where it is still manifest, especially in sin and death, the twin cohorts of evil.

For this combat he is fortified by the Eucharist. Here he can share the victory of Christ himself over Satan and death.

XVIII. 1 John   Verses 19-21 take up again ideas that have
    4:19-5:4   been already analyzed. Here then commen-
    1st reading tary will be restricted to the latter verses,
    January 10 where John points out that being born "of
    God" (1 Jn 1:1-3), sonship with the Father,
can be verified by three precise criteria. They are as it were the three witnesses required by Jewish law to verify an assertion (Dt 17:6; 19:15; Nb 35:30): faith; love, the love of God and the brethren (vv. 1-2); and observance of the commandments (v. 3).

Dispositions such as this place the Christian in opposition to the "world": he is open to God, where the world is involved with itself (cf. Jn 3:2). At this point John introduces a new idea: the *Christian has overcome the world*. This victory is at once past (v. 4) and present (v. 5); past, at the moment of conversion, present, in the faith of each day. All the time the evangelist has in mind Christ's original, decisive victory over the world (Jn 16:33; cf. 1 Jn 5:6). When he conquered the "worldly" temptation to save himself. It is for his followers to conquer every tendency towards self-divinization by entrusting their whole salvation to God. That is why their victory can be said to begin with conversion and continue so long as their lives are governed by faith in God and by love.

But however apt it is in the Johannine context, where "world" has a very particular meaning, there is a danger in our idiom of interpreting the opposition between the Christian and the world very equivocally. It could be used to foster the idea that the Church is separate from the world and to oppose any well-intentioned attempts to establish dialogue between the two. Such a dualist concept of two divided entities is wrong. The Church does not even have to "go to the world" to summon it to conversion, and bestow on the world the gifts she has of faith and love. She *is* the world in process of becoming — she points towards a humanity gathered together by the spirit of love. If she is to fulfill her function she must, like Christ, put herself at the service of mankind, become as it were the catalyst of universal brotherhood.

Whenever any Christian group — a school, a political party, a union — begins to set man in opposition to his fellow man, that group is no longer doing the work of the Church, even though it involves a wrong interpretation of 1 John 5:1-5. The Church's only task is to bring about communion among men in the name of Jesus Christ, that communion to which the eucharistic assembly, the only absolutely genuine Christian institution, explicitly refers.

**XIX. Luke
4:14-22
Gospel
January 10**
Whereas Matthew presents Christ with the traits of an itinerant rabbi (Mt 4:12-17), Luke, much more of a liturgist, begins and ends his gospel with an account of the events that took place in the temple (Lk 1:5-23; 24:50-53) and has the ministry of Christ begin with a Sabbath liturgy of the synagogue.

This comprises two readings. The first was drawn from the Law (Pentateuch), to be read and commented on by a "doctor of the Law"; the second, of later origin, was normally taken from the prophets and could be read and commented on by anyone who was 30 years old. Since Jesus was 30 years old, he claimed the right to read and comment on the second reading. His first public discourse is therefore a liturgical homily.

a) Luke has not preserved Jesus' discourse but he sums up the message in just one phrase: "today the scriptures are fulfilled" (v. 21). All the *laws of homilies* are contained in this little verse. The liturgy of the Word is not a simple moral lesson of the catechism nor the affirmation of eschatological hope; it proclaims the fulfillment of the plan of the Father in the life of the assembly today. We no longer contemplate what happened in the past, whether a golden age or a time of failure; we no longer dream of an extraordinary future; we live in the present moment as the privileged place of the coming of the Lord.

The apostles on their part respected this homiletic practice of Jesus (cf. Ac 13:14, 42; 16:13-17; 17:1-3; 18:4). The Christian liturgy is consequently daughter of the liturgy of the synagogue; it enacts the recalling of the past and the hope of the future in "the celebration of today." Yet we may ask ourselves if the sermons preached in our Christian assemblies are faithful to that of Christ or to those of the doctors of the Law!

b) Christ (or Luke) seems to have purposely stopped the reading at the moment when the prophecy of Isaiah 61 announced "a year of grace." He passes in silence the following verse which announced the judgment of nations, and "a day of vengeance for our God" (Is 61:2), no doubt in order to place emphasis exclusively on the grace of God. These words of *grace* aroused the astonishment of the assembly (v. 22) and are the cause of the incidents recorded in verses 25-30. It is again in order to reinforce the idea that his mission is all of grace and not of condemnation that Christ (or Luke) adds to the citation of Isaiah 61:1-2 a verse borrowed from Isaiah 59:6 dealing with the freedom offered to prisoners.

Christ therefore defines his mission as a proclamation of the gratuitous love of God to everyone. Such a revelation could only scandalize the Jews who looked forward to an eschatology with all the eagerness that their hatred of pagans could provoke.

c) Luke attaches great importance to the role of the Spirit in the life of Christ: at baptism it is there to confirm the messianic vocation of Jesus (Lk 4:1); it loans its power to the working of miracles by Jesus (Lk 5:17; 6:19; 9:1); it assists in the selection of the apostles (Ac 1:2) and comforts him in his mission (Lk 10:21). It is the gift of the Father (Lk 11:13) and an important element in the last days (Lk 24:49; Ac 1:4-8; 11:16; 2:1-4). One can easily understand that Luke has retained the homily of Christ at Nazareth in the measure that it constitutes a recognition by Christ of his spiritual vocation.

To say that today the Word of God is fulfilled — which is the function of the homily — does not merely signify that an ancient prophecy is fulfilled or that an inspired text is suddenly enhanced. It is not the Word of the prophets or of the theologians that is fulfilled but that Word of God more profoundly that sanctifies humanity and the life and condition of man. To say that the Word of God is fulfilled is the same as saying that today humanity is rejoined to God in Jesus Christ. It is not therefore a matter of preaching a homily which is supposed to apply to such and such an inspired text, or apply such and such prophetic words to the events in the lives of the members of the assembly; it is rather a matter of revealing, in the same way that the gospel does for the privileged event of Jesus Christ, how the events actually lived by men and Christians are revelatory of the saving design of God. The biblical sources and vocabulary should be supplemented by sociological and psychological sources and vocabulary. It is necessary therefore to disassociate the work of Jesus Christ from socio-cultural context to which it is linked, a link which is often reinforced by the "word" of the evangelist in order to see it in action in the contemporary milieu, as a response to the need of the specific people to which the homily addresses itself.

Thus it is always to the present moment of man that the

homily reunites the present moment of God and deserves to be a function of the Word of God.

XX. 1 John 5:5-13 Verse 7 of this reading is certainly apocryphal.
1st reading It originated in the fourth century in some
January 11 ancient Latin versions as a gloss. The Vulgate did not have it originally, but adopted it later from the Old Latin versions. As late as the eighth century a number of copies of the Vulgate, and liturgical formularies, were without it.

Apart from this verse, the main idea of the reading is clear enough. When the Father gave eternal life to his Son, by raising him from the dead, he gave testimony to him (v. 11). We also have to accept this testimony that the Son in truth has life (v. 9), so that it may be "in us" (v. 10). This is brought about by faith (v. 10) and by the external action of the Spirit (v. 6). In order to testify that this life is in the Son, the Spirit makes use of three witnesses, according to the procedure of Jewish courts: its own testimony, that of water and that of blood. Water and blood denote the sacramental economy (Jn 19:34).

John's doctrine is therefore as follows: *faith* consists in believing that the Son of God has eternal life, especially since his resurrection, and that this life is our inheritance. This we believe through faith in the testimony of the Spirit. And this testimony is given through "water and blood."

Jesus of Nazareth did not consider man's earthly condition as a state of fall, a time of trial; nor did he postpone the perfect encounter of God with man to some tomorrow, in "another" condition. Rather he reveals to us the fact that the perfect response to the salvific initiative of God takes shape in death itself, formerly considered as a consequence of sin (water and blood: v. 8).

Jesus' obedience unto death for the love of all men demonstrates that all is grace here on earth, that everything, objectively speaking, is a sign of the Father's paternal goodwill — including death, the death of a condemned man — even when this condemnation to death has its source in man's rejection of love. The objective reality of man's earthly condition, in the eyes of the Creator, is not and cannot be profoundly damaged by sin. On the contrary, it must be said that God intervenes as a liberator in all that happens; he is essentially good, and he bestows the blessings of his providence upon the good and the evil alike.

The presence of the resurrected Christ in the Body which is his Church constitutes the foundation and permanent source of the Church's sacramental nature. The Church is truly the Temple of God's dialogue with man. The perfect sacrifice of Jesus' death on the cross is constantly actualized in the Church. But the sacramental nature of the Church is not evident to the same degree in all domains of ecclesial life. What is it, to begin with, in the domain of "rite," where man expresses the ultimate aims of his existence? It is in this domain that the Church has the mission of visibly assembling men; it is here that he displays the face of an "Institution." It is understandable, therefore, that the sacramental nature of the Church evokes above all the "sacramental rite." We must begin with a study of this sacramental nature, but without forgetting the importance of other developments.

In the domain of "rite," this sacramental nature has precise contours which affect the whole body of the Church, taken as an institution. On the one hand, the concrete acts in which everyone must participate have an objective reality which always takes precedence somehow over personal engagement. These acts form a part of the ritual pattern of the Church, making real the action of Jesus Christ. On the other hand, the Church's sacramental dimension is not distributed uniformly. It has a central nucleus, the Eucharist, and the activity of the institution apart from this is but a development of the assembly *par excellence* in the Eucharist, convoked by the local bishop.

This said, we must not reduce the Church's sacramental power to ritual acts alone. There is nothing here comparable to the automatism of pagan liturgies! The Word which accompanies the rite reminds us specifically of this: the ritual gesture must always be the expression of inner sacrifice. Christians have a considerable responsibility. Although it is true that the ecclesial institution never ceases for a moment to be sacramental, in the sense that the Head is always present in the Body, it is also true that sacramental efficaciousness may be more or less "present" in the Body. It is all very well for our celebrations to be beautiful, but it is essential that each one of us make an offering that is acceptable to God, and that the offering include the sacrifice of our life.

XXI. Luke   The three synoptics who recount this episode
5:12-16   of the healing of lepers see in it one of the
Gospel   first manifestations of the power of the young
January 11   rabbi over evil. They place the miracle in
                  Galilee — "in a city," Luke specifies (v. 12),
which seems unlikely, owing to the stringent law governing lepers (Lv 13:45-46). Matthew mentions these regulations in his narrative (Mt 8:5), to which he adds the healing of a pagan and a woman (Mt 8:1-15), thus presenting Jesus as gatherer of categories of human beings heretofore excluded from the chosen people. Luke sees in this miracle simply an occasion of wonderment for the crowd (v. 15).

The narrative of the healing of lepers is characterized by Christ's reaction when his *power as wondermaker* is revealed.

First he takes pity on the suffering he encounters. Contrary to Mark 1:41, Luke does not mention his sentiments. Yet this "emotion" and "compassion" are significant, for through them Christ demonstrates the powerful and healing love of the Father. He wants to cure the sick he meets, and in this appears his charism as wonderworker. Without it there would be no miracle. The love of Christ for his brothers brings God's love to them.

On the other hand, Jesus fears the charism which he has; he warns the man he has miraculously healed to keep it secret (v. 14a) and asks him not to evade the prescriptions of the law (Lk 13-14). Finally he turns away from the admiration of the crowd fearing that they will misinterpret his miracles (v. 16). Furthermore, he does not examine the faith of the man who seeks his help, as he will do later. He simply discovers the divine power which is in him and looks for the best ways to put it in operation.

The contemporaries of Christ united soul and body more closely than the Greeks. Illness was regarded as a reflection or consequence of some moral sickness. By healing the body therefore, Christ was led to awareness that his preaching inaugurated the eschatological time of victory over evil and the era of consolation (Lk 4:16-20; 7:22-23).

By building his life on love for brothers and obedience to his Father Jesus of Nazareth becomes the first member of humanity who is free from sin and guilt, and thus the sole source of genuine hope for mankind.

The cures by Christ constitute a moment when all creation is rectified by his life and by his person. Today, the healing of mankind has become the monopoly of science. The Christian cooperates, because he knows that he will really heal his brothers insofar only as his own faithfulness to the Father has freed him from evil.

XXII. 1 John
5:14-21
1st reading
January 12

Conclusion of the first letter of John presented under the form of a profession of faith ("we know").

a) The man who lives in communion with God (begotten by God: v. 18) does not know sin (cf. 1 Jn 3:6-9), says St. John. This does not mean that the disciple of Christ lives automatically in a sinless state! Moreover, the apostle declares that for anyone to pretend that he is without sin would be to live a lie before God (1 Jn 2:8-10; 5:16). The impeccability of which he speaks here emphasizes only the incompatibility of sin and the life of sonship. However, John affirms as well that the Son protects the man who lives in communion with God by giving him the knowledge (v. 20: cf. 1 Jn 1:1-5) necessary to keep him from the world and from evil (vv. 18-19).

b) The choice to be made between God and idols (v. 21) is a common theme in biblical literature. The history of Israel is dominated by the theme of separation from idols (Ws 6:25-32; 1 K 18:20-40; Mt 3:8-11). The prophets constantly compared the God of life with dead idols (Is 44:9-20; Ws 13:10-14; Dn 14); they contrasted a nature dominated by idols with history directed by God (Jr 2:26-37; Ps 106/107); the lies of false gods with the truth and fidelity of the true God (Is 46:1-7; Jr 10:6-16), the dumb silence of false divinities with the knowledge given by the one true God (Ho 2:21-22) a knowledge based on the covenant and mutual love (Ho 4:2; 6:6). John brings all these arguments together in the last two verses of his letter.

The Christian is constantly tempted to idolatrous worship such as love of power, of self, loving another falsely (1 Co 10:14-22; Mt 6:24-34; Ep 5:1-20; Rv 13:11-17). His struggle, however, prepares the way for God's final victory over idols (Rv 20:1-10).

The state of sinlessness of which John speaks does not mean a capacity to avoid sin. The problem of our life is not sins but sin itself. For Saint John sin is the opposite of the "communion" he speaks of from the very beginning of his letter. Sin is separation: separation between men, division of the individual within himself, separation of men from the fundaments of their being. This last separation is the most "original," the most fundamental, and the one which is the source of all others.

We have only an instant to reconcile the fundaments of our being. Our entire existence is plagued by constant distraction to the point of disjunction from the deepest part of ourselves. This is true sin: not an act, but a state of cleavage inside, because of the superficial idols which surround us.

The state of sinlessness proclaimed by John is the opposite of this dichotomy. It means harmony with the fundaments of our being, or at least the possibility of harmony. For the Christian it now has a name: Jesus Christ and his Spirit. This union progressively transforms our sinful state into a meaningful destiny: victory over idols and guilt.

XXIII. John   The synoptics have the ministry of Christ
3:22-30   begin just when the ministry of the Baptist
Gospel   is completed (Mt 4:12). The reason for this
Jan. 12   was probably the desire to contrast their bap-
                  tisms. John is alone in presenting their ac-
tivity as simultaneous and identical.

Jesus baptizes in Judea (v. 22) and John, it would seem, further north. However, the baptism is the same: it consists of a conversion rite proposed by the Baptist which Jesus, as a disciple ("He who was with you"), believes himself able to administer. But he meets with such success that the followers of John are disturbed (vv. 25-26). The Baptist's last discourse is designed to reassure them.

a) The terms of the reply of John the Baptist are certainly in the style of the fourth evangelist. He declares that the crowds may not follow Christ without some sign from the Father (v. 27; cf. Jn 6:44-65). To follow Christ is, in effect, the initiative of faith which only God can inspire. However, this declaration might also signify that the necessary gift of God would not be given to the crowds but to the minister. Christ received a greater gift than John (cf. Jn 6:37): it would follow, then, that he must have greater success. If men abandon John to follow Jesus, it is because they have been given to Jesus by the Father.

b) John introduces into the discussion the image of the *friend of the bridegroom*, which would indicate to his disciples the difference between himself and Jesus (v. 29).

The friend of the bridegroom must present the fiancee to her bridegroom prepared and purified. Paul saw himself in the same role with the Corinthians, because his preaching was a way of conducting people to Christ, their spouse (2 Co 11:2). Christ himself is sometimes considered the bridegroom's friend, preparing and purifying the bride; at other times he is presented as the bridegroom, who in turn presents the bride all "glorious" to himself (Ep 5:27). Rabbinic tradition saw God in Genesis 2:22 as the friend of the bridegroom, preparing Eve and taking her to Adam.

In attributing this title to himself, John the Baptist recalls that his ministry has purified the bride (Israel) through the baptism of conversion, and that he himself has presented her to her bridegroom, the Lamb of God (Jn 1:29-34), by sending his best disciples (Jn 1:35-39). Far from being saddened by Jesus' success, John is overjoyed by his secondary role. He is faithful to his role of friend of the bridegroom, whose task it was to encourage joy and celebration among those attending the wedding banquet. He now encourages joy where before there was bitterness and jealousy.

Every Christian in the world, each ministry in the Church, has the function of leading men to Christ through the same self-denial exercised by the Baptist. The precursor or the Apostle who would impede this process, compromises the coming of the kingdom.

FIRST SUNDAY

Commemoration of the Baptism of Jesus

A. THE WORD

I. Isaiah
42:1-4, 6-7
1st reading

The four pieces grouped under the heading "Servant of Yahweh" are now considered to be an independent collection composed by a disciple of Second-Isaiah, which, for a reason that is not clear, were distributed through the works of the latter. Read consecutively, they might be described as a scenic presentation of the Servant's enthronement.

It is certain that the first poem consists of the first four verses of chapter 42, but whether verses 5-7 belong there is by no means certain. On the contrary they have close links with the second poem (Is 49:1-6); there are obvious similarities, principally the identification of the Servant with the people of Israel as a whole.

The Servant-Israel, light of the nations (v. 6; cf. Is 49:6), has the task of spreading his splendor to the ends of the earth (Is 42:4) by manifesting the salvation of Yahweh (Is 49:6) and bringing the Law and instruction to the nations (vv. 1, 3, 4). Of course there is no question here of a strictly missionary role, because it is only to Israel that God will bring salvation, confounding thereby the nations who should recognize the one true God (cf. Is 52:10) and the superior right of Israel. Actually the Servant-Israel rejects the role of preacher to the nations (v. 2; cf. Ac 11:19), acting by presence and witness only. Doubtless what the prophet has in mind is an Israel dispersed among the nations, but enjoying in that condition the liberty and dignity that constitute a striking testimony to Yahweh's special solicitude. Indeed in Is 49:6 more important for the Servant than re-peopling Palestine is to take advantage of the Diaspora for bear-

301

ing witness to God's light throughout the whole world. While then there *is* some suggestion of universalism in the poem, it is still rather self-centered.

The reflection suggested by the reading is one of the most important in the Old Testament. Israel's witness to the nations is seen for the first time against the background of the Diaspora. In other words her mission is no longer that of an organized nation separate from others; in the situation contemplated the nation is shorn of part of its personality and its members no more than individuals scattered among the multitude.

So too the missionary vocation of each Christian is bound up with a "hidden life" like that of Christ at Nazareth. Jesus merited the title of Servant not only because he belongs to the line of great individual servants like Moses and the prophets, but particularly because he was able to propose to all men a filial "yes" to the father. This would be independent of any sort of structures set up by Israel among the nations. Structures may of course be necessary, but they should subserve the over-all missionary objective. Too often we have seen their biggest energies concentrated on preserving themselves.

II. Acts 10:34-38   This is an extract from Peter's discourse before
    2nd reading   Cornelius and his household at Caesarea, in
                order to lead them to conversion and baptism.
In the Acts the missionary discourses differ according to the composition of the audience, Jewish (Ac 2:14-36; 3:12-26; 4:9-12; 5:29-32; 10:34-43; 13:16-42), or Gentile (Ac 14:15-17; 17:22-31; cf. 1 Th 1:9-10).

The six Jewish discourses resemble one another very much, and it seems very likely that Luke has a considerable part in their composition. Exegetes have been busy trying to determine what material is prior to Luke, and what is specifically Lucan.

We regard all the introductions (in this case verses 34-35) as specifically Lucan, as well as the resume of the public life (vv. 36-38), which is merely mentioned in this case, and which corresponds to Luke's structural plan for his gospel.

Where however the discourse gives us a description of the passion and resurrection of Jesus (vv. 39-40), a sort of "summary" of the passion is used that must have circulated among the primitive communities (cf. Mk 8:31; 9:31; 10:33). Luke was wont to add to these summaries a detail borrowed no doubt from primitive preaching. It laid the responsibility for Christ's death on the Jews, at least the Jews of Jerusalem. However this accusation is more evident in the other Jewish discourses than here.

a) One of the most important items in the passion and resurrection summaries is the mention of the *third day*. In primitive catechesis this item was very constant, and it is still found in our creed. It is really a reference to Hosea 1:2 (where the word "raise up" in Greek is the same as that used for the resurrection). The Talmud saw in the oracle of Hosea the final resurrection of the body. The three days represented the periods of time needed to raise up all the dead of Israel, and let them reach Jerusalem. Thus the resurrection of Jesus is the first of many others (cf. Mt 27:52-53); it is here and now the general resurrection of the body.

b) Christ's resurrection is presented in all these discourses not as something proceeding from Christ himself ("he raised himself up"), but as an act of God ("God has raised him up"). Thus Luke is appropriating a phrase from the vocabulary in which Israel formulated its hope in the general resurrection of the dead. He means to assert that the general *resurrection of bodies*, as foreseen by the prophets, has begun with Christ's resurrection. The doctrine then becomes not so much one of hope, as of faith. It no longer belongs to the future, but is being shaped, realized even, in the present.

Apparently it is to Luke also that verses 41-42, about witness, are to be attributed. But again, when he speaks of Christ being "constituted judge of the living and the dead," he returns to the Jewish concept of the final resurrection. He is making Jesus the central figure of the *eschatological judgment* which will separate the just from the unjust, and enable them to participate in the resurrection and the restoration of the Kingdom.

The dominant themes of Peter's discourse, faith in Christ's resurrection and our own, conversion, and bearing witness, describe admirably the course of catechumenate and Christian baptism. Baptism is the sacrament of faith, not in the sense that it automatically begets faith. It prepares each disciple to triumph over evil, and make his life a resurrected life which disposes him for a new baptism. The new baptism is that of death, the gate that opens the way to eternal life with Jesus Christ.

III. **Matthew**   Today's three gospels describe the baptism of
3:13-17   Jesus by John the Baptist. John's account,
Gospel   which is rather individual, will be treated
1st cycle   separately; but it does have elements in com-
                     mon with the synoptics. We shall deal first
with the points common to the three accounts, then with particular elements in Matthew and John.

1. Common Elements in the Gospels

a) One of the first acts of Christ's public life is the baptism (v. 13) by John, and enrollment among the latter's disciples. A novel significance is given to this decision by the first heavenly sign, the Spirit appearing over the waters in the form of a dove (Mt 3:16; Lk 3:23; Jn 1:32-33). We recall that in the Old Testament the Spirit (*ruah*) and water are associated (Is 44:3; Ez 36:25-26; Jl 3:1), as prior to that had been the wind (*ruah*) and water (Gn 1:2). The association should be understood in the Baptist's terms (Mt 3:11); the messianic times have arrived and the judgment of God, separating his faithful people from the impious, has begun. In fact Jewish tradition, basing itself on texts like Is 42:1; 11:2 and 61:1, expected that the Messiah and the new people would manifest themselves by means of a particular gift of the Spirit.

The descent of the Spirit then on the baptized Christ makes him at once the Messiah and the representative of the people of the last times. In subsequent controversy between Christians and disciples of the Baptist the phenomenon will serve to demonstrate the superiority of Christian baptism. Both rites are signs of conversion; but only the Christian signifies God's movement of encounter which inaugurates the last times. In the primitive account however this is not the sense.

The descent takes place after the "heavens are opened" (Mt 3:16; Lk 3:21). The source of this apocalyptic phrase (cf. Ac 10:11; Jn 1:51, etc.) is very probably Isaiah 63:9-19, where, according to the Septuagint version, the Spirit, grieved for a long time, is finally given to the new Moses by the "Father" at the moment of the sundering of the heavens. Thus the new people seemed to be concentrated in the actual person of Christ.

The image of the dove too suggests the same idea. There are two different attempts to clarify this image, but they are both in agreement about its ecclesiological significance. Some regard the word dove as a mistake in translation, the original being "shekinah," the divine glory that is, resting first on Sinai, then in the temple, and making the people the dwelling place of God (Ex 24:15-18; 40:34-38). Others see here a figure for the chosen people drawn from the Canticle of Canticles (1:15; 2:14; 4:1; 5:2; 6:9) where the divine spouse is calling his dove, the new Jerusalem, to be united with him in a new marriage. The appearance of the dove at the moment of Jesus' baptism could signify that the marriage is accomplished, that God has found his bride.

All these notes, the heavens opened, the Spirit and the dove combine to give the account an ecclesiological as well as a christological meaning. In the very links which bind him to the new people Christ is revealed, and so realizes the prayer of Isaiah 63:9-19.

b) Matthew 3:17, Luke 3:22 and John 1:34 all introduce into the account the detail about the *heavenly voice* enthroning Jesus as Messiah. All mention the voice but they are not in agreement about its message. Matthew and John see an allusion to Isaiah 42:1; Luke a reference to Psalm 2:7, while Mark (1:11) has a formula which combines both these sources.

Matthew's reference (3:17) to Isaiah 42:1 is not exact. He is influenced by the christology of the primitive communities and reworks the text because the figure of the Servant of Yahweh seems overly narrow. He speaks already in terms of the Son of God (Mt 17:5) and affirms the divinity of Jesus.

When he refers to the psalm of royal enthronement, Luke's purpose is to affirm the royal messiahship of Christ. But we should keep in mind the frequent use of this quotation by Christian texts for a special reason. To express that is, not the external procession of the Son in the bosom of the Trinity, but the moment of the resurrection, when Christ begins to enjoy his divine privileges and assumes his lordly power (cf. Ac 13:33; Heb 1:5; 5:5). Luke then seems to have attributed the paschal prerogatives at the baptism by anticipation, and in this transference of the quotation a certain amount of significance is lost. It can still be taken in its literal sense after the resurrection: at this moment Christ's humanity really was begotten into the divine life. At the baptism it simply designates Christ's Messiahship, which will reach its definitive stage in the divinization which resurrection means.

Jesus appears as a new prophet, a new "servant" on whom the Spirit descends as on Moses at the moment of his "emergence from the waters," on whom the heavens are opened as on Ezechiel (Ez 1:1). But as the baptism proceeds in terms of a solemn enthronement the prophetic aspect is quickly supplanted by the royal and messianic. We are turned towards the very mystery of Christ's personality by the citation of psalm 2:7 and the Christian emphasis of the title "well beloved Son." Thus while the baptism does not indeed proclaim the eternal divine sonship of the Word, the apocalyptic suggestions of theophany do focus attention on the human-divine personality.

2. Elements peculiar to Matthew's account

Matthew alone (vv. 14-15) gives us the initial dialogue between the Baptist and Christ. This suggests the subsequent controversy between followers of both rather than a real exchange. How could the Baptist have immediately perceived the personality of Christ and asked him for a baptism which he has not yet instituted (v. 14)? Then Jesus' reply (v. 15) is more an expression of Matthew's theology (Mt 5:17-18; 24:34) than a record of actual words. It is possible to discern primitive Christian apologetic against the baptism of John. A good argument for the importance of this on the part of John's disciples was the fact that Jesus himself received it. The counter argument by Christians was that the only purpose here was to fulfill the Law and the prophets, all Jewish justice that is. The rite would subsequently be transcended just as Christian justice transcended that of the scribes and Pharisees.

IV. Mark 1:7-11   All the necessary data for the commentary on
  Gospel   this gospel can be found in what is said in
  2nd cycle   paragraph 1: **Common Elements in the Gospels,** p. 304.

V. Luke 3:15-18, Verses 15-18 have already been commented
  21-22   on, p. 100. Verses 21-22 reproduce the com-
  Gospel   mon foundation of the gospels on the baptism
  3rd cycle   of Jesus as it was commented on above, p. 304,
                   in connection with the gospel of the 1st cycle.

The gospel on baptism of St. Luke is not original. Some details however permit us to examine the particular mentality of the third gospel.

We may first of all note the *prayer* of Jesus (v. 21), a theme dear to Luke (Lk 5:16; 6:12; 9:18, 28-29; 11:1; 22:41), which has Christ pray precisely at the moment when he receives the Holy Spirit, as he has Christians pray on similar occasions (Ac 1:14; 2:1; 4:31, all baptismal occasions), in order to have it understood that the baptismal ritual of the Christian is already virtually formulated at the Jordan (prayer of the community, baptismal rite by the priest, gift of the Spirit by God). This concern to discover the baptism of the Church in that of the Jordan will cause Luke to forget the role of John the Baptist. He is even thought to be already in prison (cf. vv. 19-20, which curiously enough is not read in the liturgy anymore) at the moment of Jesus' baptism. In omitting mention of the ministry, Luke accentuates still more the ecclesial meaning of the baptism of the Jordan.

B. DOCTRINE

The Meaning of Christian Baptism

Even though it makes a person a living member of the Body of Christ, Baptism, paradoxically enough, especially in old Christian countries, does not occupy the place it ought in Christian awareness. There are two main reasons for this anomaly. As many Christians are baptized immediately after birth, they do not have any natural feeling about Baptism influencing their person, or that as a result of it all their energies ought to be mobilized for the extension of the Kingdom. Secondly, a huge number of people, whose parents do not practice Christian life, have been baptized. They are estranged from the life of the Church in all essentials, from all life, one might say, that is lived in faith. So that Baptism becomes a simple ritual. And even in the case of people whose faith is profound, the manner in which the sacrament is administered fails to inculcate its full meaning in the Christian life.

Under such conditions it is easy to understand why the majority of people cannot see their baptismal initiation as the decisive moment in their lives, the genuine new birth into the Body of Christ. Nowadays, in the eyes of many, the line of demarcation between Christian and non-Christian is no longer Baptism, but the quality of the Gospel-oriented life. We are in danger of neglecting certain fundamental realities of our faith. The liturgy today provides us all with an opportunity of realizing the true meaning of baptismal initiation.

John's Baptism of water

There was, in New Testament times, a baptism for proselytes, an initiation rite for those of pagan origin who wished to join the chosen people. Some considered it just as essential as circumcision. For the understanding of Christian Baptism however, another rite, the baptism of John, seems much more important.

John proclaimed a baptism of penance: the Messianic times were at hand. By this unique rite, administered in the desert, the initiate was somehow associated with the true offspring of Abraham. In the Baptist's view the constant infidelity of Israel, over such a long period, had revealed the inadequacy of circumcision by itself. Only a small Remnant would be saved, the theme which prophetic circles had constantly developed. John was not the only proponent of such views in his time; but he was original in providing entry by means of his baptismal rite into the Remnant which would escape the wrath of God. His baptism of water required a personal acknowledgment of sin: it was a call to conversion. But all the objective value of this rite enacted in the desert was derived from the accompanying "Word": "Be converted, the hour is at hand."

The gospels regard the rite as an intermediate stage only, leading to messianic baptism in fire and the Spirit, fire symbolizing the eschatological judgment inaugurated by the coming of Jesus. It has unique significance because one day Jesus will present himself for baptism by the Precursor. Subsequent to that event, when confronted by a reality entirely new, its transitory character will become manifest.

The Messiah's Baptism in fire and the Spirit

The Gospel accounts of Jesus' baptism emphasize its profound theological significance. He asks for baptism at the hands of John and receives it. This event is sufficient for a total transformation of the rite: it takes on a radically different meaning.

Jesus, the awaited Messiah, is about to respond to God's initiative by a life of perfect obedience. The small remnant of the faithful, foretold by the prophets, is concentrated in him alone. Salvation will be accomplished by his fidelity, and the time of the Spirit will be inaugurated. When he receives baptism it denotes official messianic investiture. The Spirit descends on him, because he is the adequate focus of salvific action. But he is Messiah precisely because he is man-God, the Chosen One of

God, the well-beloved Son who has all the favor of the Father. Before John he "was."

The baptism inaugurated his public life and indicated the whole itinerary he must follow. His task will be that of the Servant, the Lamb who takes away the sin of the World. For this reason it is only on the day of his baptism in death that the rite takes on its plenary sense. "I have a baptism wherewith I am to be baptized, and how I am straitened until it be accomplished" (Lk 12:50). He will be established as the First-Born of the true people of God by baptism in death, as the cornerstone of a new world. Each man, to be incorporated in the edifice of the Kingdom, is called to the living link with Jesus, baptism in the Spirit.

Ecclesial Baptism in the name of Jesus

There is a good deal of material in Scripture and tradition concerning the rite which makes a man a member of the Church, the Body of Christ, and by virtue of that a child here below of the Kingdom, the citizen of a new world. Objectively speaking, Baptism puts a man into genuine communion with God and integrates him into the family of the Father. In it the work of the Spirit is accomplished, because man finds the capacity to develop an adequate response to God's initiative. It is new birth in the Spirit, the bath of regeneration, the exchange of universal association in sin for universal association in love. It assures our passage from the ancient world of darkness and solitude to the new world of brotherhood without limits. It is purification and illumination, and it is each of these indissolubly.

But only in the name of Jesus can this Baptism of the Spirit be conferred. Apart from the vital link with him, First-Born of the true people of God, it is deprived of all content. What takes place is altogether due to the work accomplished by Jesus of Nazareth, above all to the redemptive act of the Cross. Because it is communion in the Pasch of Christ, ecclesial Baptism absorbs a man into the cross and resurrection. Passage from the ancient world to the new has been accomplished by one only; all men can find access to the Father only through the link with Christ. So that the capital effect of Baptism is union with Christ and his eternal sacrifice, accomplished once for all in the major event of the cross. And the rite is invariably accompanied by a 'Word' which is designed to initiate the Christian into salvation history, of which the living principle is Jesus of Nazareth who died and rose again for all men.

And, last of all, Baptism is the sacrament of faith. On the soul of the baptized person the seal of the Spirit is definitively imprinted: the power to shape a perfectly structural life of faith is infused. This is not automatic. Normally a long ecclesial apprenticeship (the catechumenate) in the faith is presumed before Baptism is conferred. The recipient is engaged to conversion of life, which must be constantly deepened according to the pattern of total obedience set by Jesus. And he is turned towards a further baptism, that of death, which definitively opens the door to eternal life in the Risen Christ.

Baptism, the foundation of missionary responsibility

Baptism incorporated us into a people, which is not just another of the peoples of the earth. It is a people not of this world that will reveal its identity only after death. But even in this life the essential characteristic of the Church is that it is always in growth, always dynamic, always open. If humanity is to experience the salvation of the Kingdom in reality, it should accomplish a task on earth that is already measured in millenia, and the end of which we do not know. The task will not be accomplished until the mystery of Christ is rooted in all nations and in all cultures. If the good news of salvation is proclaimed to all men, we shall have on this earth a taste of the cosmic dimension of the universal brotherhood founded by Christ. So much does the salvation of humanity, as conceived by God from all eternity, depend on missionary endeavor, with all that it entails.

We must see Baptism then against a planetary, even a cosmic, background. Membership of the Church is not just a means to personal salvation — there is a universal missionary responsibility implied in Baptism. As members of Christ's Body, we are called to be with him saviors of humanity and of all creation. Our call is emphatically reiterated at Confirmation, which is the culmination of our baptismal initiation, and which is normally conferred by the bishop, the missionary *par excellence*.

When the baptized person takes part in the mission of the Church, he is promoting the ecclesial Act that gives meaning (content that is to say and direction) to the fruit of the Spirit already present in every man. For in exercising her universal mission, the Church directs the action of non-Christians towards Baptism, and gives it significance eventually in the growth of the Kingdom.

The purpose of mission then is not to baptize, but to lead towards Baptism, to accompany men on the difficult path that lies between unbelief and faith in Jesus Christ. For a variety of reasons, one of which has to do with the very difficulty that mission presents, many people fail to join the Church in this life. But if they are faithful to the light of the Spirit and to the voice of conscience, they will be baptized in death. Nevertheless we Christians should be always deeply conscious that the salvation of each and of all depends upon our fidelity to the missionary responsibility contracted at Baptism.

The eucharistic assembly perfected by openness

Christians often prefer to celebrate the Eucharist among acquaintances. Yet the truth is that everywhere the Word and Bread is shared the summons is universal. Indeed, for a proper celebration, it is important to have strangers who are not associated with the usual congregation: and the assembly will find itself renewed in energy precisely in proportion to its readiness to welcome strangers. The whole conduct of the liturgy ought to indicate how strangers who are baptized really belong.

The assembly that welcomes renews itself in joy, a joy that

does not spring simply from a gathering of brothers, but from a deep realization of the catholic character of the Eucharist. Brothers who are strangers can be bearers of indescribable riches, if somehow they are enabled to disclose them.

The more it expresses the mystery of catholicity, the more actually does the eucharistic community witness its fidelity to the obligation of mission. When outsiders are welcomed, each participant will find himself more aware of true encounter, and he will be a more luminous bearer of the Good Tidings.

TABLE OF READINGS